the establishment
of
empirical sociology

the establishment
of
empirical sociology
studies in continuity, discontinuity, and institutionalization

•

edited by
anthony oberschall
yale university

harper & row, publishers
new york, evanston, san francisco, london

to paul f. lazarsfeld

The Establishment of Empirical Sociology: *Studies in
Continuity, Discontinuity, and Institutionalization*

contents

foreword

A famous essay urges historians not to assess historical events from the point of view of the present but to try to interpret the past in the way the earlier participants themselves saw the events of their time. The historian is advised to try to understand the past for its own sake, though it is true that he can never entirely abstract himself from his own age. Still, his goals will be very different from those of the writer who avows to study the past for the sake of the present.

It was Herbert Butterfield who gave this counsel in an address that has greatly influenced and certainly symbolizes much of modern historiography.[1] One example he uses in developing the idea of "The Historical Process" is his own denial of the Protestant Reformation as the beginning of the fight for religious freedom in the English-speaking world. Rather, he believes that the sixteenth century saw a battle between two equally intolerant religious systems. Because neither could win, subsequent generations slowly accepted the principle that a state could contain several religious organizations which could coexist without claim to political power.

The older interpretation was tagged "Whig history" because the great British historians of the nineteenth century supposedly interpreted their material as demonstrating a steady progression to contemporary English political life. I shall presently have to say a word in defense of Whig history, but let us first look at what the idea of a mature history means to sociology.

With regard to the history of sociological thought, the application is fairly clear. We have to know what the classic writers had in mind when they began to use the term "sociology," what concrete problems they were worried about. Merton formulated such a program succinctly:

A genuine history of sociological theory must extend beyond a chronologically ordered set of critical synopses of doctrine; it must deal with the interplay between theory and such matters as the social origins and statuses of its exponents, the changing social organization of sociology, the changes that diffusion brings to ideas, and their relations to the environing social and cultural structure.[2]

Lewis Coser has carried out this program very successfully in a recent book on the life and works of a number of social theorists. Robert Nisbet has taken the same approach, though his book is organized around a set of major conceptual topics rather than around men.

Notice the central role of interpretation in all of this work. The assumption is that the basic facts are known, and once the documents have been studied, the social historian's task is to make them more understandable. But what if important chunks of the past are unknown or even overlooked? Then not even Whig history is possible.

Where there is conviction or even suspicion of incompleteness, one must go back to a still earlier narrative phase and assemble and organize the basic information. But one cannot really return in full innocence to an earlier phase of historical writing. For as the record of events is written, one will be haunted by the specter of the Whig historian—Why do you tell it at all?—and of the mature historian—What did it mean at the time?

This is actually what happened in sociology. Until recently, the history of empirical research was neither studied in its own right nor treated as a part of the standard histories. So we are in the situation just described. The present volume is part of a larger project to recapture that neglected sector of the sociological tradition. But the narrative is assembled for reasons very much rooted in the present, and this has to be explained first.

In the foreword to his monumental work *Main Currents in Sociological Thought,* Raymond Aron makes the following comments:

> The method I have followed is certainly not the only one possible. Modern sociology has two principal sources: the politico-social ideas or doctrines on the one hand; the administrative statistics, surveys, and empirical investigations on the other. For several years Professor Paul Lazarsfeld has been conducting, with the help of his students, a historical investigation of this other current of modern sociology. It is possible to argue that the empirical and quantitative sociology of today owes more to Quételet and Le Play than it does to Montesquieu or Auguste Comte. But my taste and abilities have predisposed me in the other direction.[3]

Notice how Aron points out that personal interest is an important element. But it would be unsatisfactory if a new departure were a personal whim only; something insufficient in the old state of affairs should motivate it. The trend that Aron attributes to me and in which Dr. Oberschall has played such a major part started in the United States, where empirical studies were always considered part of the graduate sociology program, but where the conventional university departments were never suited to the execution of research projects that required teamwork, division of labor, and a certain type of leadership which was different from the customary relationship between an individual teacher and his disciples. I have repeatedly commented on this problem and will not go into further details here.[4] The essence of the story is that most universities created centers, laboratories, bureaus, and organizations which were not well integrated into the academic departments, were badly financed, and yet were indispensable for the training of students. The battle for and around these hybrid centers and their financial support is still raging. My interest in the history of empirical research is part of this battle. By showing that empirical social research has a dignified intellectual pedigree, one could strengthen the claim that it should have a better academic representation. Fortunately this plan became in itself interesting to a number of students and colleagues. A brief sketch of the history of the whole project seems therefore appropriate.

In 1955 the National Academy of Sciences appointed a committee to explore topics common to the social and the natural sciences. In the course of its deliberations it was decided to support a conference on the history of quantification, which finally was held in 1959. Economics, psychology, and sociology were the social sciences involved. I was invited to represent sociology, and my report was subsequently developed into a lengthy paper with the imaginative and energetic help of Dr. Oberschall. Edwin Boring, the psychologist, had no difficulty in organizing his material; measurement and experimentation had for a long time been the central topics of his field, and the history was well documented. Joseph Spengler, the economist, solved a near-dilemma by an editorial decision. He did not discuss descriptive economics (price indices, business cycle studies), but instead only the role of quantification in economic theory where the writings of a number of major authors provided him with the main sources for interpretation. I had to point out that quantification in sociology is a vague topic because it includes mere counting, the development of classificatory dimensions, and the systematic use of social indicators.[5] The subject matter was also difficult to delineate because of extensive overlapping with other social sciences. Thus, for example, "with the economist the sociologist shares family budgets, and with the psychologist, he makes the study of attitudes a joint conern."[6] In the course of my essay I felt compelled to include the observational method of Le Play without which his use of budgets could have been misunderstood; I had to show that some of Quételet's "laws" were really multivariate analysis in the modern sense, and that Tönnies' "sociography" was an interesting effort to induce generalizations from case studies—in sum, I had to demonstrate that the history of quantification necessarily became the history of empirical social research.

In my essay and its postscript I suggested a large number of problems that required further investigation. A number of them have been carried out, and they certainly have borne out my anticipation of complexity.

The most far-reaching follow-up occurred

when the new *International Encyclopedia of the Social Sciences* accepted the history of empirical research as a legitimate field of inquiry. Oberschall and Lecuyer, one of my French collaborators, were invited to contribute an article on this topic; it is by far the best presentation available. Their bibliography contains about 100 references to work done mainly before the turn of the last century.[7] They, too, adopt a broad meaning for "empirical social research." They, as I, do not explicitly define it, but still it is easy to list what they include: studies of social problems such as poverty, health, and prostitution; of institutions for coping with these problems—prisons, poorhouses, hospitals; of crusaders for reform—charity organizations, royal commissions, semiacademic associations. Oberschall and Lecuyer also include efforts to improve governmental activities and to describe the states of agriculture and industry, the loyalty of the populace, migration, and the expanding scope of education. They touch on methodological innovations and on the role of public and private agencies which supported these empirical studies.

Already at the narrative stage one has to decide what would be included under the notion of empirical social research. The answer is not always simple. One certainly would include situations where a scholar or a government agency collects observations for the better understanding of a problematic situation; but even here it is difficult to decide what is a travelogue and what is the beginning of a social inquiry. At the other extreme one finds the collection of large-scale censuslike material. This would be relevant for our history at two points. In the early stages of social bookkeeping the appropriate methods are usually undetermined and a great deal of experimentation is neccessary—how to take a population census was a matter of argumentative debate and experimentation for a long period. But once procedures are established, it is also relevant to consider whether the data are used for new purposes. The establishment of criminal statistics in France greatly stimulated the work of Quételet and finally led to the whole new field which the French and the Germans call "moral statistics." The very subject matter investigated needs to be included. One can hardly imagine books on the leisure-time activities of British factory workers at the beginning of industrialization. We now have numerous surveys on peoples' exposure to mass media. But as I have observed elsewhere, such research can be done for very different purposes. In France many social scientists worry whether "mass culture" would endanger the workers' participation in social movements; in this country the pertinent studies are either done for commercial purposes or by people concerned with the level of taste in mass society.

In addition to methods and to the subject matter of research, institutional innovations belong in our narrative: the creation of journals and of scientific societies concerned with social research; the availability of funds and of volunteer manpower; the locus of decision to engage in empirical studies; and the institutional setting in which they are carried out.

Part of this rich information came from specific studies done by the two authors and other students in our group. The original plan was to study four countries in detail; we now have impressive records on two of these. Two dissertations were written on Germany: Oberschall on the period 1870-1914 and Suzanne Schad on the Weimar Republic. The first has appeared as a book which can be consulted directly.[8] Oberschall found that social theorists had repeatedly worked on empirical studies of contemporary problems without being able to integrate them with their primary efforts to build broad sociological systems. Schad's manuscript is not yet published, but one of her major findings was that a large amount of what we now call empirical social research was conducted in Germany between the two world wars. Schools of education and psychiatric centers carried out studies of social stratification, the structure of small groups, the influence of the family, and rural life. This research at least equals in amount and quality the work done in the United States at the same time. But this was not considered sociology in Germany, and no traces of these investigations can be found in the writing of German sociology professors at the time.[9]

The second country with which we made progress was France. Here, too, we established a division of labor. Terry Clark covered the period between 1870 and 1914. His main story was the transition from one powerful "school" to another, which embodied both political and intellectual forces: the victory of Durkheim over Le Play. Clark has published large parts of his dissertation in special articles, and a representative example is included in the present volume.[10]

The richest material was discovered for France under the *ancien régime* and during the troubled years of 1800 to 1850.

The whole French part of the project merits digression at this point. During the academic year 1962-1963 I directed a seminar at the Sorbonne. It was organized by Bernard Lecuyer, who had acquired an advanced degree in history with special honors and had then turned to sociology. His training equipped him to delve into original archive material to which other members of the group lacked access. He brought to the fore a remarkable system of reporting by the regional administrators to the court and ministers of the Bourbon kings. Not only did they write up their assessment of public opinion, but they were sometimes asked to start rumors about new tax legislation so that the central administration could predict how strong an opposition might develop.

After the Revolution and the Napoleonic era, public concern shifted to the impact of the new factories and the status of the rural population, which was beginning to form the proletariat of the urban centers. The systematic surveys done then were probably superior to the information the famous British Royal Commission collected at the same time. The narrative of this period summarized in the *Encyclopedia* article mentioned above owes much to Lecuyer's original research. We all regret that external circumstances did not permit inclusion of some of his work in the present volume.

The Paris seminar was remarkable also in enlisting the participation of a group of young faculty members who have by now acquired a high reputation of their own. Some were especially interested in a reinterpretation of Gabriel Tarde. They unearthed original statistical studies, in particular, some on delinquency trends in France. Tarde was especially concerned with the comparison and interpretation of time series data. The word "imitation," which is still attached to his reputation, is really only part of an approach that today we would call "interaction and feedback analysis." In this connection he discussed in considerable detail the measurement of intervening variables that could not be observed directly. The Tarde phase of the seminar is ably summarized in Raymond Boudon's new book *La crise de la sociologie.*[11] The work of the Paris group has recently led to the appearance of selected writings of Tarde instructively introduced in an essay by Terry N. Clark.[12]

In 1966 Robert Merton and I organized a seminar at Columbia to work on the two English-speaking countries. The papers by Cole and Elesh in this volume are a product of this seminar. Soon thereafter, Philip Abrams' book on the history of English sociology covered or at least touched upon many of the episodes we meant to explore.[13] The English situation was virtually the opposite of what we found on the continent. The social scientists there were keenly aware of their empirical ancestry. In his introduction to the present volume, Oberschall notes that Abrams describes social thought as an outgrowth of empirical work whereas continental writers treated social theory as a world of its own and were practically oblivious to its empirical sibling. The contributions by Cole and Elesh remain timely because of their richness of detail and the fact that they were prepared with a different perspective from that of Abrams.

Our Columbia seminar was also meant to cover the American scene, but time did not permit us to complete this work. The only topic covered in detail was the relation between social work and social research. An as yet unpublished dissertation by Betty Broadhurst concentrated on the work of a Johns Hopkins social scientist,

Amos Warner, who in the latter part of the nineteenth century played a considerable role in the development of philanthropic organizations while at the same time maintaining close contact with the emerging centers of midwestern sociology, particularly Wisconsin and Michigan.[14] In the present volume Oberschall has now undertaken the task of providing the main frame for the American story. Hopefully his work will lead to more specialized monographs.

Reviewing this whole enterprise raises a curious question. How is it possible that all these sketches can be written without an explicit definition of "empirical social research"? At this point we can take recourse to another idea which has recently gained prominence. Thomas Kuhn has pointed out that from time to time a fresh turn is made along an existing course of academic endeavor. He was thinking in terms of major revolutions in thought, but his general idea can also be applied to much more modest events. Kuhn speaks of the emergence of a new paradigm, but subsequent writers have stressed that he uses the term in a variety of ways. I find especially useful the part of his writings that Masterman calls the "sociological notion of a paradigm—something which can function when the theory is not there."[15] If such a new perspective evolves, it attracts "an enduring group of enthusiasts, many from competing modes of scientific activities," and is "sufficiently open-ended to leave all sorts of problems for the redefined group practitioners to solve." In short, "something sociologically describable and above all concrete already exists in actual science at the early stages when the theory is not there." And Masterman stresses that it is this "sociological" aspect of the paradigm idea that makes it attractive to scientists in new fields, especially those in the social sciences.

Substitute in all this for the "lack of theory" the lack of a well-circumscribed field and the lack of a well-conceptualized set of problems, and we shall find ourselves at home. How is this new paradigm to be characterized in our case? One way is to compare it with Merton's admonition for a better history of social theory quoted earlier. All he says there applies to our field. But much has to be added. We deal not only with individual writers but also with working teams that form and dissolve. "Sponsors" of all kinds play a major role. The discontinuity between efforts over time is marked.

It is necessary to distinguish between empirical work done for specific purposes and similar endeavors motivated by the desire to discover general laws. Methodological and technological advances (e.g., attitude scales and computers, respectively) have a much greater influence on empirical research than does a theoretical reflection. The choice of problems in empirical research probably fluctuates much

more with the changing social context, and controversies are probably
rarer and settled more quickly. And the latest but most vexing problem,
the relation between the theoretical and empirical trends, begins with a
lack of contact in the first half of the nineteenth century, then becomes
the administrative problem "Statistics and Sociology" at the turn of the
century, and now agitates all parties concerned as "Social Theory and
Empirical Social Research."

But as such information accumulates, the need
for a more stringent intellectual approach becomes ever more pressing.
And indeed it was found in the notion of "institutionalization" which
the papers in this volume and Oberschall's introduction bring out so
strongly. It is a timely new phase in the collective enterprise. In my
introduction to Oberschall's first book I made a preliminary but feeble
effort in stressing three levels of inquiry:

The program as it is now proceeds on three levels. First, what is the intrinsic development of research ideas and techniques from one period to the next? Second, what
are the social networks—institutions, personal contacts, controversies—within which
progress was promoted or hindered? Finally what are the broad cultural and historical factors that shaped the birth and growth of empirical social research as we know
it today?[16]

The emphasis of the group changed to the
second level, and in a much enriched version—not the role of institutions
and social networks as they existed at the time, but their very evolution,
the way ideas interplayed with social forms, the latter being sometimes
the result and sometimes the crucial backups of the former. As can be
seen from this volume, the idea of "institutionalization" has become the
conceptual core of the whole program, probably very much through
Robert Merton's influence. Earlier it had been used by Ben-David in his
impressive writings on the history of the university structure in various
countries.[17] Shils applied it specifically in a sketch of the recent history
of sociology when he compared the relative public success of two German social scientists and of several American university departments.[18]

In his introduction Oberschall gives a very
clear picture of the phases through which such institutionalization
moves: a new topic of inquiry attracts a small group of students; funds
and more people become mobilized; finally an organized and continuous
tradition is established. Other contributors to the present volume analyze relevant episodes in the light of this model, and thus this volume is
a great step forward in the whole program—the new paradigm for the
full study of the history of sociology. But it still is Whig history because
it looks at the past as steps to contemporary achievement. In view of
the administrative confusion about research institutes mentioned above,

this is an important contribution indeed. I shall be most satisfied if the spirit of the present volume begins to penetrate into today's college courses.

But the mature historian looks over our shoulders, and it is tempting to guess what he would want us to do. First, he would probably say that phases do not follow each other automatically; every new step is the result of preceding conflicts. I can think of a technical and an ideological example. For the first, look at the "budget" as a social research device. When Le Play wanted to gauge the religious attitudes of his families, he asked them how much they spent on contributions to the church. Some of his successors objected that this was the technological approach of a mining engineer; it would be equally important to know how often they prayed and went to church. So the time budget was born. But when work, education, or even leisure activities were transferred to organizational settings, time alone became less important. With whom was the time spent? The "contact budget" became a standard tool of research.

On the ideological level we can observe a more important case. When Booth quantified the concept of poverty, he intended to settle an argument with socialist friends. When quantification had become part of American sociological training the tables were temporarily turned: Doctoral candidates looked for problems to quantify rather than for the burning issues of the day. Now this "quantifying establishment" is being attacked by a strange coalition of macrosociological Marxists and ethnomethodologists who want to explore the "true" existential meaning which lies behind measurement techniques. I am convinced that new types of empirical research will evolve, probably much concerned with underdeveloped countries where linguistic analysis and the study of social change under the impact of industrialization will be bound together. As a matter of fact, we have on hand an illustrative case which only on the surface looks very different. Empirical social research is experienced in Germany as an American invention though in fact it was a European import to America. A distinguished German colleague, Heinz Hartman, has raised a fundamental question about this situation. If empirical research claims to describe social reality, to which ontological philosophy does it belong? Materialism? Dialectics? Phenomenology? It does not match any of them, but Hartman deems it crucial that the question be answered. Out of this conflict between an old German university tradition and a new technology has come one of the best discussions of empirical social research.[19]

The theme of conflict and contradiction as the source of a historical process appears at still another point. Who are the agents who press forward the movement to new institutional forms? I have elsewhere tried to make the point that they are often "marginal men," people between two social strata or two cultures, but not quite at home in either. They are searching for an institution with which they can fully identify.[20] This theme has been developed through a Columbia program on innovation in higher education where we have analyzed the history of major reformers of European and American universities. But here again one is wary of attributing the same meaning to "institutionalization" with different forms and within different historical contexts. As a matter of fact—to voice one slight note of dissent to parts of this volume—I am not even sure whether the term "institutionalization" applied to the teaching of sociology at the turn of this century has quite the same meaning when applied to empirical research institutes fifty years later. But I feel quite optimistic regarding one point. I think that ideas are much more subject to change than concrete research procedures. With regard to empirical research, the gap between Whig and mature history might not be that large. Still, the more we know, the more difficult it becomes to know more.

It has been said that only at its peril does a social science forget its history. But it is even more dangerous to have left such a lopsided history as that which sociology has written. Perhaps soon a historian of empirical sociology will be an acknowledged specialist of his own, where familiarity with contemporary work, skill in archival inquiry, and creativity in interpretation will be equally required. For the moment we should be grateful to the young scholars who have invested some of their intellectual and academic capital in the present volume.

Paul F. Lazarsfeld

notes

1. *The Whig Interpretation of History* (London: Bell, 1950).
2. Robert K. Merton, "On the History and Systematics of Sociological Theory," in *On Theoretical Sociology—Five Essays, Old and New* (New York: Free Press, 1967), p. 34.
3. Raymond Aron, *Main Currents in Sociological Thought,* Vol. 2 (New York: Doubleday Anchor, 1970).
4. "The Sociology of Empirical Social Research," *American Sociological Review,* 27 (1962), 732-741.
5. "Notes on the History of Quantification in Sociology," *Isis,* 52: 2 (1961), 277-332. The *Isis* article owes a great deal to an earlier work on the history of sociography reported in 1933 in the appendix of *Marienthal.* Hans Zeisel played a crucial role in this effort. Our monograph has now been translated into

English: cf. Marie Jahoda, Paul Lazarsfeld, and Hans Zeisel, *Marienthal* (Chicago: Aldine, 1971).

6. *Ibid.,* p. 277.

7. The entry "sociology" in the *Encyclopedia* consists of three parts: 20 pages on the field in general, 13 pages on the "development of social thought," and 14 pages on the "early history of social research," as just mentioned. The first part, written by Albert Reiss, Jr., is as far as I know the first general statement that gives equal weight to "two roots" of sociology, social research and social theory. Reiss accords generous credit to Oberschall and to me when he talks of the empirical origins of sociology.

8. Anthony Oberschall, *Empirical Social Research in Germany, 1848-1914* (The Hague: Mouton, 1965). Lazarsfeld and Oberschall also wrote a special paper on the untranslated German material of Max Weber: "Max Weber and Empirical Social Research," *American Sociological Review*, 30 (Spring 1965), 185-199.

9. Suzanne Schad, *Empirical Social Research in Weimar Germany,* unpublished Ph.D. dissertation, Sociology Department of Columbia University, 1971.

10. "Discontinuities in Social Research," *Journal of the History of the Behavioral Sciences*, 3:1 (January 1967), pp. 3-16. "Emile Durkheim and the Institutionalization of Sociology in the French University System," *European Journal of Sociology*, IX (1968), pp. 37-71.

11. Cf. Raymond Boudon, *La Crise de la sociologie* (Genève-Paris: Droz, 1971).

12. *Gabriel Tarde on Communication and Social Influence* (Chicago: University of Chicago Press, 1969).

13. Philip Abrams, *The Origins of British Sociology, 1834-1914* (Chicago: University of Chicago Press: 1968).

14. Betty Broadhurst, *Toward Graduate Education in Social Work,* an unpublished Ph.D. dissertation, Sociology Department of Columbia University, 1971.

15. Margaret Masterman, "The Nature of a Paradigm," in Imre Lakatos and Alan Musgrave, eds., *Criticism and the Growth of Knowledge* (London: Cambridge University Press, 1970), pp. 68 ff.

16. Paul F. Lazarsfeld, Preface to Oberschall, *op. cit.,* p. vii.

17. Joseph Ben-David and A. Zloczower, "Universities and Academic Systems in Modern Society," *Archives Européennes de Sociologie*, 3 (1962), 45-82.

18. Edward Shils, "Tradition, Ecology and Institution in the History of Sociology," *Daedalus*, 99 (Fall 1970), pp. 760-825.

19. Heinz Hartman, *Empirische Sozialforschung-Probleme und Entwickelungen* (Munich: Juventa, 1970).

20. Paul F. Lazarsfeld, "An Episode in the History of Social Research: A Memoir," in Donald Fleming and Bernard Bailyn, eds, *The Intellectual Migration* (Cambridge, Mass.: Harvard University Press, 1969), pp. 270-337.

introduction:
the sociological
study
of the history
of
social research
•
anthony oberschall

        The contributors to this short volume dealing with the history of empirical sociology were not primarily concerned with describing and listing all the instances of empirical social research conducted in the past, although the reader can form a good idea of the extent and type of research performed in nineteenth-century England from the papers of David Elesh and Stephen Cole. Nor were we primarily concerned with tracing the history of specific techniques and methodological innovations, how they originated and how they became adopted outside of the circle of originators, although here again the reader will find some relevant information in several papers, for instance on the diffusion of regression techniques in American sociology in the 1920s and 1930s. Rather, we were concerned with the twin questions of the institutionalization of sociology and of social research, or to put it more accurately, the lack of continuity and institutionalization in some countries and their more partial or successful institutionalization in other contexts. We were also interested in why sociology and social research became closely identified in some situations but not in others.

an outline of the
history of social research

        By now it has been well documented that empirical social research has a long, distinguished, and interesting history antedating that of academic sociology and even that of social and

evolutionary theorizing.[1] What is meant by social research? For our
purposes, it consists of broadly systematic empirical investigations by
means of social surveys, field observations, and the secondary analysis
of demographic, socioeconomic, and institutional data. Even excluding
studies based on historical and archival data, anthropometric and psychological experiments, ethnographic and linguistic investigations, and
those based on the myths, customs, and religions of nonliterate peoples,
it is apparent that the list of social researchers and of empirical investigations is a long one, international in scope. The major episodes, foci of
concern, and twists and turns in the history of social research can be
mentioned briefly.

Political arithmetic started in England in the
late seventeenth century, flourished there and in France in the eighteenth century, and became slowly but progressively institutionalized as
demography and census activity in the mid- and late nineteenth century
in Europe and in the United States. During the *ancien régime* in France
considerable descriptive, fact-finding social research was conducted by
government agencies to facilitate the formulation and administration of
socioeconomic policies. Findings were, however, kept secret. In France
also, at the time of the French Revolution, the idea of applying probability theory to problems of social organization and policy such as the
decisions of juries and the deliberations and methods of voting in political assemblies was clearly formulated by Condorcet with his call for a
"mathématique sociale" and pursued by him and several other mathematicians in some depth.[2] These efforts at applying mathematical probability models to areas other than gambling problems and demography
were not pursued. Eventually, and without reference to this early development, the notion of mathematical models was reintroduced in each of
the social science disciplines.[3] The most interesting and prolific period
of social research in France occurred between 1815 and 1848, when
public hygienists and medical reformers became concerned with the
condition of the working and lower classes in the urban and increasingly
industrial environment.[4] It is to the public hygienists that we owe such
a classic as Parent-Duchatelet's treatise on prostitution, which still stands
as the most thorough and empirically documented work on that topic.[5]
During the reign of Napoleon III, this research tradition disappeared, yet
for a time Le Play's field studies of working-class families throughout
Europe kept empirical research topical. The weaknesses in Le Play's
approach to social research and the factors that distracted him and his
followers from establishing an empirical research tradition are described
in Walter Goldfrank's contribution to this volume.[6]

In Britain, in the 1830s, an era of statistical
enthusiasm witnessed the creation of numerous statistical associations,

two of which survive to this day. Long before Booth, these societies pioneered the technique of the large-scale social survey as a fact-finding instrument for studying the problems of the lower classes. The papers of Cole and Elesh in this book describe and explain the rise and eclipse of their research activities. In midcentury, a vigorous movement of moral statistics lead by Quételet flourished in several countries. Many moral statisticians sought to establish inductive laws and quantitative empirical generalizations about population, society, and social processes. Crime, suicide, pauperism, education and literacy, military conscription, religious and political behavior, and numerous other topics on which numerical data became increasingly available from many countries were scrutinized and analyzed in quantitative ways. In the United States, the controversy over slavery was conducted by some of its defenders and detractors by marshaling quantitative evidence.[7] In Germany, moral statistics sparked a prolonged controversy over free will and determinism, which proved detrimental to social research, yet later investigators such as Tönnies were inspired by the moral statistical tradition, undertook detailed social statistical investigations, and sought to incorporate them into the discipline of sociology as it was then taking shape.[8] In Germany also, in the 1880s and 1890s, an association of university economists and civil servants, the *Verein für Sozialpolitik*, undertook a whole series of empirical investigations on agrarian questions and later on industrial workers. In the latter studies Max Weber played repeatedly an important role.[9] In the United States, at the turn of the century, the social reform activities associated with the Progressive movement, the social gospel, municipal reform, charities and corrections, and social settlements provided the occasion for numerous empirical investigations about urban problems, the assimilation of immigrants, crime, delinquency, dependency, working conditions, and so on, just at the time that sociology as an academic discipline was being established in some American universities. Only the most important episodes and research groups could be listed in this brief summary.

Empirical social research, up to very recently, has been episodic and noncumulative. It was undertaken for reasons other than the testing of theory and development of science. Efficient public administration, social reform, legislation, ameliorism are in need of facts, and social research is a major means of providing the data. Social researchers are not university scholars but officials and concerned reformers for whom social theory is a luxury and social research but one of many competing activities that make demands on their time and energies. It is true that in every country certain associations and societies which bring together separate individuals interested and engaged in social research flourish for a time, that journals are published and a rudimentary communication network does develop so that later investigators are to a limited extent aware of, and are influenced and stimulated by, earlier social researchers. Yet time and again a promising research tradition melts away, techniques of research discovered and fruitfully applied at a particular time are soon forgotten and fall into disuse only to be rediscovered quite independently by later investigators, and even within the same research groups the high quality of earlier research deteriorates over time. In short, until recently social research was an uninstitutionalized activity. Much research performed depended on the fortuitous combination of financial means, interest in certain topics, reforming outlook, and research skills, found in single individuals. Intellectuals and scholars who called themselves sociologists were seldom interested in social research, and even more rarely engaged in it. Yet at some point efforts were made to combine sociology and social research into the same role, and some academic sociologists came to define social research as one of the important and legitimate activities of their discipline and of their role. I shall show in my paper in this volume that this occurred first at the University of Chicago in the 1920s. In the remainder of this introduction, I wish to present a simple theoretical scheme based on the work of Joseph Ben-David and his associates to explain what it was that blocked or favored the institutionalization of both sociology and of social research and how it was that these two activities came to be performed in the same role only in the United States, and discuss the scheme briefly referring to France, Germany, England, and the United States.

a theoretic scheme of the institutionalization of empirical sociology

Simplifying somewhat, Ben-David's view is that the establishment of a new scientific role and discipline proceeds in four steps.[10] First, there is some differentiation in subject matter, method, and techniques from earlier disciplines. Second, this hitherto peripheral subject matter comes to be regarded by some social strata or groups as a meaningful part of culture. In the case of natural science these were groups with interests and an outlook opposed to the established order, opposed to the upper strata of society. Third, these beginnings lead to increasingly patterned recruitment of talented people into the new scientific activity which thus gains in numbers, in its resource base, and in stature. In his treatment of the establishment of physiology and psychology as separate academic disciplines, Ben-David shows that an emerging discipline attracts scholars and others not solely because it represents an intellectual challenge; for some groups the discipline becomes a means of professional advancement and career mobility.[11] The fourth and final step consists of the successful consolidation of a distinct scientific community with its own subculture, a broad organizational base, a communications network, publications, and scientific associations. At this point the members of the new discipline have developed a separate identity, and the new science becomes a self-perpetuating domain of culture and to a large extent independent of its environment. It is now assured of a resource base and it generates its own problems and concerns from within the discipline. In another paper especially relevant for the case of social science, Ben-David shows that the manner in which a national system of higher education is organized can decisively facilitate or impede the process of differentiation.[12] In the more decentralized and competitive higher education systems of the United States and of Germany, disciplinary innovation is more likely to be successful than in the more centralized and hierarchic French and British systems.

The first step in the process of differentiation is not problematical, and in the case of sociology and of social research, it is not difficult to demonstrate that it has occurred in all four countries sometime in the nineteenth or twentieth centuries. The heart of the scheme consists of the second and third steps. They can be conceptualized somewhat differently in the context of a supply-demand model. Neither the demand for a new discipline such as sociology, nor the supply of potential sociologists can be taken for granted. On the demand side, apart from the intellectual and scientific interest it awakens, the emerging discipline must acquire a sponsor group which backs it with its resources. Only thus can vested interests, both ideological and organizational, be overcome during the process of differentiation. On the supply side, there should exist a group of people whose professional advancement and career chances are enhanced by engaging in the new activity, who assure recruitment into the new discipline, who fight to defend and expand the initial institutional footholds gained, and who themselves become a powerful lobby in favor of institutionalizing the new role in addition to the original sponsor group. The model clearly posits that the fate of the emerging discipline is linked with fairly cohesive, large, and identifiable groups that have a stake in its establishment, on both the demand and supply sides. Weakness on either side, and especially weakness on both, will defeat or delay the process of differentiation and of institutionalization. If the demand is to some extent being met by the incumbents of established roles and disciplines, the demand for a new role and discipline will be weaker, and the supply of potential recruits will be siphoned off by established channels of professional and career advancement.

This model is applicable to the case of a new role and discipline for which there are neither precedents nor sources of support outside the country. The diffusion of an already established role and discipline to other countries, for example, the establishment of sociology in Asian, African, and Latin American universities, might have to include further variables and processes. The purposive adoption of an existing organizational model for a system of higher education and the provision of resources, both financial and manpower, from outside the country would have to be considered, among other things. No claim is made here that the model identifies all the variables and processes that play a part in disciplinary differentiation and establishment, only that the most important have been spelled out and incorporated into it.

The demand for social research arises in several ways, which can be broadly grouped into three categories. (1) Basic information about population and resources are needed for purposes of efficient administration and the formulation of public policy. This demand is usually generated and sustained by the government primarily. In British history, for instance, first the political arithmeticians and later the government itself through numerous statistical agencies fulfilled this demand. The role of statistician, in the sense of descriptive census statistician, with a clearcut career pattern, becomes established well ahead of the role of social researcher in all countries. (2) Social problems resulting from rapid social change during a period of industrialization and urbanization generate a demand for more extensive and more detailed information than government agencies are prepared to provide. This information is needed by social reformers, civic groups, philanthropists as part of their ameliorist activities and as a baseline for suggesting concrete solutions to social problems. In the history of social research, this is the dominant source of demand. In Britain, it was wealthy reformers, philanthropists, concerned professionals, and the voluntary associations they formed that fulfilled this demand by engaging in social research directly. (3) Another source of demand for social research is the need for empirical data to test scientific theories and to provide insights and understanding for social processes. This source remains very weak until sociology as a university discipline has actually been established.

The demand for sociology also arises in several different ways. (1) It can result from purely intellectual concerns, from reflection and wrestling with philosophic and scientific questions; this is the aspect that is usually emphasized in histories of sociology and of social thought. Consideration of this factor does shed light on the systems of thought of sociology's founding fathers and on their convergence and concern with certain topics; but intellectual demand itself has a

small impact on the processes of role differentiation and institutionalization. In many countries, this demand is present for a long period of
time. It corresponds to step 1 of Ben-David's scheme, and can be taken
for granted if one narrows his time and space perspective to nineteenth-
and twentieth-century Europe and North America. (2) Sociology can
fulfill the demand for an ideology, a religion of humanity, a moral and
social philosophy, a secularized system of scientific ethics, and so on,
opposed to existing systems of thought, which certain groups find useful for political reasons. They may become the sponsors of sociology on
the demand side. The systems of thought of Comte and Le Play, to mention but two early sociologists, were seized upon by many groups at
different times and places because they provided just such an ideology.
Terry Clark's paper and my own in this volume demonstrate that this
source of demand was very powerful in the successful establishment of
Durkheimian sociology in France and of American sociology. (3) Sociology can also be stimulated by demand for a course of instruction,
either because the subject matter is thought to contribute to broad,
humanist learning, or because it is thought to be vocationally useful to
social workers, administrators, philanthropists, social reformers, teachers,
civil servants, in providing them with an inventory of practical skills and
techniques and an occupational outlook. This last source of demand was
strong only in the United States.

        The demands for sociology and for social
research are to a large extent independent of each other until after sociology has been successfully institutionalized. Efforts by sociologists to
establish their discipline in the university do not necessarily lead them
to engage in empirical social research when they seek to demonstrate the
validity and usefulness of their theories and their approach. The primary
foci of intellectual concern in the late nineteenth and early twentieth
century were with broad, universal schemes of evolution and of social
change. Sociologists bent on legitimizing their discipline sought to demonstrate the originality and superiority of their approach with reference
to these questions. To accomplish this goal they relied mostly on ethnographic data, the history of religions, readily available institutional and
census-type statistics, and on historical and ethnological techniques. On
the applied side, the demand for social research stemming from reformist,
ameliorist movements did not stimulate a demand for sociology because
those engaged in social action were engaged in solving concrete and practical problems and not in elaborating a theory of society and of social
processes. Only in the United States did a peculiar alliance of social
reformers and academic sociologists bridge this gap and did a mutually
reenforcing demand for both theory and social research arise.

applying the model

The main facts about the history of sociology and of social research in Britain are well established in the excellent book by Philip Abrams[13] and further elucidated in the papers of Sir G. N. Clark, Elesh, and Cole in this volume. It should be recalled that as late as the years between the two world wars, there was a department of sociology that awarded an undergraduate sociology degree only at the University of London, but even there sociology appeared to be a specialty within economics and economic history, and attracted only a small number of undergraduates. Practical and vocational instruction was offered in a separate department of social science and administration. The precarious foothold of sociology in the British university system before the World War II is beyond dispute. Throughout the nineteenth century, the ameliorist and reformist demand for social research was the predominant one. Reformers, philanthropists, civil servants, politicians, and professionals who engaged in social research either on their own or banded together in voluntary associations were wealthy and high-status amateurs. They had little interest in social theory and looked upon research as a necessary preparatory activity for reform and legislation. Research was but one of many activities they were concurrently engaged in, and not the central one at that. When social conditions improved, when legislation had been passed, when the government expanded its information-collecting activities, and when competing and more compelling political and administrative matters demanded their attention, their interest in social research diminished. Those who were inclined to pursue a long-term career in social action could do so as statisticians, civil servants, and politicians in existing political and administrative roles for which there was well-established precedent and institutionalized support. In Abrams' view

[British] society provided numerous outlets for social concern of a legitimate, satisfying, and indeed, seductive character. . . . it provided for a large and apparently open class of "public persons," access to government. . . . Statistician, administrator, reform politician—these were the roles systematically encouraged. The ancient universities offered a fourth possibility, that of social philosopher.[14]

Thus there did not exist pressures for the creation of a professionally and organizationally distinct role of social researcher linked to a new academic discipline. The one discipline that dealt with wages and thus also with the material condition of the working classes and that concerned itself with questions of public policy was political economy; but political economy was laissez faire in orientation, deductive in its theorizing, and consequently hostile to the interventionist legislative orientation of private charity and reform governments and the inductive

approach of social researchers. Under the circumstances, the organization of social research remained linked to voluntary associations whose
weaknesses for providing a base for sustained and cumulative social
research is the central concern of Elesh's paper.

British sociology suffered equally from a lack
of demand and from weaknesses on the supply side in a higher education system marked by the dominance of the Oxbridge tradition not
favorable to disciplinary innovation. In a system concerned with the
classical and humanist education of gentlemen destined for leadership
in public life, the existing and entrenched disciplines of history, philosophy, and economics were considered quite sufficient. Moreover, no opposition group outside the walls of the university needed the elaboration
of a new moral and social philosophy opposed to establishment thinking because socialism was already available. Within the university, young
aspiring scholars concerned with the intellectual problems of social
theory and evolution, which were somewhat marginal to established
disciplines, were attracted to anthropology, social biology, eugenics, and
demography. These new disciplines had established a firmer, broader,
and more promising university base than that provided for sociology by
a few wealthy amateurs such as Victor Branford or T. Martin White, who
financed sociology as an academic subject at the University of London.[15]
The separation of sociology from social administration as a field of
instruction reenforced the speculative tendencies of some sociologists
and contributed to "the diversion of other promising sociologists early
in their careers away from social analysis and research and towards
administration, party politics, or one or another kind of institutional
innovation."[16] Divorced from both government and university sponsorship, the meager resource base of sociology attracted either marginal
academics or wealthy amateurs. A critical mass of sociologists did not
arise under those circumstances. In the long run, the combination of
theory and method represented by eugenics and social biology was to
provide the point of departure for a rebirth of British sociology, and was
to stamp it with its characteristic concerns: the demographic emphasis,
questions of opportunity and ability, mobility, stratification, education,
and social waste.[17]

In Germany, both social research and soci-
ology underwent a slow and steady growth without however becoming
firmly institutionalized or linked up until after World War II.[18] Had it
not been for Hitler and the Nazis, a continuation of the trends and
forces at work during the Wilhelmian and Weimar periods into the
1930s was to be expected. Before World War II, the demand for social
research, as in Britain, arose in connection with the "social question"
because factual information on the rural and urban working and lower

classes was needed to formulate public policy. Unlike Britain, the structure of higher education was decentralized and competitive and therefore receptive to innovation. Unlike Britain again, the individuals who banded together into the major voluntary association concerned with social research and policy formulation, the *Verein für Sozialpolitik*, were professors and were firmly rooted in the historical school of economics. There were also other associations as well as isolated individuals ranging from independent scholars to clergymen and self-educated workers who engaged in research at one time or another, but it was the *Verein* that remained the largest such body. Because its members possessed some of the skills necessary for conducting social research and for perfecting research techniques, the *Verein* had the potential for continuous and cumulative empirical social research, yet this potential was not realized. The reasons for this are several.

The German academic and intellectual milieu, especially in the social and cultural sciences, was characterized by frequent controversies and fights (*Streiten*) over philosophic issues, which easily led to prolonged personal polemics, open hostility, and intense rivalries among the very professors who were meant to collaborate in the *Verein für Sozialpolitik* surveys. The *Verein* did not have a permanent, central staff and a continuous source of funds for research at its disposal. Collective research undertakings depended on enlisting the cooperation of individual professors who would then recruit students through their research seminars to get the fieldwork done. The students in turn would write a report, which would become a dissertation and then be published in the social science journals attached to various universities or professors, or in the *Verein's* own publications. Economics students typically were not scholarly oriented, tended to spend but a short time at any single university, and in any case were required to produce only a modest piece of research in order to obtain a Ph.D. degree. This organizational structure was not suited to produce large-scale empirical investigations and a high quality of output.

Moreover, the *Verein für Sozialpolitik,* as the National Association for the Promotion of Social Science in Britain in the midnineteenth century, was explicitly concerned with suggesting practical measures for social reform, social engineering, and legislation. After a study was completed, members passed resolutions at the large annual meetings. The attention of the members was centered on political debates rather than on a critical review of the quality of the findings and on the techniques of research utilized. The university professor concentrated in his own professional work on philosophic and historical topics, or engaged in more narrow, specific, economic investigations. Empirical social research was thus important to the German professor

in his capacity as citizen but not in his disciplinary role. Several independent efforts to provide a more secure financial and professional base
for social research by means of alternative structural arrangements such
as institutes or observatories, to use Tönnies' term, were all unsuccessful
before World War I.[19] During the Weimar period, the volume of output
of social research increased considerably.[20] In addition to the condition
of the working class, the topics studied dealt with child development,
youth, the position of women in society, salaried employees, and many
others. Few researchers were university sociologists, and the link between
academic sociology and social research remained tenuous. A research
institute for social science was created in 1919 and was attached to the
newly founded University of Köln, but its financial backing was modest,
depending as it did on the municipal administration of Köln. According
to one of its original and senior members, Leopold von Wiese,

In the present condition of sociology as a science, it still does not possess a costly
research organization. Almost everything still depends on the intense, personal
dedication of individual researchers.[21]

In 1924, the *Institut für Sozialforschung* was
created at Frankfurt University as a result of a local businessman's generous gift. Subsequently, an important and theoretically relevant
research project was conducted at the Institute by university professors.[22]
It remained, however, a unique undertaking, and in any case the Hitler
era cut these developments abruptly off.

Sociology in Germany suffered from a weak-
ness in demand outside of the circle of university professors who were
sociologically oriented within their respective disciplines. The founding
nucleus that created the German Sociological Society in 1910 included
some distinguished professors of history, economics, law, religion, and
philosophy, yet these disciplines were so broadly defined in Germany
that scholars with a sociological disposition could fit into existing career
patterns. Many traditionalists opposed sociology because of its allegedly
positivist, foreign, and socialist orientation, and sociology lacked support
in the civil service and the government, an important weakness in a state-
run university system. After World War I, the Social Democrats were
more favorably inclined to establish chairs of sociology and courses of
instruction, and some progress was made in this direction, but economic
recovery, inflation, and later the economic depression and political tur-
moil preceding the Nazi seizure of power certainly represented an unu-
sually unfavorable environment for institutional innovation backed by
resources.[23] The sociologists themselves were primarily concerned with
academic legitimation and with defining and delimiting their discipline,
which in the German academic milieu could only be done by engaging

in philosophic debates over method, values, and objectivity in the cultural sciences. These concerns largely determined the content of German sociology in the Weimar years.

The cases of France and the United States need only detain us briefly because they form the topic of two papers in this volume. In the United States, sociology and social research were both successfully institutionalized in the university by the mid-1920s, and most successfully at the University of Chicago. The demand for sociology and social research originated in the same source: the powerful and broadly based reform movement at the turn of the century and its subsequent offshoots which included the Protestant social gospel movement, the Progressives, muckrakers and municipal reformers, the charities and corrections movement, the social settlements, and others as well. The large number of social workers, investigators, administrators, and philanthropists demanded training in a higher educational setting and the prestige of a college degree, and a scientific justification for the reform movement itself because ameliorism was contrary to the tenets of laissez-faire economics and Social Darwinism, the dominant ideologies of the age. The early American sociologists obligingly fulfilled this instructional and ideological demand. In return they got the powerful backing of the reform movement for establishing a firm departmental foothold in the university. The fact that the institutions of higher education were recent, highly competitive, and generously financed certainly contributed to the speed and success of role and disciplinary differentiation. On the supply side, the somewhat earlier professionalization of economics made it attractive for a variety of Protestant ministers, journalists, reformers, and social scientists with a scientific inclination and academic aspirations to throw in their lot with sociology when they found economics as a discipline closed to them.

In France, the crucial demand for sociology came from the republican political leaders and administrators in the Third Republic who wished to secularize the secondary-school curriculum hitherto strongly influenced by a Roman Catholic outlook. In their view, *lycée* teachers needed to acquire a secular, republican, anti-clerical, and nationalist outlook which the existing system of producing secondary-school teachers was not accomplishing. For this purpose, they were searching for and willingly backed a new discipline that was founded on a secular moral philosophy and that could provide courses of instruction in it in a systematic and scientific manner. Increased political and scientific competition with Germany also made educational reform imperative, and resources for university innovation were more readily made available than would have been the case otherwise. The highly centralized, state-controlled French university system did not impede but favored this process because a small group in top authority positions could overcome the vested interests within the system opposed to sociology as a new discipline. Durkheim was the right man at the right time and place. His republican, nationalist, secular outlook and academic credentials were beyond dispute, and his conception of sociology filled the bill for a positivist, scientific, secular moral philosophy. His competitors were either pro-Catholic, monarchists, anglophiles lacking in nationalist zeal, foreigners, or part-time academics lacking the proper academic degrees and career patterns expected of university professors. Some did secure positions in peripheral higher education institutions, but Durkheim and his followers occupied center stage. They used their influence to exclude all outsiders from desirable positions and to sponsor members of their own school. The intellectual brilliance and originality of Durkheim certainly helped his success, but it was not the decisive factor. There is no need to pursue the topic further because Terry Clark's paper in this volume covers the ground with greater detail and authority.

It is hoped that the theoretic scheme outlined in this introduction will provide one way in which the reader can profitably approach the contributions included in this book.

notes

1 See "Sociology: Early History of Social Research," *International Encyclopedia of the Social Sciences* (New York: Macmillan and Free Press, 1968); Heinz Maus, "Zur Vorgeschichte der empirischen Sozialforschung," in *Handbuch der empirischen Sozialforschung,* 1 (Stuttgart: Enke Verlag, 1961); and Paul F. Lazarsfeld, "Notes on the History of Quantification in Sociology—Trends, Sources and Problems," *ISIS*, 52:2 (June 1961).

2 G. G. Granger, *La Mathématique Sociale de Condorcet* (Paris: PUF, 1956).

3 In economics, one of the earliest exponents is F. Y. Edgeworth, *Mathematical Psychics: An Essay on the Application of Mathematics to the Moral Sciences* (London, 1881). In sociology, it took over a century: James S. Coleman, *Introduction to Mathematical Sociology* (New York: Free Press, 1964).

4 The most comprehensive account of the public hygienists and medical topographers is George Rosen, *A History of Public Health* (New York: MD Publications, 1958).

5 J. B. Parent-Duchatelet, *De la Prostitution dans la Ville de Paris* (Paris: 1837), 2 vols.

6 See also Lazarsfeld, *op. cit.,* especially pp. 311-332.

7 See for instance Hinton R. Helper, *The Impending Crisis of the South* [New York: Collier, 1963 (first published in 1857)]. Much of it is based on a quantitative comparison between slave states and free states. He writes (p. 40): "To

say nothing of the sin and the shame of slavery, we believe it is a most expensive and unprofitable institution. . . . Few persons have an adequate idea of the important part that cardinal numbers are now playing in the cause of liberty. . . . Intelligent businessmen from the Chesapeake to the Rio Grande are beginning to see that slavery, even in a mercenary point of view, is impolitic, because it is unprofitable. Those unique, mysterious little Arabic sentinels on the watch-towers of political economy, 1, 2, 3, 4, 5, 6, 7, 8, 9, 0, have joined forces, allied themselves to the powers of freedom, and are hemming in and combatting the institution with the most signal success. If let alone, we have no doubt the digits themselves would soon terminate the existence of slavery."

8 Anthony Oberschall, *Empirical Social Research in Germany, 1848-1914,* (Paris: Mouton, 1965), chap. 3.
9 *Ibid.,* pp. 21-27 and chap. 4.
10 Joseph Ben-David, "The Scientific Role: The Conditions of Its Establishment in Europe," *Minerva,* 4:1 (Autumn 1965), 15-54.
11 Joseph Ben-David and Randall Collins, "Social Factors in the Origins of a New Science" *American Sociological Review,* 31:4 (August 1966), 451-465.
12 Joseph Ben-David and Awraham Zloczower, "Universities and Academic Systems in Modern Society," *European Journal of Sociology,* 3 (1962), 45-84.
13 Philip Abrams, *The Origins of British Sociology, 1834-1914* (Chicago: University of Chicago Press, 1968).
14 Abrams, *op. cit.,* pp. 4-5.
15 *Ibid.,* pp. 109-111.
16 *Ibid.,* p. 149.
17 *Ibid.*
18 Oberschall, *op. cit.*
19 *Ibid.,* pp. 60-63, 141-145.
20 For the Weimar period, I relied on Suzanne P. Schad's unpublished seminar paper, "Empirical Social Research in the Weimar Republic," Columbia University, Sociology Department, 1965. She has now completed a dissertation on this topic.
21 Leopold von Wiese, *Kölner Vierteljahrshefte für Soziologie,* 4 (1924/25), 123.
22 *Studien über Autorität und Familie* (Paris, Alcan, 1936).
23 A list of sociology courses and university positions was published from time to time in the *Kölner Vierteljahrshefte für Soziologie.* See in particular Vol. 1 (1921), 86-90, and Vol. 4 (1924/25), 316-329. Typical of the many statements of opposition to sociology on the part of university professors is Georg von Below, "Sociologie als Lehrfach" *Schmollers Jahrbuch,* 43:4 (1919), 59-110.

social science
in the age
of
newton

•

sir g.n. clark

The economic writers in the age of Newton
showed few traces of the scientific spirit. They, and their contemporaries who wrote about similar subjects, were not patient, thorough, and
impartial like the scientists, yet in various ways the manner and even
the methods of science cast a reflection on what was written about economics and other social questions. Various writers began to hope that
they might discover social truths by the same processes which were laying bare so many hidden physical truths. In every period the active and
progressive branches of thought are bound to exercise this influence
outside their own borders. As theology provided medieval thought with
its framework and its language; as biology dominated the thought of the
later nineteenth century; so physical science left its impress on seventeenth-century thought. It could not, indeed, simply be extended without alteration to cover social facts. These offered no opportunity for
experiment, nor for observation with instruments. Social science, when
it came, had to be different in these and other ways from natural science, and no one yet used the name "social science" in any language;
but the thing was coming into existence.

A number of English and continental writers
laid it down that politics was a science. In the year of the foundation of
the Royal Society, for instance, Saint-Évremond, a Frenchman living in

Reprinted from G. N. Clark, *Science and Social Welfare in the Age of Newton* (London: Oxford University Press, 1948), with the permission of the author and the publisher.

Sir G. N. Clark is the British historian and authority on the seventeenth century. His books include *The Seventeenth Century* (1929), *The Later Stuarts* (1934), *Science and Social Welfare in the Age of Newton* (1937), and *War and Society in the Seventeenth Century* (1958).

London, wrote a letter in which he included it among the sciences which particularly deserved the attention of gentlemen.[1] The others were ethics and polite learning, so that what he had in mind was not science in the narrower sense; but other authors applied the idea more strictly. About the same time economists and political writers began to use phrases which had originally expressed mechanical notions. The metaphor of the balance of trade was probably derived from the balance in bookkeeping; but in the late seventeenth century it was used along with several similar expressions connected in people's minds with another kind of balance, equilibrium as the physicists studied it. There was the balance of property, a balance of parties,[2] the balance of power. It is even said, though I have not seen any proof of it, that the mere use of the word "powers," to describe states in their mutual relations, springs from this habit of thought. It was not a mere matter of language. There were writers who hoped that the new knowledge would be extended systematically over the whole universe, and they did not ignore the life of men in societies. Bacon included it equally with physical nature in his great program for the future of learning. In this, as in many other respects, he did not foresee the exact course which the future was to take; but he was right in thinking that thought about man would advance in some sort of connection with thought about nature.

In the century which began with Bacon and ended with Newton, the most tangible product of this connection was the rise of statistics, the quantitative study of social facts. It is well known that modern statistical studies trace their continuous history back to the publication in 1662, once again the year of the foundation of the Royal Society, of John Graunt's *Observations upon the Bills of Mortality*. Among the earliest fellows of the Society there was an active group who were interested in this new study, which was then called "political arithmetic." There are many textbooks of the history of statistics in which the new study is connected with the immediately preceding advances in mathematical knowledge, and with the scientific interests of that generation; but it is quite wrong to think that it arose from the sudden application of mathematics to the investigation of society. Statistics did not start from nothing; it built higher a long-standing structure. To understand its relation to the scientific movement as a whole, we must make a rapid survey of the use of quantitative methods in social matters over a long preceding period.

We cannot assign to this, any more than to any other great historical phase of thought, a definite beginning. Far back in the Middle Ages tables of figures were constructed for certain specific purposes of government. The Anglo-Saxon systems of government were based on enumerations of families: several of these are

preserved in Bede's *Ecclesiastical History*.[3] The "Tribal Hidage," a tabular statement of the number of "hides" in England, by districts and with
totals for larger areas, probably goes back in its original form to the
seventh century.[4] For military and financial purposes statesmen necessarily thought in terms of figures; but in the Middle Ages such special
concerns were few, and numerical calculation was not extended beyond
them or used as an instrument of thought except in very narrow departments. Domesday Book, that wonderfully minute and complete review
of the resources of a kingdom, does not contain estimates of their totals,
and modern antiquarians have had to make their Domesday statistics
for themselves. For William the Conqueror the totals would have had no
practical value. What he wanted was to know his precise rights in each
place. Whenever any payment fell due he wanted to exact the full
amount, and the information he collected enabled him to do this at the
time and place where, but for this knowledge, he might have been
cheated. He did not attempt or need to see what the whole amounted
to, because the money he received did not form a whole, a single fund.
Each payment, as it came in, was earmarked for a specific purpose. The
money was only a small part of his dues: his army was provided by tenants owing military service, and many of his other needs by tenants who
owed service in the administration, or by payments of food and other
goods in kind. There was no public revenue in the modern sense, to be
added up in a single total and allocated to the different needs of government.

In the later Middle Ages there are signs that
people connected with government were beginning to use collections of
figures as the framework of their thoughts about policy. Common medieval thought, as exemplified for instance in the chronicles, handled figures as carelessly as Herodotus; but there is a type of naive curiosity
which likes to collect figures, and in the fifteenth century, if not earlier,
this was coming into alliance with political knowledge. There was, for
instance, an Englishman, apparently concerned with administration in
East Anglia, who jotted down, as he came across them, figures of the
length and breadth of England, the length of the coastline, the number
of parish churches, of villages, of counties, of bishops, the number of
dioceses in the world.[5] He cannot very well have had any practical use
for them, but his curiosity about figures was already leading to comparisons, and this obscure Englishman was only one step away from the
point of view of one of his most famous contemporaries, the central
figure of the political thought of the Italian Renaissance. Machiavelli
used a figure whenever he could. His figures are few, and they are not
all good,[6] but he had a grasp of the value of figures in shaping policy.
They are one of the elements in his comparisons of the resources of

different states, data in those calculations of strength which are characteristic of the modern tendency in his age.

This modern tendency affected the attitude of
princes to the government of their states. If Domesday Book is compared with the surveys of their resources made by princes in the sixteenth century, it will be seen that the social foundations of the state
had changed so that a public revenue was now the main contribution of
a country to the upkeep of government, and this revenue had to be estimated, not perhaps as a single whole, but in a few large branches, and
not merely in each year but with rough forecasts for the future. Armies
were now hired for pay; civil servants were salaried officials; military
stores, far more expensive than before, had to be bought from contrac-
tors, and so on through most of the activities of the state. In a more
complicated economic system the ascertainment of a prince's right had
to be done with a more advanced method, the more so because opposition was becoming more ingenious and itself rested sometimes on special
legal or economic knowledge.

As an illustration of this stage of development
we may take the statistical work of a German ruler, the Landgrave
William IV of Hesse-Cassel, who ruled from 1567 to 1592.[7] Like some
of his contemporaries he made a thorough survey of his revenues, and
he had two special reasons for doing it; he had inherited a territory
diminished in area and therefore needing reorganization, and in contests
with his feudatories and with popular rights he wanted to equip himself
with the unbreakable weapon of exact figures. The result is embodied
in a composite volume known since the eighteenth century as the *Economic State*. At first sight it appears almost miscellaneous. It begins
with a very detailed list of fiefs, giving even fuller particulars than
Domesday Book, of the agrarian arrangements, mills, fisheries, taxes,
and saltworks. It continues with estimates for the expenses of the court
and administration, tables of dietary and purchase prices for the court,
of the equivalent values of coins, of wages, and finally a survey of military arrangements, including estimates of expenses based on two actual
campaigns in the past. Some things are embedded in it which do not
concern us now, but with these exceptions it is all taken up with counting and measuring. The technique is much more developed than that of
Domesday Book. There is a table for the conversion of measures of
capacity and weight. The estimates of the values of properties are based
on averages for three, six, or nine years.

This last point shows that simple mathemat-
ical calculations were being used in public affairs.[8] In this instance it is
significant that William IV was not only a good administrator with able
ministers to help him, but also one of those Renaissance princes who

made use of science in their work. He was an astronomer of repute and he showed interest in various branches of science and mathematics. His revised book of fiefs was accompanied by a set of estate maps which are notable in the history of cartography. About the same time English land-owners were ordering those beautiful and accurate maps of which hundreds still survive in their muniment rooms. The advance in map-making in the late sixteenth century resulted very clearly from a convergence of economic needs and intellectual progress. There had been great changes in the ownership of land, in its use, and in tenures: there was a need for the defining of rights. At the same time the art of surveying was improved: there were better instruments and better books on their use. This new cartography was used in the service of the state, for instance by the great Cecil in Elizabethan England, who employed more than one map-maker.[9] In all its aspects it was closely allied to statistics. The estate maps often had in the corners tables of the amounts of land held by different owners, or the numbers of beasts they had a right to pasture. The county maps of Saxton, the most notable of Cecil's cartographers, were accompanied by descriptions which gave figures. This was no accident but arose from the nature of the two methods. A map is an abstract statement based on measurement; statistics are abstract statements based on measurement, counting, and calculation. If this appears to be a farfetched identification, let it be remembered that two of the pioneers of statistical science, Petty and Gregory King, were surveyors before they were statisticians. Neither of them, at any point of his work, got very far away from the geographical point of view.[10]

Thus we find from the early days of the Renaissance the two always intermingling currents of science and *Wirtschaft*, private and political, bringing with them a more extended use of figures. In England statesmen made an increasing use of commercial information which we can hardly refuse to call statistical. Statistical information is collected because it is believed that quantitative knowledge will be useful in shaping policy: the sort of knowledge desired will depend on the prevailing economic conceptions. Once it has been obtained, this knowledge becomes one of the component factors of ideas and policy, so that statistics are historically always both a product and a determinant of thought and action. From the early seventeenth century the figures desired by politicians were those which would throw light on the balance of trade, for economic thought regarded that balance as the key to commercial policy. We possess several documents from the reign of James I in which experts in customs matters made calculations of English imports and exports.[11] Some of them are accompanied by polemical notes maintaining that certain ways of making these calculations are right, and other ways fallacious. In comparison with modern trade figures all these calculations are, to be sure, extremely rough. Even supposing that the customs returns on which they were based were fairly accurate, the margin of error was far too large for any but the most elementary conclusions to be drawn. In spite of this such figures continued to be prepared all through the seventeenth century, not only in England, but in those other countries which had a customs system capable of providing suitable materials.

This point had already been reached when Bacon gathered together many prevailing ideas in his project for a conscious advance of universal science. With him indeed it was no more than a project, and some of his followers only added a formal rigidity to the project without advancing it in substance. This seems to me to be true of the best-known representatives of the "pansophic" tendency, such as Comenius, whose *Triertium Catholicum* is an overelaborate scheme for correlating all branches of knowledge.[12] If, however, the attempt to work out a comprehensive system of all the sciences proved to be barren, it was closely related to two other attempts which yielded abundant fruits.

Of these the first was the encyclopedic tendency. We may indeed talk about an encyclopedic tendency in various senses. It may be understood as meaning simply universal curiosity, and in this sense it flourished exuberantly in the early seventeenth century;[13] but it is more commonly taken to mean something more systematic. Curiosity, indeed, can hardly ever be utterly indiscriminate; the merest collector of information usually collects information of some particular kind. Compilers and collectors of information were very active, among them collectors of political and social information. The politics of the time, especially its international politics, created a new demand for political information. Machiavelli's studies of foreign countries were followed by a growing mass of diplomatic *relazioni*, spreading, as the scope of alliances widened, over all Europe, Asia, and America. The wars and religious movements brought the newsletter and the newspaper, and along with them there came into existence books which gave the background of the news for the statesman and the general reader, as the diplomatic reports had given it for the statesman alone. Some were superficial and, for the distant countries, even fabulous; but by the middle of the century it was possible to buy a tolerably good Latin account of the constitution of every important European country, and of the social economy of some of them.[14] Material of this kind was used by teachers in some of the continental universities, and it is of it that the adjective *statisticum* was first used.[15] Attempts were made, in a uniform series of books, and even in single folio volumes, to give this sort of survey of the whole world.

The collection and arrangement of data led, as it often has done in the history of thought, to systematic interpretation, and it did so in this instance because the spirit of the scientific movement penetrated to social studies. Descartes himself, who brought the scientific movement to maturity in his mathematical, determinist, materialist physics, did not include man and social relations in his own scope; but it was easy for others to bring them in. His contemporary Hobbes constructed a system of determinist and materialist ethics and politics. In the middle and the second half of the seventeenth century there were many discussions as to how far the Cartesian method could be extended to man. The greatest of all philosophical problems were involved in these discussions, and it is no part of our present task to trace how they ultimately led to the separation of science from philosophy and theology which was impending in the time of Newton. What we now have to observe is that at one stage of the discussions there definitely emerged a determinist and materialist tendency in historical thought.[16] We find it fully developed in the works of Sir William Temple. As a young man he was, at least nominally, the pupil of Ralph Cudworth, one of the Cambridge Platonists, and the Cambridge Platonists were in the thick of the controversies about the metaphysics of Descartes. Temple conversed with many of the leading men in Holland, especially his friend John de Witt, whom we shall mention again, and it was in Holland that Cartesianism was first taught in universities. It would be oversceptical to doubt that these influences helped him to the view that "most national customs are the effect of some unseen, or unobserved, natural causes or necessities." He studied politics and economics with the starting point of science, that the same cause will produce the same effect.[17]

Another stream which may be traced from the "pansophism" of Bacon's time was "pantometry," the belief that all things can be measured. The old desire for a scheme of all knowledge was bound to take this form when, with Descartes, the scientific movement came under the domination of mathematics. Descartes himself, in his philosophy, sought for certainties like those of mathematics. There were soon others who tried to reach certainty by the same method in other spheres, even the most unlikely. Spinoza's *Ethics* were *ordine geometrico demonstrata*; Newton's friend Craig and the physician George Cheyne tried to make a mathematical theology. These three attempts came some years after the beginnings of political arithmetic, but they will suffice to show that political arithmetic was not an isolated innovation but part of a wide intellectual movement.

In considering its antecedents we must look not only at the intellectual movement but also at its effects in everyday thought and practice. While, at the summit of the intellectual world, the leaders of thought were engaged with mathematics and the quantitative study of nature, the use of figures was becoming commoner and more skilful on the lower levels. Universities and schools spread the knowledge of elementary mathematics through the workaday world. In the commercial countries more and more "writing schools" taught the practice of bookkeeping by double entry. More and more people learnt to carry out measurements and simple calculations. The history of such knowledge among ordinary men is naturally hard to trace; but it seems clear that in this respect the second half of the seventeenth century showed a marked advance from the first half, at least in England. The school books were better and they indicate that a higher standard was required. It will be enough to mention one instance of this. In the first half of the century two systems of calculation were in use in private business. There was the method of written or mental arithmetic which we use now, and there was the more primitive system of manual arithmetic, reckoning by moving counters on a counting board. This latter now does not survive in England at all except that something like it is used as a means of teaching children to count with the abacus. We know with reasonable certainty that it ceased to be used by adults in the second half of that century.[18]

By all these processes the way was prepared for political arithmetic. The event usually taken as marking its beginning was indeed the emergence of a new kind of statistical inquiry, more ambitious and more exact than anything that had been attempted before. Graunt's book was called *Natural and Political Observations . . . upon the Bills of Mortality . . . with Reference to the Government, Religion, Trade, Growth, Ayre, Diseases, and the several Changes of the said City* of London. The Bills of Mortality were returns of the deaths which occurred in London. They were prepared by the Parish Clerk's Company, one of the city livery companies, and the first published specimen goes back to 1592. From 1603 they were published uninterruptedly once a week, and the number of parishes included in them was from time to time increased. The only plausible reason that can be assigned for their publication is that they were meant to give warning, or to allay false apprehensions, of outbreaks of the plague, and this is confirmed by a number of circumstances, such as the dates 1592 and 1603, which were both plague years. Sprat, the historian of the Royal Society, was, however, justified in writing that before Graunt's time these papers "went about so many years, through every Tradesman's hands, without any manner of profit, except only to the Clerks that collected them."[19] We may notice that their end was worse than their beginning. In the nineteenth century a number of parishes ceased to make returns to the Company and the Company, having no means of compulsion, continued to make increasingly defective returns. From 1840 the registrar general's office published complete weekly bills; but the old series, though now utterly valueless, continued to appear year after year.[20] The energy devoted to publishing economic information is not always well directed. So little is known about Graunt's life that it is impossible to say either how he got his mathematical training or how he came to study vital statistics. His election as an original member of the Royal Society, and the publication of a third edition of his book in 1665 for the use of its members, prove that it at once found an appreciative audience among the scientists.

There has indeed been a controversy as to whether Graunt deserves the credit for this work or whether it should go to the extraordinary man with whom he was closely associated, Sir William Petty. That such a doubt should be possible is an added proof, as we saw in the case of disputed technological inventions, that the innovation was *partus temporis*; but the grounds for questioning Graunt's claim are not sufficient.[21] Graunt was a cautious, critical worker who, so far as he could, tested the value of his figures and limited his inferences to what appeared reasonably probable. Petty was a man of tumultuous versatility, who flung out a hundred suggestions for one that he considered in detail. He had been in touch with many currents of thought. Educated partly by the Jesuits at Caen, and partly in the medical schools of Leyden and Oxford, he had been amanuensis to Thomas Hobbes, the great English materialist and determinist philosopher. He was full of the idea that numbers could elucidate all sorts of practical affairs, and he gave the new science the name that it kept throughout the eighteenth century: "political arithmetic." In what he wrote, about population, trade, revenue, and defence, he used any figures that came to hand, however defective, and his conclusions were for the most part worthless. He convinced his contemporaries of the value of a study which he had not the patience to pursue.[22]

One particular piece of work in which Graunt showed his more scientific attitude was an attempt to construct from the London figures a "life-table," a table exhibiting the number of persons who survived at certain ages. Such tables are nowadays in constant use in the offices of insurance companies and are printed in such books of reference as *Whitaker's Almanack*. Then they were a new invention, and life insurance was not yet a practical possibility, because its basis in calculation and known fact had not been laid. What method Graunt used is not quite clear, and as a mathematical exercise his attempt is inferior to those already made by the two great thinkers Pascal and Huygens about the calculation of chances in games of hazard, to which the same principles apply. Down to this time vital statistics were the concern only of private inquirers, and they had not reached the stage of practical application. In 1671 another step forward was taken. The great Dutch statesman John de Witt had to find money for a war against Louis XIV. He had been trained in mathematics and had written a book on geometry. With the advice of another mathematician he now tried to calculate the capital value of state annuities. He had to rely on conjecture for the figures of the expectation of life; but he followed the method of Huygens, and his confidence in that method heralds a new era in finance.[23] The first really sound table was that by Halley, derived from the figures of mortality in Breslau, and printed in the *Philosophical Transactions.*[24] The primary interest of such calculations was still that of state finance; the government of William III raised various war loans for which it paid in the form of life annuities; but within a few years the history of the true life insurance began, with its far-reaching social consequences, and its great incidental reinforcement of the belief in statistical method.[25]

Statistics as we know them in modern life are very different from these crude anticipations. They are manipulated by means of a highly specialized technique, designed to test the data thoroughly and to extract from them everything that they can be legitimately made to prove. This technique would not have grown up if it had not been for the development of the external machinery by which the data are provided. In the social and economic sphere the large numbers appropriate for it have been for the most part collected, and in the eighteenth century could only be collected, by the state. The beginning of the modern period may be put at 1801 when both England and France for the first time took a census of population, for the census figures are the measuring scale of all our other immense statistical accumulations. Yet, although the connection is indirect, some light is thrown on the transition from the early to the modern statistics by the history of commercial statistics from the time of Petty. These were collected not by private inquiries but by the state. During the period of Colbert ministers, both in France and England, sometimes tried to get better and fuller trade figures. In France there was a serious obstacle in the way: even after the reforms of Colbert the tariff system was so complicated that the government could not construct satisfactory national figures. England, however, was a single unit for customs purposes. In 1671 the government took over almost all the customs administration from the farmers and soon afterwards the increasing demand for more accurate figures at last brought about a striking advance. What decided it was the financial crisis of 1695-1696. This was one of the worst moments of the wars against Louis XIV: there had been heavy losses of shipping, the currency was in a bad way, and a recoinage had to be undertaken.

Parliament inquired with alarming pertinacity into the causes of the mis-carriages, and one of the permanent results of these inquiries was the creation of the office of the inspector general of imports and exports, the first special statistical department successfully created by any western European state.

The inspector general was an official of the customs, and he reported regularly to parliament, the treasury, and the newly created board of trade. He and his clerks drew up, from materials supplied by the customs officers, full and minute annual accounts by quantities and estimated money values, of all English imports and exports. From time to time they extracted, as they were called for, returns of special commodities or of trade with particular countries. Their methods, though in some ways open to criticism from the start, were at any rate much more satisfactory than those that had previously been known. Mr. R. M. Lee has shown that the initiative which led to the statistical work of the board of trade came from the economist Charles Davenant.[26] It seems certain that the new office was not copied from any foreign model. There is nothing to connect it with the names of any of the early statisticians. Petty and Graunt were dead; Halley was employed in 1696 in the recoinage but seems never to have worked at trade figures; but Gregory King, the most important economic statistician of his day, appears to have been employed by the treasury at or about this time.[27] It would, however, scarcely be rash to say that the foundation of the new office was partly due to the popularity of political arithmetic. The same crisis which brought it into existence also caused the foundation of the board of trade, and the board of trade, of which Locke was a member, also exemplified the now prevailing belief in the value of figures. When it turned its attention to the poor law, it obtained, through the archbishops, returns from the clergy of the amounts paid in each of their parishes in poor relief.[28] The number of replies received was only 4415, less than half that of the parishes in England; but the attempt, for which there was no precedent, was a symptom of the new intellectual attitude to social questions.

There is another instance, close to these in time, of the exact quantitative study of economic facts. These were facts of the past, including the remote medieval past; but the impulse to study them probably came partly from the currency problems of the reign of William III. The facts themselves, with much in the way of interpretation, were given in 1706 in a book called *Chronicon Preciosum* by William Fleetwood, afterwards bishop of Ely. It was the first noteworthy European book on the history of prices, and it remained for many years the best book on that new subject. Like the books on political arithmetic it had roots in various earlier lines of inquiry, but in a general way it belongs, like them, to the movement towards quantitative social science.

At the beginning of the eighteenth century this social science seemed to have an established position and a great future. The hopes of that time are well stated by Arbuthnot in his *Essay on the Usefulness of Mathematical Learning*. For the most part that essay follows familiar lines; but it contains one claim that Arbuthnot's predecessors had not made.

Arithmetic is not only the great instrument of private commerce, but by it are (or ought to be) kept the public accounts of a nation; I mean those that regard the whole state of a commonwealth, as to the number, fructification of its people, increase of stock, improvement of lands and manufactures, balance of trade, public revenues, coinage, military power by sea and land etc. Those that would judge or reason truly about the state of any nation must go that way to work, subjecting all the forementioned particulars to calculation. This is the true political knowledge. In this respect the affairs of a commonwealth differ from those of a private family, only in the greatness and multitude of particulars that make up the accounts. Machiavel goes this way to work in his account of different estates. What Sir William Petty and several other of our countrymen have wrote in political arithmetic, does abundantly show the pleasure and usefulness of such speculations. It is true, for want of good information, their calculations sometimes proceed upon erroneous suppositions; but that is not the fault of the art. But what is it the government could not perform in this way, who have the command of all the public records?[29]

This passage shows much wisdom. It is perhaps a little overcolored, for instance in the reference to Machiavelli; but in the main it represents the attitude of judicious men at that time. Leibniz, who had perhaps a wider outlook on the state of thought than any other man of his generation, wrote his view about another aspect of "pantometry" a couple of years later. He said that various authors had promised mathematical demonstrations in metaphysics and ethics but few had succeeded in them, because of the great trouble involved in carrying them out with rigor. They never could appeal to a wide audience; but investigators who undertook them in the proper way were not likely to repent it.[30] These hopes were not fulfilled. During the greater part of the eighteenth century the attempt to apply quantitative thought to human affairs made no substantial progress. It was allowed a place, if a modest place, in the general work of science, but the idea of an all-inclusive, mathematical study of the universe receded.

This may be illustrated from the form then taken by the encyclopedic tendency. In the early eighteenth century the standard encyclopedias began to take the form, familiar to us, of a number of separate articles arranged in alphabetical order. We expect, indeed, to find in an encyclopedia articles on philosophy and on the sciences

which shall show how they are related to one another; but the advantage
of the arrangement is, not only that it is convenient for ready reference,
but also that, when each branch of knowledge is growing in its own way
and without regard to its supposed place in an ideal whole, it can be
summarized by itself as a separate unit. Alphabetical order, as the plan
not merely of the index but of the whole work, means that, while the
attempt at comprehensiveness is still made, the systematic correlation
is relegated to a subordinate place. We may expect it to arise when knowledge is growing in many directions, and not in the framework of an
accepted interpretation of the whole. It was in such a condition of economic knowledge that Savary des Brulons planned his *Dictionnaire uni-
versel de commerce, d'histoire naturelle, d'arts et métiers*, posthumously
published in 1723 and afterwards adapted into English by Malachi
Postlethwayt. The conditions were similar in a wider sphere at that time,
when the Newtonian system was elbowing the old metaphysics aside,
and when the positive sciences were following divergent paths of observation and experiment. John Harris, a fellow of the Royal Society, published in 1704 the first edition of his *Lexicon Technicum*, an alphabetical dictionary of mathematics, science, and technology. Ephraim
Chambers, also a fellow, brought out in 1728 the first edition of his
still more comprehensive *Cyclopaedia*, from which all our many modern
encyclopedias are lineally descended.

On the practical and administrative side, as on
Chambers's two folio volumes were more com-
prehensive than those of Harris; they included a good deal, for instance,
about law and heraldry, which went beyond the boundaries of science;
but with one remarkable exception they let the social sciences alone.
Economics had not then reached the status of a science, and there is
only one economic article, on "Political Arithmetic." That social statistics won a place in this early encyclopedia was due to its having a mathematical form. But there was nothing in the rest of the encyclopedia to
connect it with any other branch of knowledge. It had no place except
its alphabetical place; its ascertained results were summarized in one
short article, and there was no sign of its possessing a living principle
capable of further great advances.

On the practical and administrative side, as on
the side of theory, the start made by statistics in the late seventeenth
century was hardly more than a false start. The English administration
methodically collected its figures of foreign trade, and they were increasingly used to support the arguments of pamphleteers and politicians.
The French and other governments found it convenient to set up similar
statistical offices; but the English commercial statisticians discovered no
important economic truth which was not otherwise known. At the most
they prepared the way for true quantitative thinking. They worked

usually in a spirit of unenterprising routine, and the best economic thinkers made little use of their materials, rightly considering that they were not
prepared with sufficient critical care. Adam Smith was in line with the
best of his predecessors when he dismissed the possibility of making accurate estimates of trade with the plain statement: "I have no great faith in
political arithmetic."[31] By this time the high hopes of Petty and Arbuthnot
were dead, and quantitative methods in economics and in social thinking
generally had to make a fresh start in the late eighteenth century.

       How are we to account for this interruption in
a movement which had seemed so powerful a century before? A full
answer would, no doubt, have to draw upon many factors of eighteenth-
century history, some of which have not been sufficiently explored for
a full answer to be possible as yet. Three things may, however, be said
which would form parts of the answer. First, the slack period of social
thought came at much the same time as a slack period of scientific
thought: the central eighteenth century was not, like the seventeenth, a
time of cardinal scientific discoveries. Second, on the side of practice,
the inactivity in exploring social facts was part of the general administrative torpor of England in the eighteenth century. In France, where
social administration was vigorous and intelligent, quantitative study
appears to have made more progress both in method and in achievement.
The third point is the most important, for it concerns the potentialities
of the quantitative method itself. The attempt was made to apply it
separately, not as one element in an all-round examination of human
and social life by all the methods that can explain them. Quantitative
study did not begin as part of a comprehensive social science, embody-
ing the knowledge that ethics, political thought, and theology had
already attained. It was not continuous with the main tradition of
thought on human problems; it even deliberately broke away. It did so
at a time, the late seventeenth century, when the old unities of thought
and action were everywhere falling apart; when science and philosophy,
philosophy and religion, religion and government were drifting away
from their old, sometimes quarrelsome, intimacies into estrangements,
mutual indifference, profound hostility. It began in isolation precisely
at the time when isolation was certain to make it sterile. Its disappoint-
ments were typical of an age in which Western civilization was breaking
up into parts that no longer made a whole.

notes

1   *Letters of Saint-Évremond,* ed. Hayward (1930), pp. 35-36. This is earlier than
    the other and more significant passages which I have cited in *The Seventeenth*
    Century (1929), p. 216.

2   This phrase corresponds to the practical aims of King William III in the earlier part of his reign, and is used by Defoe in his *Appeal to Honour and Justice* (1715), near the beginning. For the other phrases see *The Seventeenth Century*, p. 214.

3   Bk. II, c. ix; III, cc. iv, xxiv; IV, cc. iii, xiii, xvi, xix, xxiii; v, c. xix.

4   See J. Brownbill in *English Historical Review*, xxvii. 625, xl. 497: the latter article has a facsimile of the "English" text.

5   Bodleian MS. Tanner 70, fos. 37 v, 64, dating from *c.* 1484-1500.

6   At the end of the *Ritratti delle cose della Francia* he gives the number of parishes in England as 52,000; the Tanner MS. has 52,080. The real number is about 9000. The exaggerated estimate was current in the fourteenth century: see Stubbs, *Constitutional History*, 4th ed. (1906), ii. 442-443.

7   See Dr. Ludwig Zimmermann's excellent edition, *Der ökonomische Staat Landgraf Wilhelms IV*, 2 vols. (1933-1934).

8   I do not know whether the use of averages in calculations of the annual value of estates was practised earlier in Europe or in Asia. It was the basis of the land-revenue system of Mogul India at the beginning of the seventeenth century: see W. H. Moreland, *India at the Death of Akbar* (1920).

9   See Nowell's letter to him in R. Flower, *Laurence Nowell* (1936), p. 16. Sir Thomas Wilson, another protégé of Cecil and of his son, makes considerable use of figures in his State of England of 1600 printed in *Camden Miscellany*, xvi (1936).

10   Cf. Y. M. Goblet, 'Un précurseur anglais de la géographie humaine . . . Sir William Petty' in *Mélanges de géographie offerts á Vádar Švambera* (1936). This argument, however, should not be pushed too hard. Petty had also been an anatomist, and his *Political Anatomy of Ireland* is not different in method from his other books.

11   Brit. Mus. MS. Lansdowne 152, fos. 175 ff. (calculations of Sir Lionel Cranfield for London, 1605-1911, and of John Wostenholme for England, 1612-1614); *Acts of the Privy Council,* 1615-16, p. 479.

12   It was published in 1681, eleven years after the author's death; I have used the facsimile edition, with an epilogue by J. V. Kléma, which was published at Prague in 1920.

13   See, for instance, the admirable and entertaining chapter in which the Abbé Bremond showed its place in humanistic devotionalism: *Histoire littéraire du sentiment religieux en France,* i (1916), 255 ff.

14   For references see *The Seventeenth Century*, p. 215.

15   For instance in the title of the *Microscopium Statisticum, quo Status Imperii Romani Germanici representatur*, by Helenus Politianus. I have not been able to find a copy of this work in England.

16   Isolated instances of this tendency were, of course, known long before, such as the doctrine of the influence of climate on institutions, which was derived from Aristotle and other Greek writers.

17   *Observations upon the United Provinces* (1673), Introduction.

18   Barnard, *Casting-Counter and Counting-Board* (1917), pp. 87-88. It may be worth considering whether the intensified economic competition of the period of Louis XIV encouraged the increased use of mathematics, as it did other kinds of rationalization; but it would be difficult to find direct evidence on this question.

19   *History of the Royal Society* (1667) p. 243.

20   J. S. Wharton, *Law Lexicon*, 3rd ed. (1864), p. 121. For the bibliography of the Bills see N. G. Brett-James, *The Growth of Stuart London* (1935), pp. 534 ff.

21   For the present state of the discussion it is sufficient to refer to two convincing, though unnecessarily emotional, articles by Professor M. Greenwood in the *Journal of the Royal Statistical Society*, xci. 79 and xcvi. 76.

22   In addition to *The Economic Writings of Sir William Petty*, ed. C. H. Hull, 2 vols. (1899), which also contains Graunt's pamphlet, the *Life* by Lord Fitzmaurice (1895) and two publications edited by the late Lord Lansdowne, *The Petty Papers*, 2 vols. (1927), and *The Petty-Southwell Correspondence* (1928) should be used.

23   For references to expert discussions of this work see N. Japikse, *Johan de Witt*, 2d ed. (1928), p. 312, n. I.

24   Vol. xvii (1694) for 1693.

25   For its beginning see W. R. Scott, *History of Joint-Stock Companies to 1720*, iii (1911), 366 ff.

26   *English Historical Review, liv* (1939), 38 ff. For the foundation of the board, see P. Laslett in *William and Mary Quarterly*, xiv (1957), 370 ff.

27   This I infer from a number of papers in the important bundle of his unpublished "Exercises in Political Arithmetic" in the Public Record Office, T 64/302.

28   The papers relating to this matter are among the records of the old board of trade in the Public Record Office.

29   *Life and Works*, ed. Aitken (1892), pp. 421-422.

30   *Nouveaux essais* (1765), II, c. xxix, 12. This posthumously published book was written in 1703.

31   *Wealth of Nations*, ed. Cannan, ii. 36; see also i. 439.

the manchester statistical society: a case study of discontinuity in the history of empirical social research

•

david elesh

Recent research into the history of empirical social research has revealed, contrary to common assumption, a long chronology before Booth's classic study of the London poor. In England empirical interest in social statistics can be traced back to the political arithmeticians of the early seventeenth century. On the continent it developed, though to a far lesser extent, under the German "statisticians," who sought to establish a factual foundation for statecraft. As an approach to the study of social life, empirical research has a history reasonably continuous to the present day. But if one tries to find an articulated tradition of research through specific individuals, groups, and institutions, he is immediately confronted by a bewildering array of discontinuities and intellectual deadends. A typical instance is to be found

David Elesh is Assistant Professor of Sociology and a member of the Institute for Research on Poverty at the University of Wisconsin (Madison). Born in 1940, he received his B.A. from Reed College in 1962 and Ph.D. in Sociology from Columbia University in 1968. The author of a number of journal articles on methodology, organizational analysis, and poverty research, Elesh currently is completing a book on the factors affecting the distribution of physicians within cities, and analyzing the data from the urban negative income-tax experiment in New Jersey and Pennsylvania.

in the history of the English statistical societies. Founded in the period 1833-1838, these groups were organized to collect, analyze, and disseminate statistical information on the populations in their areas. In terms of the history of quantitative social research, their work is particularly significant insofar as it appears to represent one of the earliest uses of the social survey. Yet within ten years of their founding, all of these groups had ceased empirical work and most ceased to have any effective function at all. Today, quite transformed, only the Manchester and Royal (London) Societies remain. By 1887, Booth, their lineal descendant, could publish his studies of the London poor as if nothing like them had been known before. The question that immediately arises within the history and sociology of science is why the earlier researchers discontinued their work, why the empirical social research of the statistical societies failed to become institutionalized.

The question is applicable to larger problems than English social research in the first half of the nineteenth century. The history of science is full of discontinuities, of rediscoveries of older theories and methods. Examples are easily found. Harvey's "discovery" of blood circulation some years after the work of Servetius, determination of the principles of thermodynamics years after Gibbs, and Mendel's discovery of the laws of heredity years before all illustrate the often discursive course of scientific progress. It should not be surprising, then, that the history of social research follows patterns long established in natural science. And, no less than the history of natural science, the history of social research may help us to understand the conditions under which new ideas and social forms are accepted into existing intellectual traditions.

In this case study of the first and prototypical statistical society, the MSS, I shall suggest some reasons as to why the statistical societies failed to institutionalize empirical research as a means of dealing with social questions. It is in the nature of historical research that such an analysis is necessarily incomplete and provisional, yet I believe there is enough evidence to indicate that its essential outlines are correct and that the concepts here employed may be useful for the study of scientific discontinuities more generally.

The remainder of this paper is divided into three sections. The first describes the founders of the Society and the membership prior to 1841, the period of surveys. The second investigates the nature of their research, and the final section presents and applies a general scheme for analyzing the degree of institutionalization in a science from its published record and relates the findings to the specific set of external factors which hampered institutionalization.

the manchester statistical society

the founders

The founders and early members of the Manchester Statistical Society were men united by common social ideology, politics, religion, group affiliations, and kinship.[1] Foremost was a commitment to social reform. In their first *Annual Report* the founders stated that the Society owed its origin to

a strong desire felt by its projectors to assist in promoting the progress of social improvement in the manufacturing population by which they are surrounded. Its members are not associated merely for the purpose of collecting facts concerning the condition of the inhabitants of this district, as its name might seem to imply, but the first resolution entered on its minutes pronounces it to be a "Society for the discussion of subjects of political and social economy, and for the promotion of statistical inquiries, to the total exclusion of party politics."[2]

Benjamin Heywood, one of the founders, expressed himself as follows:

The improvement of the working classes is an object of paramount and urgent importance; and as it is the duty of every man to mark out for himself some sphere of active usefulness to his fellowmen, I would select the furtherance of this object for mine.[3]

The founders were five in number: William Langton, James Kay-Shuttleworth, Samuel Greg, William Rathbone Greg, and Heywood. All were friends, under 40 years old, and all were engaged in either philanthropy, cotton manufacture, or banking. All were Unitarians, and because of the lack of educational opportunities for dissenters, all were educated outside the country (four in Scotland, the other on the continent). Politically they were Whigs, and all had a history of active involvement in reform movements.[4]

The idea for the Society came from William Langton, born in Yorkshire in 1803, the son of a Preston merchant, who was educated in Switzerland, France, Italy, and Germany. From 1821 until 1829 he was active in business in Liverpool where he joined the Provident Society, bringing him into firsthand contact with the conditions of the poor. In 1829 he went to Manchester as cashier in Benjamin Heywood's bank, and together with Heywood and Kay-Shuttleworth established the Manchester and Salford District Provident Society in March 1833.[5] It was his work in this society that convinced him of the need for some agency to collect social data and he suggested to Kay-Shuttleworth that a Statistical Society be founded. This work was, however, but one facet of Langton's activities. In the same year he established the Manchester Athenaeum and lectured at the Manchester

Mechanics' Institute founded by Heywood with Heywood's brother
James. The following year he sat on a parliamentary committee to study
educational conditions in Manchester, and in 1837 he was active in
establishing the Manchester Society for the Promotion of National Education. He was a member of the Manchester Literary and Philosophical
Society and held office in the Chetham (historical) Society. In 1846 he
became the secretary of a committee organized to look into the possibility of a university for Manchester.

        The second founder, Kay-Shuttleworth, was
born in 1804; after serving in a bank for a time, he attended the University of Edinburgh where he was granted the M.D. degree in 1827. That
same year he came to Manchester and took the position of senior physician at Ancoats and Ardwicks Dispensary, which brought him into contact with the poorest parts of the population. His published work during
this period indicates a definite change of interests from medical questions to the conditions of the poor.[6] He believed the Reform Bill a necessary step toward improving these conditions, and in 1831 joined the
attack on Parliament with his *Letter to the People of Lancashire Concerning the Future Representation of the Commercial Interest.*[7] These
political activities were interrupted by the outbreak of a cholera epidemic, but it was during this epidemic that he prepared an indictment
of the conditions in the cotton industry, *The Moral and Physical Conditions of the Working Classes Employed in the Cotton Industry in Manchester,* published in 1832.[8] Earlier in the same year Kay-Shuttleworth
had accepted the secretaryship of the Manchester Board of Health and
used this position to collect some of the first statistical data on the conditions of the working classes.[9] His method was to create a subordinate
board of health in each of the 14 police districts of Manchester. The districts were then divided into sections and two or more inspectors
appointed from the inhabitants of the sections. These inspectors were
provided with "tabular queries" and went about inspecting the residents.
The residents themselves were asked few, if any, questions, and it may
be that Kay-Shuttleworth did not believe such interviews helpful. Two
of his "tabular queries" are reproduced in tables 1 and 2. Whatever the
value of this study, it is clear that Kay-Shuttleworth was actively interested in survey research before the Statistical Society came into being.
Where this interest might have led is impossible to tell, for Kay-Shuttleworth left Manchester to become assistant poor law commissioner in
East Anglia in 1835. He retained his membership in the Society even
after leaving the area but gave no more papers to it and his subsequent
influence on its development appears negligible.

        Shortly after Langton suggested the Statistical
Society, Kay-Shuttleworth discussed the matter with his friends, Samuel

table 1 · inquiries concerning the state of houses

district no._____

(name of street, court, etc.)	(no.)	(no.)		(name of street, court, etc.)	(no.)	(no.)
1 Is the house in good repair?			11	What is the state of the beds, closets, and furniture?		
2 Is it clean?						
3 Does it require whitewashing?			12	Is a private privy attached to the house?		
4 Are the rooms well ventilated, or can they be without change in windows, etc.?			13	Will the tenants assist in cleansing the streets and houses?		
5 Is the house damp or dry?			14	Will they allow the Town's Authorities to whitewash them, if they cannot conveniently do it themselves?		
6 Are the cellars inhabited?						
7 Are these inhabited cellars damp or ever flooded?			15	Are the tenants generally healthy or not?		
8 Are the soughs in a bad state?			16	What is their occupation?		
9 Who is the proprietor?			17	Remarks concerning food, clothing, and fuel		
10 What number of families or lodgers does the house contain?			18	Habits of life		
			19	General observations		

and William Rathbone Greg. Both men were cotton manufacturers devoted to improving the conditions of the working classes. Samuel had, two years before, established a model village along the lines of Robert Owen's New Lanark. Until 1846, he devoted the major portion of his time to improving the living conditions of his workers. In that year a strike forced him to give up the business, and embittered, he would have no more to do with the working class during the remainder of his life. Like all of the founders, he was also a member of the Manchester Literary and Philosophical Society.

William Rathbone was more politically minded than his brother and was active in the anti-corn law and antislavery movements. He also contributed to *Edinburgh* and *Pall Mall*, two literary periodicals of the time. In 1856 he became commissioner of customs, and in 1864 comptroller in Her Majesty's Stationery Office.

This conversation led to an organizational meeting at the home of Benjamin Heywood, a major force in Manchester civic affairs. Heywood had been active in organizing the Manchester Mechanics' Institute (1824) and the Provident Society already mentioned.

table 2 · inquiries concerning the state of streets, courts, alleys, etc.

district no. _____	inspectors _____		
names of streets, courts, alleys, etc.:	(name)	(name)	(name)
Is the street, court, or alley narrow, and is it ill-ventilated?			
Is it paved or not?			
If not, is it under the Police Act?			
Does it contain heaps of refuse, pools of stagnant fluid, or deep ruts?			
Are the public and private privies well situated and properly attended to?			
Is the street, court, or alley near a canal, river, or marshy land?			
General observations			

In 1831 he was elected to Parliament as the candidate of the Manchester Reform Committee and ruined his health fighting for the Reform Bill of 1832. He was an active member of the British and Foreign School Society and a founding member of the later Manchester Society for Promoting National Education (1837). He encouraged, financially and organizationally, savings banks, other provident associations, exhibitions of art and industry, the building of public baths and parks, and friendly societies.[10]

the early membership

These, then, were the founding members of the Society; for them the Society was a means to an end: social reform. They were bound together by similar educational background, group affiliations, perspectives, and kinship. In fact, the degree to which they were related to one another is a peculiar feature of the early members of the Society. The kinship ties of the founding members are diagrammed in table 3.

If the group of founders is expanded to include those figuring most importantly in the early surveys, it numbers 13.[11] The similarity of background and perspective found among the founders is reflected in the larger group as well. Of the 13, 10 were Nonconformist in their religion[12] and Whig in their politics.[13] Of the remaining three, one is known to have been an Anglican and no data on the remaining two were available. Eight of the group were related to at least one other member; eight found their relationships in the Statistical Society strengthened by a joint membership in the Manchester Literary and

table 3 · kinship in the manchester statistical society, 1833–1841

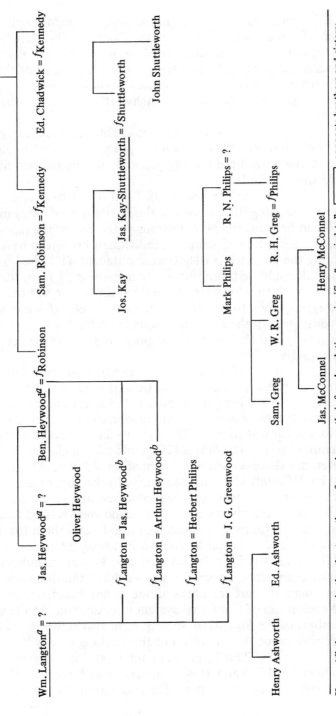

Key: All the names in the chart are those of members or their female relatives. = signifies "married to"; [connects brothers and sisters; vertical lines denote "son or daughter of." Founders of the Society are underlined.
a Officeholder.
b Two Heywood sons married two Langton daughters, but the evidence is not conclusive that the sons were James and Arthur.
f Female.

Philosophical Society. Six were active in the Manchester Mechanics Institute; five were also members of the Provident Society. The Manchester Chamber of Commerce claimed four members, one of whom, Robert Hyde Greg, served as president. Greg also served as president of the Anti-Corn Law Association in 1839; the Association found at least six active supporters in the group, and one, Henry Ashworth, was one of the founders of it.

Thus the same broad aim of social betterment linked all of those active in the early survey work, and it may be said that this goal characterized the Society generally during the period of surveys, 1833 through 1841.

In the year 1839-1840 the Society contained sixty members—assuming little attrition, this figure incorporates most of those who had been members in previous years. By culling names from various sources, some 55 names of individuals known to have been members during the period 1833-1840 were obtained. Of these, no information at all could be found for 4; the remaining 51 form the basis of the following analysis. However, it should again be stressed that these were not the type of men to be found in the *Dictionary of National Biography*; consequently the amount of data available for a given individual varies greatly and the figures to be presented are, at the very least, highly tentative.

Of these 51, 42 were active in some form of social reform activity aside from their participation in the Statistical Society. This is not to say that the remaining 9 did not engage in reform activities, only that there was insufficient information to characterize them. The Nonconformists numbered 25 of the 51, members of the established church, 6, and the others (20) could not be classified. On political preference there is even less information; 23 were Whigs, but only 1 could be definitely classified as a Tory. In the larger membership, too, the same pattern of kinship that was observed before can be found: no less than 23 of the members during this period were related to at least 1 other member. Common associations also bound them together; 16 were active in the Manchester Mechanics Institute, 29 held membership in the Literary and Philosophy Society, and 11 were members of the Chamber of Commerce. Education was a subject that interested many of these men: 19 were members of one or more societies to encourage the adoption of a national system of education. At the same time, 20 members of the Statistical Society were also active in organizations concerned about the condition of the working classes.[14]

This brief characterization of the general membership between 1833 and 1840 is in accord with those of the founders and early survey researchers. Their backgrounds and patterns of association and interests clearly indicate the same basic concern with social policy and social reform. It included nine members of Parliament, two mayors of Manchester, six city aldermen, two newspaper editors, and nine assorted federal and local officials from the secretary to the Committee of Council (forerunner to Board of Education) to the Director of the Manchester Gas Works.[15]

With this introduction, the Society's research itself will be discussed in the following section. The noninstitutionalization of survey research will be demonstrated on the internal evidence of this work. Subsequently, a final section will offer an attempt to account for the lack of institutionalization.

the work of the
manchester statistical society

the surveys—an overview

It is possible to obtain some estimate of the general nature of the research in the period 1833-1863 by taking the papers presented at the annual meetings of the British Association for the Advancement of Science during this period as an index of the Society's work. While this index provides a slightly better time series than the available reports of the Society, it is least informative in the 1840s, where it need be most. From 1834[16] to 1863, members of the Manchester Statistical Society read 56 papers before the British Association, but only 7 of these were given in the years 1843-1853, and from 1847 to 1851 no papers at all were read (see Column 1 of table 4). Column 4 gives the total number of papers presented. Table 4 shows that the Manchester men concentrated their contributions in the early and late parts of the period. There is no apparent reason for the distribution. It may have represented a conscious decision not to participate in the British Association on the part of the Society or a change of emphasis in its mode of publication; there is simply no evidence to account for it.[17]

Column 2 of table 4 gives the number of papers read before the British Association reporting "original survey research" by year. As can be seen, 14 such surveys were reported from 1834 to 1841, but none thereafter. This, of course, is the basic problem of this paper: why did they stop. But while some suggestions will be offered as to why no further original research was done, there are none to indicate why it ended so abruptly.[18]

Column 3 documents the shift after 1841 from original surveys to secondary analyses. A typical example of such secondary analyses is Henry Ashworth's "Statistics of the Present Depression

table 4 · number of papers read before the statistics section of the british association for the advancement of science by members of the manchester
statistical society by year, 1834-1863

year	total	original surveys[a]	secondary analyses[b]	total (including non-manchester papers)
1834	1	1	–	4
1835	5	2	–	14
1836	1	–	–	12
1837	5	5	–	17
1838	–	–	–	–
1839	3	3	–	11
1840	1	1	–	21
1841	3	2	–	13
1842	9	–	8	18
1843	1	–	1	1
1844	–	–	–	–
1845	3	–	3	17
1846	2	–	2	14
1847	–	–	–	–
1848	–	–	–	–
1849	–	–	–	–
1850	–	–	–	–
1851	–	–	–	–
1852	1	–	1	1
1853	–	–	–	–
1854	1	–	1	1
1855	–	–	–	–
1856	–	–	–	–
1857	2	–	–	40
1858	3	–	–	30
1859	–	–	–	–
1860	2	–	–	17
1861	9	–	2	34
1862	2	–	2	16
1863	2	–	1	17
Total	56	14	21	287

[a] Four papers were unclassifiable.
[b] Original surveys and secondary analysis do not add to the total number in the
first column because other types of papers read were not separately classified
above.

of Trade at Bolton; showing the mode in which it affects the different
Classes of a Manufacturing Population."[19] The paper is based upon Manchester Chamber of Commerce statistics, the written reports of various
trade committees, and returns made by mill proprietors to a parish

officer. Ashworth's social classes are really occupational categories such
as mill owners, iron founders, engineers, millwrights, machine makers,
carpenters, weavers, cotton hands, laborers, and the like. Because his
data differ for different occupational groups, his mode of analysis is
also varied. Mill owners are analyzed in terms of their losses under conditions of full and slack production, the more skilled occupations in
terms of their unemployment, and the less skilled in terms of their unemployment, general living situation (presence of furniture, bedding, use of
pawnshops, etc.), and relief.

An especially interesting aspect of Ashworth's
analysis is the inclusion of a table comparing the weekly budget for four
families of six. Expenditures are broken down into amount spent on
specific categories of food, drink, soap, tobacco, medicine, clothing,
education, sick societies, and the like (see table 5).

This information appears to have been col-
lected by the Bolton Poor Protection Society, and Ashworth gives no
indication of the manner of collection or its original use. Such budgets
anticipate Le Play, but Ashworth actually carried his analysis further
than Le Play by arranging the several budgets in a table with respect to
increasing income. Thus he is able to observe the changes in life style
produced by greater income. In his own words:

The first range of this table shows the amount of each kind of agricultural food
consumed by the various families from the lowest point of No. 1 to the trebled
allowance of the family No. 4. By the second item, the exciseable articles, it is seen
at what point of their earnings that description of their luxuries begins, and the rate
at which it increases and comes in aid of the revenue. The third item, clothing and
incidentals, advances rapidly in amount after 15s per week; and with this enlarge-
ment of income we observe the prudential habits, money savings, benefit societies,
a dread of pauperism, and an inclination to education, and take every care to provide for their offspring.[20]

But this is the extent of Ashworth's commen-
tary, and it appears that this remarkable table went unnoticed and unex-
ploited.

The shift to secondary analyses was not the
only change after 1841 for the late 1850s and early 1860s show a distinct trend toward historical essays and discussions of more general
questions of political economy, for example, the introduction of deci-
mal coinage or the relation of jurisprudence to commerce. In fact, of 18
papers read after 1857, 13 represent such essays and discussions. Table
6 shows a change of subject, too; while education is still the dominant
topic, papers on working conditions, criminality, vital statistics, and
religion steadily diminish in number. On the other hand, the number of

table 5 · four budgets: depression of trade at bolton (statement of four cases, showing the manner in which a man and his wife with four children spend their weekly earnings)

commodities	amount of earnings							
	no. 1 5s. 6d.		no. 2 10s.		no. 3 15s. 6d.		no. 4 26s. 6d.	
	s. d.	s. d.	s. d.	s. d.	s. d.	s. d.	s. d.	s. d.
Bread and flour	1 9	– –	2 6	– –	3 6	– –	4 0	– –
Oatmeal	1 0	– –	1 10	– –	1 6	– –	2 0	– –
Potatoes	0 10	– –	1 8	– –	1 9	– –	1 8	– –
Milk	0 11	– –	0 6	– –	0 9	– –	0 10	– –
Butter	– –	– –	– –	– –	0 10	– –	1 4	– –
Butcher's meat	– –	– –	– –	– –	0 9	– –	1 9	– –
Bacon	0 2	– –	0 8	– –	0 4	– –	0 3	– –
Cheese	– –	– –	– –	– –	0 7	– –	0 10	– –
Ale or beer	– –	– –	– –	– –	– –	– –	0 6	– –
Total of agri-cultural food	– –	4 8	– –	7 2	– –	10 0	– –	13 2
Sugar and treacle	– –	– –	0 5	– –	0 11	– –	1 9	– –
Tea and coffee	– –	– –	– –	– –	0 7	– –	1 2	– –
Soap and candles	0 4	– –	0 6	– –	0 8	– –	1 0	– –
Tobacco, snuff, and condiments	– –	– –	0 2	– –	0 4	– –	0 11	– –
Medicine and attendance	– –	– –	– –	– –	– –	– –	0 4	– –
Total of excise-able articles	– –	0 4	– –	1 1	– –	2 6	– –	5 2
Clothing	– –	– –	0 6	– –	0 9	– –	2 0	– –
Education	– –	– –	– –	– –	– –	– –	0 6	– –
Sick societies	– –	– –	– –	– –	0 6	– –	0 6	– –
Coal	0 6	– –	0 9	– –	0 9	– –	1 4	– –
Rent	– –	– –	0 6	– –	1 0	– –	2 6	– –
Savings	– –	– –	– –	– –	– –	– –	1 4	– –
Total of articles needful and incidental	– –	0 6	– –	1 9	– –	3 0	– –	8 2
Total	– –	5 6	– –	10 0	– –	15 6	– –	26 6

papers on commercial and economic questions increases as do those in the miscellaneous category—probably indicating a greater range in what was considered acceptable subject matter at this time.[21]

These changes could not go unnoticed, and in 1863 they became the subject of Alfred Aspland's presidential address to the Manchester Statistical Society. Aspland, however, limited himself primarily to changes in methodology rather than subject matter.

... It was held as a reproach against us that our transactions were more of the nature of Social Science essays than Statistical inquiries. But you cannot separate the two; the latter establish the facts upon which the former is based, and the discovery of anomalies and abuses, of shortcomings or overaction, will enable us to

table 6 · number of papers given by members of the manchester statistical society before the british association for the advancement of science, by subject and year, 1834-1863[a]

year	education	working classes	criminality	vital statistics	religion	misc.[b]
1834	–	–	–	1	–	–
1835	2	–	–	1	2	1
1836	–	–	–	–	–	1
1837	2	3	–	–	–	1
1838	–	–	–	–	–	–
1839	1	1	–	–	–	–
1840	1	–	–	–	–	–
1841	1	2	–	–	–	–
1842	2	1	2	3	–	1
1843	1	–	–	–	–	–
1844	–	–	–	–	–	–
1845	2	–	1	–	–	–
1846	1	–	1	–	–	–
1847	–	–	–	–	–	–
1848	–	–	–	–	–	–
1849	–	–	–	–	–	–
1850	–	–	–	–	–	–
1851	–	–	–	–	–	–
1852	–	–	–	–	–	1
1853	–	–	–	–	–	–
1854	–	–	–	–	–	1
1855	–	–	–	–	–	–
1856	–	–	–	–	–	–
1857	–	–	–	–	–	2
1858	2	–	–	–	–	1
1859	–	–	–	–	–	–
1860	1	–	–	–	–	1
1861	1	–	1	1	–	6
1862	1	–	–	–	–	1
1863	1	–	–	–	–	1
Total	19	7	5	6	2	18

[a] Some studies covered more than one subject and were multiply classified.
[b] Four of the miscellaneous papers for 1861 and the paper for 1862 are on economic topics.

take a clear purview of the scene, and determine the most valuable field for the operation of numbers.[22]

It may be noticed that Aspland does not distinguish between numbers gained from primary and secondary analyses, and in fact the remainder of his address indicates that he is referring only to secondary analyses. It would appear that by this date original surveys were so much past history that they were not even worth mentioning. Aspland asserts that the work of the Society lay in eliminating error in existing statistics by critical commentary and advice to the data-gatherers in order that proper inference could be made—and this inference was to be made by members of the Society.[23]

the surveys—a detailed analysis

In his view that social research should be directed to "the discovery of anomalies and abuses, of shortcomings and abuses"—in short, to the formulation of policy—Aspland represents a clear continuity with the Society's founders. In the founders' statement of purpose quoted earlier, several themes were revealed: social reform, nonpartisan social inquiry, and the discussion of political and social economy. Much of this could characterize the purposes of the many statistical societies appearing in England and abroad at this time. In some the goal of social reform was more explicit: for example, the full title of the Birmingham Society was the "Birmingham Statistical Society for the Improvement of Education." In others, like the Irish Society for Statistical and Social Inquiry, discussions of political economy received greater emphasis. But probably none were as free from party politics as their statements of purpose might suggest—if only because the prior purpose of social reform necessarily raises political questions.

There is thus an inherent contrast between the objectives of nonpartisan social inquiry and social reform. In this section, which deals with the structure and methodology of the Society's work, the importance of the contrast will not be developed, but it will be useful to keep it in mind in the ensuing exposition. The contrast itself will be dealt with more fully in a later section.

The earliest complete and available paper, that of Samuel and William Rathbone Greg read before the Society in March 1834, is entitled an "Analysis of the Evidence Taken before the Factory Commissioners, as far as it relates to the Population of Manchester and the Vicinity, Engaged in the Cotton Trade."[24] The study is a secondary analysis of the data gathered by a parliamentary committee in 1832 and designed to refute the committee's conclusions. The original report of this committee was evidence for the Factory Act of 1833 which fixed a minimum age of employment and regulated the hours of persons under eighteen. The Gregs, both cotton manufacturers, arranged the data under the following rubrics: (1) the health of the factory population; (2) the alleged fatigue arising from long hours of labor; (3) alleged cruelty toward the factory children; (4) state of education; (5) state of morality; and (6) wages and poor rates.

The authors state there is a great deal of data on the operatives' health, much of it "various and conflicting," and that they choose to rely on the study made by the then medical commissioner, Dr. Hawkins. They begin by presenting the following table from Hawkins (table 7) which indicates the sorry effects of factory conditions—a fact not explicitly stated by the Gregs. Indeed, they fault Hawkins' evidence as representing too few cases and being "too vague and general," and argue instead from a methodologically weaker table (table 8) from which no valid inference as to the effects of factory work really can be made because there is no comparison with nonfactory employees. The Gregs argue that the two tables are contradictory because "by the first table . . . *one-fifth* of the factory children had bad health, and by the second only one-twelfth." The same reasoning permeates the rest of their analysis. In summarizing Hawkins, they state

. . . Dr. Hawkins seems to state that the defective health which he conceives, *does* exist amongst the factory population generally, is *not* a necessary result of their occupation; for he states, that in some factories he could see no desire nor necessity for legislation, and no dark shades in the condition of the people.[25]

The strongest evidence on the question, the Gregs assert, comes from the secretary of a sick club (health insurance society). The club, consisting of 563 persons, drew half its membership from factory operatives. Yet, they argue, little more than one-fourth of the sick are operatives, and the death rate among them is only one-fifth of the whole.

The evidence on fatigue, cruelty, and morality was gathered from informants rather than respondents, as were the data on education and poor rates. The information on wages was obtained by a mail questionnaire.

The earliest original survey covered educational conditions in Manchester and was undertaken in April 1834 by a special committee of seventeen men.[26] This was an inquiry into the number of day, Sunday, charity, and infant schools in Manchester and the nature and quality of the instruction. Once again, there was reference to

table 7 · health by type of employment

health	factory employees	not factory employees
Bad	86	22
Middling	153	106
Good	161	272
Total	400	400

table 8 · health of operatives in 13 factories

health	operatives
Good	787
Middling	311
Bad	92
Total	1,190

parliamentary action as the committee was directed to compare their
results with those provided Parliament the previous year. Almost no
explicit statement of methodology is given; in a later study mention is
made of an agent employed to make interviews at this time, but no
information is given in the present report.

      The primary result of the comparison with the
returns made to Parliament was to show that the latter underestimated
the number of schools in existence. The analysis proceeds with a qualitative description of each of the several types of schools, and tables are
relegated to an appendix with little or no exegesis.

      In structure, however, the study was clearly
formulated as a multistratum survey of organizations, and the authors
report tables on the characteristics of the students and teachers as well
as institutional characteristics. In three cases these institutional attributes are used as contextual measures. The most interesting of these on
teachers' characteristics—relating years teaching, whether only occupation, birthplace, education, and religion to type of school—is reproduced
in table 9. The most immediate aspect of this table is that it summarizes
a great deal of information that today would be separated among several
tables for ease of exposition. This point suggests that where the committee desired to discuss findings, it would present them more simply and
in the main body of the text. A review of ten studies indicates that this
is true, but so few tables receive comment that the finding is not very
meaningful.

      Particularly interesting are tables in which the
schools are differentiated along several indices of quality (see table 10).
In table 10a the schools are ranked according to those that use maps
and globes for instruction, maps alone, or neither. In table 10b the
schools are grouped according to the presence or absence of a library,
savings bank, benefit society, and clothing society.

      The number of subjects taught forms a third
index, and the mode of instruction, the fourth. The latter encompasses
the following indicators: whether the students are divided into classes,

table 9 · teacher characteristics by type of school (information relative to the teachers of borough of manchester day and evening schools)[a]

	have no occupation but that of their school	number of years engaged in teaching								where born and educated				religious profession			
		less than 1	1 less than 2	2 less than 3	3 less than 4	4 less than 5	5 less than 6	6 less than 7	7 and above	England	Scotland	Ireland	abroad	establisd. church	Catholics	dissenters	not ascertained
Dame schools	165	44	24	31	20	21	12	8	70	219	2	7	2	93	19	108	10
Common boys' schools[b]	112	17	4	12	8	13	3	7	51	98	3	11	1	37	16	55	8
Common girls' schools	61	3	7	14	6	3	3	2	24	50	–	2	1	32	3	28	–
Superior boys' schools[b]	33	–	1	–	3	5	–	3	23	25	3	–	1	16	1	18	1
Superior girls' schools	76	8	4	10	5	8	3	3	35	68	1	1	–	43	–	34	1
Infant schools	5	1	–	2	1	–	–	–	1	4	1	–	–	3	–	2	–
Charity[b] and endowed schools	14	1	–	–	1	2	1	–	8	11	2	1	–	12	1	6	2
Evening schools	73	14	5	9	6	6	1	3	40	73	3	7	1	26	11	43	6
Totals	539	88	45	78	50	58	22	26	252	557	15	28	6	262	51	294	28

Totals: 619 { number of years } 606 { where born and educated } 635 { religious profession }

Not ascertained: 16 (number of years)   29 (where born and educated)

None of the teachers of the dame schools
16 only of the teachers of the common boys' and girls' schools
25 only " " " of the superior " " " "
7 only " " " of the evening schools
2 only " " " of the infant school
5 only " " " of the endowed and charity schools.
55 only " " " of all the schools in the Borough of Manchester.
} were educated for the employment.

[a] The information contained in this table applies only to the principal teacher of each school.
[b] There are 60 common boys' schools, 2 superior boys' schools, and 2 charity schools, the teachers of which have also evening schools under their direction.

47

table 10 (a and b) · tables illustrating indices of school quality (day and evening schools in the borough of manchester: course and mode of instruction pursued)

a

There are 3 common boys' schools,
" is 1 " girls' "
" are 28 superior boys' "
" " 30 " girls' "
" " 2 evening "
——
64

in which maps and globes are used.

There are 12 common boys' schools,
" " 17 " girls' "
" " 4 superior boys' "
" " 41 " girls' "
" " 2 charity "
" " 3 evening "
——
79

in which maps alone are used.

b

There is 1 infant school having 160 scholars, to which are attached a clothing society, a benefit society, and a lending library.
" " 1 " " 133 " " " " " " is a lending library.
" " 1 " " 43 " " " " " " are a lending library and a clothing society.
" " 1 charity school " 94 " " " " " " is a lending library.
" " 1 " " 1041 " " " " " " is a clothing society.
" " 1 " " 170 " " " " " " are a clothing society, a benefit society, and a lending library.

1 day school connected with the mechanics institution " 210 " " " " " " is a lending library.
1 superior boys' school " 50 " " " " " " is a lending library.

There are therefore 4 schools, having 1,414 scholars, to which a clothing society is attached.
" " 2 " " 330 " " " " " benefit society is attached.
" is 1 " " 160 " " " " " savings' bank is attached.
" are 7 " " 700 " " " " " lending library is attached.

48

whether a teacher or monitor system of instruction is used, whether the students are questioned on their lessons, whether there are examinations, and whether there are outside inspectors.

None of this, however, merits comment by the authors. Their outline of the report passes from descriptions of the general categories of schools to the conclusions with the tables appended. The conclusions are based upon the tables but without clear reference to them. Thus, from the tables, the authors conclude

That the number of children returned [in the parliamentary reports] as attending different schools, affords a very imperfect and fallacious criterion of the real state of education in any town or district where such returns are made.[27]

That of the children between the ages of 5 and 15, one-third appear to be receiving no instruction whatever in school.[28]

The same format was followed in all of the available studies of education that the Society undertook from 1834 to 1841. They assert that the material was gathered by an agent of the Society (generally the same man), describe their categories of schools, present the tables without comment, and conclude that the education of the working classes requires great improvement. Methodological notes are generally nonexistent—although in their report of a survey made in York, the Society remarked that their agent encountered resistance to his inquiries because the teachers suspected that the information was being gathered for political or sectarian purposes.[29] The York survey is also interesting because it was undertaken to provide comparative data on a city in which the economy was not dominated by either manufacturing or mercantile interests, and in which the distribution of classes differed. However, no concrete information is given on what the economic organization was based upon or what the class distribution was— although scattered remarks indicate a much smaller working-class population. On the other hand, two tables compare Manchester, Salford, Bury, Liverpool, and York as to the percentage of the population and the percentage of the total number of scholars attending the various types of schools (see table 11). Save for the last column of table 11b, these tables are not discussed in the text. The last column is used to characterize the various types of schools. The lack of exposition poses a contradiction in the study, for the authors begin by arguing that the "greater comfort" and lesser density of the population of York (28,000) creates a generally higher level of education. Yet the comparative columns show that York is reasonably matched in the quality of its educational offerings by Liverpool, the largest city in the study (230,000).[30]

For unknown reasons, the studies of the working-class conditions among the poor have fuller accounts of the

table 11 (a and b) · school attendance in different community contexts

a					
estimated population	200,000	55,000	20,000	230,000	28,000
percentage of the population who	Manchester	Salford	Bury	Liverpool	York
Attend dame schools	2.36	2.81	4.20	2.28	2.66
Common day	3.40	3.30	4.04	2.65	1.96
Superior private	1.47	1.60	0.87	1.77	2.56
Infant	0.32	0.68	1.42	0.96	1.48
Evening	0.73	0.96	0.75	0.24	0.15
Endowed and charity	1.78	2.55	1.84	4.91	8.15
Total who attend day schools	10.06	11.90	13.12	12.81	16.96
Total who attend Sunday schools only	11.59	11.53	15.51	1.62	3.01
Total who attend any schools	21.65	23.43	28.63	14.43	19.97

b					
percentage of the total number of scholars who	Manchester	Salford	Bury	Liverpool	York
Attend day schools	10.90	11.97	14.67	15.79	13.33
Common day	15.68	14.08	14.11	18.37	9.82
Superior private	6.77	6.85	3.03	12.30	12.80
Infant	1.50	2.89	4.96	6.64	7.44
Evening	3.37	4.08	2.64	1.65	0.75
Endowed and charity	8.24	10.89	6.43	34.04	40.80
Total who attend day schools	46.46	50.76	45.84	88.79	84.94
Total who attend Sunday schools only	53.54	49.24	54.16	11.21	15.06
Grand total	100.00	100.00	100.00	100.00	100.00

methodology employed and problems encountered. It is possible that different individuals were responsible for the studies of working-class conditions than had charge of the surveys of education; the published reports often do not list the names of the individuals involved in these studies. Ashton's discussion of these early surveys suggests that there was considerable overlap of personnel,[31] but this does not mean that responsibilities were not differently allocated. Of six surveys of working-class conditions, two are available for detailed analysis.

The earlier of the two is entitled *Report of a Committee of the Manchester Statistical Society on the Condition of the Working Classes in an Extensive Manufacturing District in 1834, 1835, and 1836.*[32] The survey grew out of an 1834 study by Benjamin Heywood, which reported data on 4102 families in two Manchester police districts.[33] Four agents were hired to interview the working classes (ostensibly a census) in Manchester, Salford, Bury, Ashton, Stalybridge, and Dukinfield. Rather than an interview schedule, they were given a list of questions which were modified to deal with contingencies in the course of the 17-month investigation. In what appears to be final form, the list is shown in table 12. The Society's committee began by daily reading these reports and attempting to assess their accuracy by comparison with other (unspecified) data and the use of informants. In some cases a second agent reinterviewed selected samples to check the reliability of the first interviews. The committee pointed out that some tabulations reflect the observations and judgments of the interviewer, others the interviewees' responses.

Unlike in some of the educational surveys, the interviewers found little suspicion of their motives, although there was reluctance to answer questions on wages and hours of labor. Interestingly, this was foreseen by the committee and they adopted three indirect measures of income: the number of working adults, the number of working children, and weekly rent.

This was a survey of the working class, defined by the authors to include all those below the rank of shopkeeper. But how the agent determined that a given occupation was below the rank of shopkeeper is not stated, although there seems to have been one:

In that district, the agents profess to have visited and recorded *every house* belonging to the Working Population, and there is every reason to believe this to have been the case. In the case of Manchester, however, the Committee feel less confident as to the completeness and universality of the visitation; and generally they wish it to be distinctly understood, that they do not present these Tables as perfectly accurate and invulnerable. . . .[34]

In those instances where the interviewer made a rating—for example, the condition of the dwellings—he seems to have been provided with rough indices. In the latter case a house was "well-furnished" if it contained "a table and chairs, a clock, a chest of drawers, and a fair stock of necessary utensils"; a "comfortable" house was "clean, neatly arranged, and protected from the external air, even where somewhat bare of furniture."

In contrast to the reports on education, the tables themselves receive some discussion. Generally these discussions either qualify the findings or attempt to clarify possible misunderstandings of the categories used. Thus a table on the number of persons able to read and write is dismissed because the information was reported by informants rather than by the individuals themselves. While one cannot be certain, their hesitance in accepting the informant reports probably

table 12 · interview schedule from 1834-1836 survey of conditions in the working class

Left section			Right section		
Can read	*Attainments of both adults and minors*		Street or district		
Can write			Number of each distinct entrance		
Can cipher			Cellar, house, or room		
Can sew				*Name of parent or of any independent individual*	
Mark if tested					
Adults or minors, A. or M.					
Having seats	*Denomination of sect*		Country		
Not having seats				*Occupation of adults, viz., 21 and upwards*	
Attendance regular or irregular, or not at all					
Are there any books in the house			Partly or wholly out of work		
Dwelling comfortable, middling, or uncomfortable			Never have been at school		*Resident population*
Dwelling clean, middling, or dirty			Males	*Of adults, the sex only to be marked / Of minors the age also*	
Dwelling well, moderately, or ill-furnished			Females		
Total weekly payment for schooling of children			Males	*Age of non resident minors*	
Weekly rent			Females		
Number of rooms in the dwelling			Day or evening, and Sunday school	*Now under instruction*	*Under twenty-one years of age*
Number of sleeping rooms			Day or evening school only		
Number of beds			Sunday school only		
Sufficient or insufficient supply of water			Regularly instructed at home		
State of drainage			Attendance regular or irregular		
How long has the family been resident in the town or parish			Occupation of minors		
Does the head of the family belong to any benefit society			Now in receipt of wages		
Rate of earnings now			Day or evening, and Sunday school	*Formerly instructed*	
Rate of earnings 7 to 10 years ago			Day or evening school only		
	Remarks		Sunday school only		
			Regularly instructed at home		
			Age of leaving school		
			Attendance regular or irregular		

stems from the fact that these indicate that more than half of the population could read and write while their studies of education showed that approximately the same number never attended school.

The authors draw no conclusions from this study despite many worthwhile tables, for they assert that many more comparative data are required before any sound inference can be made. This perspective is interesting; a lack of comparative data did not keep the educational researchers from drawing conclusions. Perhaps it only strengthens the suspicion that another individual or set of individuals bore the responsibility for the educational surveys.

It is useful to compare this early survey with one done in 1839.[35] The purpose of the 1839 survey was to obtain comparative data on a town that was neither manufacturing nor agricultural (thus commercial?). However, the comparability of the two surveys is moot largely because the second survey represents a technical advance over the first. For example, it is possible to compare the interview schedules used in the two studies (see table 13). The 1839 inquiry is more comprehensive, delving more deeply into religion, education, condition of dwelling, and furnishings than the former. Earlier questions about wages met resistance and had to be answered indirectly, but evidently the researchers developed ways of dealing with the problem, for the 1839 schedule asks directly about present and past income. Whereas the earlier study relied upon informant reports of abilities to read and write, the latter study had the interviewer test the subjects. (It is worth mentioning here that the authors report a good deal of reluctance to answer questions.) Absent from the later schedule are the precodes built into the earlier.

Another innovation in this study is the use of percentages: prior work almost universally presented only raw numbers, but virtually all textual references to the data are given as percents. The utility of the device was apparently unrecognized, however, for it is not found to any significant extent in later work.

Like the earlier study, the 1839 survey also contains data based upon the subjective estimates of the interviewer. But unlike the former study, no guides were established for him, and the authors realize that this renders comparison with other data impossible. The agent was simply instructed to record how he defined his terms, for example

The word *comfortable* must always be a vague and varying epithet, to which it is impossible to attach any precise definition. In filling up this column, I was guided by observing the condition of the dwelling apart from any consideration of order, cleanliness, or furniture. If I considered it capable of being made comfortable by the tenant, I set it down accordingly; if it were damp, the flooring bad, and the walls ill-conditioned, I reported it uncomfortable.[36]

table 13 · interview schedule from 1839 survey of conditions in the working class

Data		Item
H		House or cellar
17		Number of persons in the house or cellar
8		Number of rooms in the house or cellar
4		Number of families in the house or cellar
J.G. T.S. O.T. N.G.		Name
1 1	2	Male	Number of adults
3	1 1	Female	
1	1 3	Male	Number of children
1	1 1	Female	
1	3 7	Church of England	Religious profession of the head of each family
				Protestant Dissenters	
6 1			Roman Catholics	
1	3 7	English	Country of the head of each family
6 1			Irish	
				Scotch	
				Welsh	
				Foreigners	
Carpenter	Bricklayer — Labourer	Occupation or trade of the head of each family
Carpenter		Occupation or trade of any other members of the family
1 1	2	Number of adults in the family earning wages
				Number of children in the family earning wages
1 2	Male	Number of children attending a day school
1	Female	
1	2	Male	Number of children attending a sunday-school
2	1	Female	
2s. 6d.	Total weekly payment for schooling of children
Yes Yes No No	Are there any books in the house?
Yes Yes Yes Yes	Dwelling comfortable
Yes Yes No No	Dwelling well furnished
3s.0d 2s.0d 1s.6d 2s.0d	Weekly rent
3 2 1 2	Number of rooms for the family
2 1 1 1	Number of sleeping rooms for the family
3 2 1 2	Number of beds for the family
Yes Yes Yes Yes	Sufficient supply of water
6 years Native 4 years 3 years	How long has the family been resident in the town?
Yes No No No	Does the head of the family belong to any benefit society?
Clarence-Street		Name of street

54

At least a vague definition of the "working class" was given in the 1834-1836 study, but none appeared in 1839. Furthermore, while some attempt was made to check the completeness of returns in the first survey, this was ignored in the second.

". . . [As overcrowding is] not only a signal proof of destitution and discomfort, but [also] a fruitful and certain source of evil," the authors present tables on the number of individuals per bed in a household. The importance of this index occurred to the authors in the midst of the earlier inquiry—after the Manchester interviews were completed—consequently the data were gathered for the remaining samples only. In both studies the authors report difficulty in obtaining replies on this point, and in the second case, one-third of those interviewed refused to answer.[37]

the failure to institutionalize

the internal evidence

Much of this paper has been devoted to the context of research, and it is from the context that many of the explanations for the failure of research to become institutionalized shall come. But a great deal can be said on the internal evidence of the early surveys themselves. The most rudimentary step toward institutionalization is the creation of channels of communication, for every science must have some means of keeping both its practitioners and interested laymen informed of developments in the field. Yet even on this level the Manchester Statistical Society did not progress very far in the period 1834-1841; the first reports of the Society were not published until 1835, two years after the Society's founding. Prior to the beginning of the regular journal of the Society in 1853, the *Transactions*, only six of ninety papers read before the Society saw print.[38] Recall, too, that the period of original surveys extends only to 1841. Thus by the time the *Transactions* begin, they serve research of a quite different character. Contributions were made to the *Journal of the London Statistical Society*, but not in such numbers that it could be termed a substitute outlet: from 1839, the first year of the *Journal*, to 1853 the Manchester Society or its members published only 16 of the 339 papers in it.[39] Finally, while many members of the Society joined the British Association for the Advancement of Science and played an active role in its statistics section, it must be said that the Association did not advance the cause of social research in the nineteenth century.[40]

A second indicator of growing institutionalization is reference to the work of others in the field. During the period

1834-1841 only three references to prior research could be found. The first was the parliamentary study of education mentioned earlier and with which a number of the Manchester educational surveys sought comparison. Second, there was the 1826 Society of Friends study of education briefly mentioned in an addendum to one report. The third was a secondary analysis, "On the Social Statistics of the Netherlands," written by W. R. Greg on the basis of some of Quetelet's published material.[41] Thus this second criterion of institutionalization also suggests little development.

A third indicator might be the cumulative nature of research within the Society. Here also the Society fares poorly. The surveys of education show no appreciable development of methodology in the five cases reviewed. Indeed, over time there was less attention paid to a formal statement of the conditions under which the data were collected and analyzed. Late surveys present findings without any methodological preface. Almost without exception the same information was collected and reported in the same format. One might say that the Society created a "set piece" which served their purposes and with which they were unwilling to tamper—hardly the indication of a developing science.

On the other hand, the surveys on the conditions of the working classes do evidence some increasing sophistication. Over time the questionnaire became more specific in wording and more elaborate in construction. The direct questions on income point to newfound techniques of handling reluctant respondents. The use of percentage represents a major breakthrough in the treatment of data. At the same time the abandonment of precoded responses and guides for interviewer judgments are definite backward steps.

There is, too, the fact that there is no continuity between the two types of surveys. The reports on the working classes are written with an eye to methodology; the means of data collection, the definition of indicators, and problems of interpretation are all treated in the text. Only the definition of indicators is found in the surveys on education. While the format of the working-class studies is adapted to the particular problem at hand and the use of new descriptive devices, the format of the surveys on education is constant. Inferences as to the quality of instruction, qualifications of teachers, and the like were made from the first findings, yet the writers of the first report on the working classes preferred to await further evidence before drawing conclusions.

In the early stages of institutionalization, sciences often have their problems defined for them by practical interests or other areas of investigation. As they mature, they begin to generate

their own problems. This ability is a fourth criterion of institutionalization, one that marks the Manchester Statistical Society in a very early
phase. As the introduction to this paper pointed out, the two problems
specifically dealt with in the research reviewed above were central to the
thinking of reform-minded men of the time; and the rest of the subjects
investigated by the Society—sanitation, religion, criminality, and the
like—could find their roots in the same social conscience. Nor did these
problems give rise to new problems investigated in their own right, for
all of these studies were descriptive of a very limited set of externally
defined subjects.

These four indicators characterize the incipi-
ent stage of institutionalization prior to the development of a distinctive scientific personnel, and encompass the level of institutionalization
the Manchester Statistical Society attained. On the internal evidence,
then, it is clear that there was little movement toward institutionalization. But the internal evidence provides few clues as to an explanation
of why research did not become institutionalized. The answer to the latter question lies in the external evidence about the men who did the
research, their motives, and their social context. The analysis of this
external evidence forms the concluding section.

the external evidence

The Society's failure to institutionalize survey
research appears to have several causes operating independently and
jointly. They are (1) the emergence of an inability to agree on common
goals, (2) a diversion of interests, money, and manpower to other interests, (3) the development of governmental institutions to gather statistics on problems of social importance, (4) the cooptation of the membership by governments, and (5) the researchers' limited aim of social
reform. Because the evidence behind it does not provide empirical clo-
sure, this list should be seen as provisional and possibly incomplete.

1. The inability to agree on common goals /
The greatest number of surveys undertaken by the Society centered on
education; of 23 surveys made between 1834 and 1841, 13 dealt with
education. The improvement of education was a cause for which many
members had worked since the early 1820s, and perhaps before. It was
a major theme in the middle-class program of social reform. It was also
a political issue and weapon.

As suggested earlier, reform in the early nine-
teenth century was not entirely seen by its authors as a response to
democratic pressures. The extension of the franchise in 1832 was a move
to placate the middle classes, not the working man, and the middle

classes were in no hurry to grant them the vote. Educational reform was a double-edged sword. It might cut down the barriers standing in the way of greater opportunities for working people, and might endanger the exclusive middle-class franchise. As Sir Benjamin Heywood told the Manchester Mechanics' Institution in 1840,

If the working classes desire to raise their condition, they must do it by exerting themselves for their own moral and intellectual improvement. Instead of seeking, in the first instance, an extension of their political privileges from the legislature, let them seek a system of rational and liberal education for themselves and their children.[42]

Or as J. E. Taylor, a member of the Society and editor of the Manchester *Guardian* put it: "Let the people have a good education and, with the habits it would induce, the bribe of intoxicating draught would be less powerful. Till then the elective franchise could not with safety be extended."[43]

But most important, education was a political issue on a religious base. The controversy dated from the early years of the century: should a national system of education be controlled by the established church? Prior to 1837 there was little effective agitation for national education, but in that year Richard Cobden, then an important figure in the Manchester Society, together with other Manchester manufacturers and merchants, began lobbying for a national system.[44] Cobden and his friends ranged themselves on the side of nonsectarian education behind Thomas Wyse, a Catholic M.P. and the most prominent member of the newly established Central Society for Education.[45] In Cobden's words, the new system "must be based upon liberal principles, untinged by sectarian prejudices; having its management carefully guarded from partiality of every kind, and its funds securely protected against corrupt applications.[46] Wyse was even more forthright: "Above all, let every class and every persuasion have access to this education. ... I know not of a Unitarian nation, or a Methodist nation, or a Catholic nation, or a Protestant nation: I only know of a British Nation."[47]

The established church immediately objected, and certain Nonconformist groups also felt that they should control the religious instruction of their children. Most of this opposition organized itself under the leadership of the Rev. Hugh Stowell, a widely respected Anglican minister. It was Stowell's view that while increased education was sorely needed, its administration should be placed entirely in the hands of the church "without its being sullied by the tampering of laymen, who do not understand the question they are meddling with."[48] The plan of the nonsectarian reformers would be "only elevating man from the brute to approximate him to the fiend, only putting power into the hands of evil."[49]

On the nonsectarian side, a series of town meetings were held which led to the formation of the Manchester Society for Promoting National Education on November 16, 1837. The new organization installed William Nield, a member of the Statistical Society, as president and placed four members of the Statistical Society on its eight-member General Committee.[50]

The opposition party was not without Statistical Society support as well. While the sectarians did not create their own organization, the Manchester Church Education Society, until 1845, their influence was strong. At least two members of the Statistical Society were active in the Church Education Society and at least five more supported the opposition party.[51]

Thus the cleavage that hampered effective national agitation for education split the Manchester Statistical Society as well. With its membership divided on political and ideological grounds, the Society could not formulate any clear policy on its educational research. That the Society's goal was to set down guides for social reform already has been demonstrated, but in the case of education action was impeded by the religious factionalism within its membership. It is perhaps not too far afield to suggest that this division contributed to the static quality of the Society's educational research and its failure to carry it forward after 1841. This, then, is one basis for the failure to continue survey research in Manchester.

2. The diversion of interests, money, and manpower to other causes / The same fall that saw the creation of the Manchester Society for Promoting National Education was also a period of intense agitation for the reform of local government in Manchester and the beginning of the movement that was to lead to the Anti-Corn Law League. These two movements were probably the two chief diversions of interests, money, and manpower from the survey research of the Manchester Statistical Society. But they did not create an immediate drain of men and energies, for the most active phases of these movements did not come until the early 1840s,[52] thus coinciding with the demise of original survey research in the Statistical Society. The most striking fact about these movements is that usually the same group of men led them both and were or had been leaders in the Statistical Society.

How then do these facts relate to the activities of the Society's membership? By and large, it can be said that the Anti-Corn Law League drew its leadership and most active supporters from the Manchester Statistical Society. Of the 13 members most responsible for the early surveys, 6—Kay-Shuttleworth, James Heywood, R. H. and W. R. Greg, Henry and Edmund Ashworth—were closely affiliated with the anti-corn law movement. Henry Ashworth was, together with Richard

Cobden and S. D. Darbyshire, one of the founders of the Manchester Anti-Corn Law Association. Darbyshire, as mentioned previously, was also an early survey researcher; and J. A. Turner and W. Raynor Wood, other early researchers, were also important figures in the anti-corn law movement. The contribution of these men was heavy. Robert Hyde Greg, for example, was president of the Anti-Corn Law League in 1839. Edmund Ashworth, as well as Henry, devoted much of his time and energy to the movement. The motives that had led these men to base their programs for political and social reform on statistical fact do not seem to have carried over into the context of the Anti-Corn Law League when a committee, including Henry Ashworth, published a survey on the effects of the corn laws on the condition of the working class.[53]

        Considered in terms of the total membership of the Statistical Society, the anti-corn law movement drew 26 members into its activities. But the actual effect of involvement in anti-corn law agitation is yet greater, for the League was closely allied with the Manchester Chamber of Commerce. It was in the Chamber of Commerce that Cobden, Ashworth, and others began to think about repeal of the corn laws, and Cobden originally suggested that the Chamber be used as the organizational base for agitation.[54] An independent organization was established due to Ashworth's arguments against its suitability,[55] but the continued close affiliation of the two organizations in spirit and purpose is demonstrated by the fact that in 1839 Robert Hyde Greg concurrently served as president of the Manchester Chamber of Commerce and the Anti-Corn Law League; and in 1840-1841 J. B. Smith held the same positions.[56] Moreover, in 1838 the Chamber petitioned Parliament to repeal the corn laws.[57]

        The corn law agitation was an enormous drain on the time and funds of its supporters. In 1839 the Manchester men were unable to meet the demands for assistance from newly founded chapters of the League in other sections of the country and resorted to hiring special speakers to make the rounds.[58] In the same year lack of funds forced the League to curtail its activities drastically.[59] The problem arose periodically until 1842 when fund-raising was more effectively reorganized on a national basis.[60] Efforts to establish new branches, prepare pamphlets, negotiate with members of the government, find suitable parliamentary candidates, form alliances with other organizations, and respond to the charges of still others, represented a sizable investment in time, money, and labor for the League's Manchester supporters who virtually alone kept the League alive during the critical period prior to 1842.[61] And, to stress once more, the majority of the most significant supporters of the League were members of the Manchester Statistical Society.

To be sure, not all of these men were active in the early survey research, but their general stature suggests that they were probably among the most influential in the Statistical Society as well as being significant in the anti-corn law movement. Apart from those already mentioned, these were such men as Thomas Potter, M.P., and William Nield, the first and second mayors of Manchester; Mark Philips and Thomas Bazley, both members of Parliament; J. E. Taylor, the editor of the Manchester *Guardian*; W. R. Callender, a Manchester alderman and founder of the Society for Promoting National Education; and Edward Herford, Manchester coroner and, like Callender, a founder of the Society of National Education.

These men were no less important in the movement to incorporate Manchester as a borough. Once again, Cobden and the Ashworths played leading roles.[62] The early survey researchers appeared to have been somewhat less involved, the Ashworths being their only representatives. Darbyshire, however, was active and the other prominent figures included Thomas Potter, William Nield, J. E. Taylor, Mark Philips, and W. R. Callender. In all, 19 members of the Society were active in civic reform. This was again a political struggle, although perhaps more clearly along Whig-Tory lines.[63] The Whigs, representing the rising middle class of cotton manufacturers, sought borough reform as a means of increasing their own franchise and the efficiency of the town administration.

The incorporating charter was quickly gained, though not without some effort, as Cobden wrote:

For three weeks, I was incessantly occupied at the Town Hall. By dint of hard work and some expense, we got at the filth in their [the Tories] Augean stable, and laid their dirty doings before the public eye. . . . They pretended to get upwards of thirty thousand names [on a petition] for which they were well paid. But the voting has shown that four-fifths were forgeries. So much for the unholy alliance of Tory and Radical.[64]

But the Tories denied the validity of the charter. Because they controlled the churchwardens, who collected the taxes, this was no small matter: for they refused to transfer the treasury to the new borough council.[65] By August 1839 the corporation was overdrawn £3000, and a year later, more than £11,600—of which £4000 had been spent defending the legality of the charter.[66] Until the fall of 1841 the credit of the borough was maintained by the personal bond of the leading incorporators. Thomas Potter was one of three who guaranteed £1000 each; William Nield, Richard Cobden, and J. E. Taylor together guaranteed £500 each.[67] The incorporators' financial outlay was matched by the time spent in slow negotiation for the transfer of the police, taxation, sanitary, judicial, and other functions from the manorial Court Leet to the new borough council.[68] It was not until the fall of 1842 that the borough council was able to assume full control over the administrative functions of the town.

The two movements described above appear to have been the chief diversion of men and interest during this time. It is less clear that they diverted money that otherwise would have financed survey research. There is no clear indication that there was a lack of funds for research, and if there was, it was more likely the consequence of a change of interest in one man: Sir Benjamin Heywood. Heywood provided the financial support for most—if not all—of the early surveys.[69] In 1834 Heywood was the archetype of the Society's early membership: a liberal Whig, Unitarian, reform-minded, devoted to the cause of national education, and active in many charitable organizations. As time progressed, however, Heywood became somewhat more conservative in action if not in outlook. His name is conspicuously absent from the rolls of the reform movements of the late 1830s and early 1840s, save for the movement for national education. He became increasingly attracted to the Church of England and in 1842 joined the church.[70] Shortly thereafter, he began contributing heavily to the support of the church; he built the Church of St. John at a cost of £5000.[71] The following year, 1843, he gave £1000 for the purchase of land for public parks. These sums represent a great deal of money for those days; together they bettered half the borough budget for 1840. While Heywood might still have had ample funds to finance further studies,[72] he was not a man of unlimited wealth. Taken together the trend of his actions in the late 1830s and early 1840s suggests a change in his interests. It is perhaps worth noting that Heywood gave no papers before the Statistical Society after 1836.[73]

The most conclusive evidence for the diversion of interests, men, and money from the Society to other areas is the testimony of those then present. Edward Herford reported that the question of *dissolving* the Society was raised at the annual meeting in 1849 "on the ground of the meetings called during the last few years having been seldom attended by a quorum of the members, and no Committee appearing to be in operation."[74] This statement is, of course, simply descriptive of the change of interests away from the Society, but it does demonstrate that the membership did not and probably could not devote themselves to so many competing causes.

3. The development of governmental institutions to gather statistics / The Reform Bill of 1832 produced a Parliament that began collecting information on an unprecedented scale.[75] This information came chiefly from two sources: the statistics section of the Board of Trade, established in 1833, and the creation of large numbers of royal commissions. From the former, economic statistics were obtained; the functions of the latter were to (1) consider legislative policy, (2) inquire into the activities of the administration, and (3) investigate social conditions.[76] For the present purposes, the social investigations of the royal commissions represent the important development.

In the three years 1833-1835, 28 new commissions were appointed and empowered to investigate such subjects as the poor laws, factory conditions, the Irish poor, religious instruction, and vital statistics.[77] However, the great rise in the number of commissions took place in the decades 1841-1850, when 54 commissions were created, and 1851-1860, when 74 were established. In addition to the areas previously mentioned, the commissions looked into such fields as education, frame-work knitters, court facilities, and election procedures.[78]

Not all of these agencies were concerned with the collection of statistical data, but many were. And it is known that on at least one occasion members of the Manchester Statistical Society were employed as assistant commissioners to gather the data.[79] These men, W. Raynor Wood and John Kennedy, were engaged—along with such members of the London Statistical Society as Jelinger C. Symons and J. Fletcher—to gather data on the condition of children working in mines.[80]

These commissions had their faults, for it was quite easy to "pack" them in order to obtain the desired report, and it was quite often done.[81] At the same time an "acceptable conclusion" was likely to be a reform-minded one because the commissions were generally conceded to be tools of the Whig reformers.[82] Thus as far as the Manchester Statistical Society was concerned, the commissions were likely to report acceptable conclusions, however obtained. Given the steadily increasing use of the commissions from 1833 to 1860, it is perhaps not surprising that the thrust of the Society's interests changed from original survey research to secondary analysis and critical commentaries on official statistics.

4. The cooptation of the membership by governments / The Statistical Society's membership was drawn into the service of both Parliament and the local borough council. The most notable example of cooptation was the appointment of Sir James Kay-Shuttleworth to the position of assistant poor law commissioner in 1835, largely on the basis of his *Moral and Physical Condition of the Working Classes* and his work in the Manchester Statistical Society.[83] In 1839 he became secretary to the Committee of Council on Education, and high sheriff of Lancashire in 1863.

Lt. Col. James Shaw-Kennedy, the first vice-president and second president of the Society, left Manchester in 1837 to assume the position of inspector general of the Irish Constabulary.

Five members of the Society were elected to Parliament during the period of the early surveys: R. H. Greg, James Heywood, Mark Philips, J. A. Turner, and G. W. Wood. Of these, three were involved in the early surveys. Two more members, Richard Cobden and Thomas Potter, were elected shortly after this period. Potter and William Nield served as the first and second mayors of Manchester. The work of W. Raynor Wood and John Kennedy for the royal commissioner on children in mines has already been noted.

5. The researchers' limited aim of social reform / The primary motive of the members of the Statistical Society was social reform: Their expressed ideology, their patterns of association, their topics for research all testify to this overriding purpose. Despite their professed devotion to nonpartisan inquiry, they often found themselves dealing with political issues. In 1837 W. R. Greg and William Langton were severely reprimanded by their colleagues in the British Association for a report on the state of education in Salford, Bury, and York, which concluded that

For the attainment, therefore, of this object (vis., a system which should provide a good and suitable education for every child of the state), of which every one in the present day will admit the paramount importance, what resource is left but in the active agency of the Government? an agency which surely might be so conducted as in no degree to interfere with the spirit of British institutions. The task is certainly one of great magnitude, and cannot fail to meet with both honest and interested opposition. But the country ought not, on this account, to shrink from it; and we feel persuaded that the establishment of a Board of Public Instruction would be hailed by all who have seen the glaring deficiencies of the present state of education as the first step in the performance of a duty which is imperative with every enlightened government.[84]

They were, said their critics, confounding objective science with political controversy.

The combination of objective inquiry with questions of political and social importance was, however, an intrinsic characteristic of the Society, as indicated by the passage from its statement of purpose given earlier in this discussion, and its methodological precepts. An 1836 methodological paper by W. R. Greg on "statistical desiderata" argued the deficiency of statistical data on questions of "national importance."[85] Quite simply, the available data were inaccurate and thus no "philosophical inferences [could] safely be drawn"— philosophical inferences, it must be stressed, on questions of national importance. Much of this deficiency could be remedied, Greg asserted, by the use of interviewers rather than mail questionnaires. Thus, the policy aims of the Society intrude even to methodological questions, and the latter arise insofar as they impede the solution of policy questions. The validity of this conclusion stems not simply from Greg's paper but also from the studies reviewed above. Here research is a tool, not a subject with intrinsic interest. The fact that it never took on this interest must be understood in the context of the broader aims of these reform-minded men.

The Manchester Statistical Society was largely an attempt to satisfy the reform impulses of its founders and early membership. It could be expected to flourish insofar as it provided satisfaction. But the Society's inability to act on the problem of education, the diversion of its membership to the pressing issues of incorporation and the corn laws, and the increased availability of official statistical data on the social questions of the time all contributed to its inability to satisfy these desires.

As its membership's interests and energies drifted elsewhere, the Society underwent a general decline in the 1840s. By the time it recovered in the 1850s, the survey research tradition had been broken for a decade and many of its early supporters were gone. The 1850s saw a new generation take control of the Society to lead its program in a different direction.

notes

1 T. S. Ashton, *Economic and Social Investigations in Manchester, 1833-1933* (London: Staples, 1934); *Manchester Guardian,* 1836-1839; *Transactions of the Manchester Literary and Philosophical Society,* 1829-1863.
2 Quoted in Ashton, *Investigations,* p. 13.
3 Quoted in Edith and Thomas Kelly, eds., *A School-Master's Notebook* (Manchester: The Chetham Society, 1957), p. 3.
4 Active though they were in reform movements, their devotion was not entirely uniform. Thus the physician, Kay-Shuttleworth, could condemn working conditions in the cotton mills while the cotton manufacturers, the Greg brothers, could temporize and see little use for factory legislation to improve conditions. For the latter men, reform really meant that the government should provide opportunities for the exercise of individual initiative to better one's condition. Thus, they supported universal elementary education but not laws to shorten working hours or safeguard health. As Thomas Ashton, a cotton manufacturer and Statistical Society member, put it: "The authority of an employer should be absolute. A government should be despotic if it would be paternal." [Quoted in Gerald Berkeley Hertz, *The Manchester Politician 1750-1912* (London: Sherratt and Hughes, 1912), p. 49.] Naturally, it was paternalistic to regulate factory conditions. Such differing views of reform characterized the Statistical Society's general membership as well as the founders.

For a radical perspective, one may turn to Frederick Engels, himself a Manchester cotton manufacturer in the early 1840s. For his view, see the appendix.

5 The Provident Society was organized for the purpose of visiting the poor to recommend "sobriety, cleanliness, forethought, and method." See Ashton, *Investigations*, p. 4.

6 *Ibid.,* p. 20.

7 *Ibid.,* p. 24.

8 London: James Ridgeway, 1832.

9 *Ibid.,* p. 5.

10 Kelly, *Notebook*, p. 4.

11 The criterion for choosing these men was either that they bore the chief responsibility for a survey or that they served on more than one survey committee. Since the Society's reports rarely give the committees' memberships, the criterion is probably conservative. Eleven others are known to have served on at least one survey committee. Of these, nothing is known of three, and next to nothing of another three. The remaining five were S. D. Darbyshire, Peter Ewart, Rev. J. J. Taylor, J. A. Turner, M.P., and W. Raynor Wood. Ewart left Manchester in 1836 to become inspector in His Majesty's shipyards at Woolwich, but the others played active parts in the movements for education, incorporation, and repeal of the corn laws.

12 Benjamin Heywood joined the Church of England in 1842.

13 The terms Liberal and Conservative were coming to be substituted for Whig and Tory, but to minimize confusion the older terms will be used throughout.

14 Members of the Manchester Anti-Corn Law Association account for 12 of the above 20.

15 The list contains a small amount of overlap.

16 The statistics section of the British Association was organized in 1834.

17 Two years, 1842 and 1861, stand out for the large number of papers (18) read before the British Association; this may have something to do with the fact that the Association met in Manchester in those years. Also, in 1842, the Manchester Society controlled the statistics section of the Association: G. W. Wood was the section president and eight of the nineteen positions on the section committee were filled by Manchester men.

18 See also Stephen Cole's chapter in this book.

19 *Journal of the Statistical Society of London,* 5 (1842), 74-81.

20 *Ibid.,* p. 78.

21 This change in the nature of the Society's work was paralleled by changes in the statistics section of the British Association. In 1857 the title of the section became "Statistical Science," and in 1863, "Economic and Statistical Science."

22 "Inaugural Address," *Transactions of the Manchester Statistical Society,* 1863-1864 (1864), i-xxvi.

23 *Ibid., passim.*

24 Manchester: Bancks, 1834.

25 *Ibid.,* p. 7.

26 *Report of a Committee of the Manchester Statistical Society on the State of Education in the Borough of Manchester in 1834* (London: James Ridgeway and R. H. Moore; Manchester: Bancks, 1835).

27   *Ibid.*, p. 18.
28   *Ibid.*, p. 19.
29   *Report of a Committee of the Manchester Statistical Society on the State of Education in the City of York* (London: James Ridgeway and R. H. Moore; Manchester: Bancks, 1837), p. 4.
30   Included as an addendum to this report is a table drawn from an 1826 study on the state of education among the working class performed by the Society of Friends. It might be worth investigating how many other studies were done by religious groups.
31   Ashton, *Investigations*, chap. 2.
32   London: James Ridgeway and R. H. Moore; Manchester: Bancks, 1838.
33   An abstract of this paper, together with one table, appear in the transactions of the statistics section of the British Association for 1834.
34   *Working Classes*, p. 6.
35   "Report on the Condition of the Working Classes in the Town of Kingston-Upon-Hull," *Journal of the Statistical Society of London*, 4 (1841), 156-175.
36   *Ibid.*, pp. 4-5.
37   These questions have had a varied history: Kay-Shuttleworth also reported difficulty with questions of this sort, but Joseph Adshead apparently found none. See his *Distress in Manchester* (London: Henry Hooper, 1842). The latter is a study done in 1840-1841 by a member of the Manchester Statistical Society for the Manchester Relief Committee and is an extension of a previous study by the same author.
38   It is interesting to note that five of the six were published before 1838, and none of them involve material from the Society's surveys. The total of ninety papers does not include two sessions of which there is no record.
39   The figures are only approximate because the data for 1841 were not available.
40   In 1877 the British Association considered disbanding the statistics section because of concern that the papers contributed did not represent true scientific achievement. See Karl Pearson's *The Life, Letters and Labours of Francis Galton*, Vol. 2 (London: Cambridge University Press, 1924), p. 347.
41   An abstract only is available: W. R. Greg, "On the Social Statistics of the Netherlands," *Transactions of the British Association for the Advancement of Science*, 5 (1835), 125.
42   Quoted in Donald Read, "Chartism in Manchester," in Asa Briggs, ed., *Chartist Studies* (London: Macmillan, 1959), p. 38.
43   *Ibid.*, p. 39.
44   The timing of events during this period is somewhat vague, and it was not possible to ascertain how many of this original group were also members of the Manchester Statistical Society. The evidence of S. E. Maltby [*Manchester and the Movement for National Elementary Education, 1800-1870* (Manchester: Manchester University Press, 1918), pp. 49-50, 141] suggests that at least nine members played important roles in this movement.
45   *Ibid.*, p. 48.
46   Manchester *Guardian*, September 27, 1837.
47   Quoted in Maltby, *Manchester and Elementary Education*, p. 44.
48   *Ibid.*

49   *Ibid.*, pp. 53-54.
50   *Ibid.*, p. 141.
51   *Ibid.*, p. 154.
52   The Anti-Corn Law League suffered a decline during the prosperous years of 1843 to 1845, rose again after the bad harvest of 1845. On the point of timing, see Arthur Redford, *The History of Local Government in Manchester*, Vol. 2 (London: Longmans, 1959), pp. 3-63; and Henry Ashworth, *Recollections of Richard Cobden, M.P.* (London: Cassell, 1876), pp. 24-30.
53   Anti-Corn Law Conference, *Report of the Statistical Committee of the Anti-Corn Law Conference* (London: C. Fox, 1842).
54   Ashworth, *Recollections*, pp. 24-25.
55   *Ibid.*, p. 25.
56   *Ibid.*, p. 43.
57   W. E. A. Axon, *Annals of Manchester* (Manchester: John Heywood, 1886), p. 204.
58   Ashworth, *Recollections*, p. 36.
59   Norman McCord, *The Anti-Corn Law League 1838-1846* (London: Allen and Unwin, 1958), p. 65.
60   *Ibid., passim.* The data are approximate. It marks the end of the worst of the League's financial problems and the beginning of the corn law question as a political issue upon which elections were fought.
61   *Ibid.*
62   Ashworth, *Recollections*, pp. 28-29.
63   The Radicals, a Chartist-oriented group, did not trust the "cotton manufacturer" Whigs and often voted with the Tories.
64   Quoted in Redford, *History*, p. 24.
65   *Ibid.*, pp. 38-40.
66   *Ibid.*, p. 40.
67   *Ibid.*, p. 41.
68   *Ibid.*, pp. 32-51.
69   Ashton, *Investigations*, p. 9.
70   Kelly, *Notebook*, p. 5.
71   *Ibid.*, p. 6; Leo G. Grindon, *Manchester Banks and Bankers* (Manchester: Bancks, 1877), pp. 190-192.
72   The average cost of the studies was about £140, or about £2800 over the period 1833-1841. None of these figures are in constant pounds.
73   Ashton, *Investigations*, pp. 142-144.
74   Quoted in Thomas Read Wilkinson, "On the Origin and History of the Society," *Transactions of the Manchester Statistical Society*, 1875-1876, p. 17.
75   Sir Llewellyn Woodward, *The Age of Reform 1815-1870* (2d ed.; Oxford: Clarendon, 1962), p. 93.
76   H. D. Clokie and J. W. Robinson, *Royal Commissions of Inquiry* (Stanford, Calif.: Stanford University Press), 1937, p. 2.
77   *Ibid.*, p. 76. A detailed breakdown of the number of studies on particular subjects was not available.
78   *Ibid.*, p. 79.
79   More is not known because it was only possible to find two commission

reports dating from the period 1833-1850.

80   *Report of the Commission on the Condition and Treatment of Children Employed in the Mines and Colleries of the United Kingdom* (London: William Strange, 1842). Kennedy was the second vice-president of the Society.

81   Woodward, *Reform*, p. 91.

82   Clokie and Robinson, *Royal Commissions*, p. 91.

83   Smith, *Kay-Shuttleworth*, pp. 24-29.

84   Wilkinson, "History," p. 15.

85   W. R. Greg, "Outlines of a Memoir on Statistical Desiderata," *Transactions of the British Association for the Advancement of Science*, 1836, p. 151, abstract.

appendix
•
frederick engels
and the manchester
statistical society

The fact that Engels' *Condition of the Working Class in England*[1] is based in large part on his experience as a Manchester manufacturer in the early 1840s makes his work relevant to the present study. He knew of—if he did not know personally—the three Greg brothers, the two Ashworths, John Kennedy, John Roberton, and Richard Cobden. He founded a good deal of his material on Kay-Shuttleworth's *Moral and Physical Condition of the Working Classes*, and to a lesser extent, on the work of another member of the Statistical Society: Canon R. Parkinson's *On the Present Condition of the Labouring Poor in Manchester.*[2]

His references to all of the above men—save Kay-Shuttleworth, Parkinson, Roberton, and Cobden, whom it seems certain he did not know—were disparaging. Of Kay-Shuttleworth and Parkinson, he apparently thought very highly. The others were simply pawns in the class struggle:

Let us suppose that a visitor comes to Manchester and wants to know something of the state of affairs in England. . . . The visitor indicates that he is interested in securing information concerning the condition of the factory population. He is referred to the leading progressive manufacturers, such as Robert Hyde Greg, Edmund Ashworth, or Thomas Ashton [all members of the Statistical Society]. . . . The manufacturer shows his visitor through an imposing, well-appointed building, which is perhaps fitted with ventilators. . . . The mill owner shows his guest a row of newly erected cottages which, from the outside, present a clean and attractive appearance. . . . He is naturally careful to select only houses occupied by overlookers and skilled mechanics, so as to be sure that the family is one completely devoted to the manufacturer's interests.[3]

Or:

In October 1844 there was a strike of the operatives in Messrs. Kennedy's mill in Manchester. Kennedy prosecuted them [for breach of contract] on the grounds that there was a notice displayed in the factory that no more than two workers in each room could give in their notice at the same time. The court decided in Kennedy's favor. . . .[4]

notes

1   W. O. Henderson and W. H. Chaloner, trans. and eds. (Oxford: Blackwell, 1958).
2   London and Manchester: no publisher given, 3d ed.; 1841.
3   Engels, *Condition*, pp. 210-211.
4   *Ibid.*, p. 201.

references

1. books

Ashton, Thomas S., *Economic and Social Investigations in Manchester 1833-1933* (London: Staples, 1934).

Ashworth, Henry, *Recollections of Richard Cobden, M.P.* (London: Cassell, 1876).

Axon, W. E. A., *Annals of Manchester* (Manchester: John Heywood, 1886).

Clokie, H. D., and Robinson, J. W., *Royal Commissions of Inquiry* (Stanford, Calif.: Stanford University Press, 1937).

De Montmorency, James E. G., *State Intervention in English Education* (London: Cambridge University Press, 1902).

Grindon, Leo G., *Manchester Banks and Bankers* (Manchester: Bancks, 1877).

Hertz, Gerald Berkeley, *The Manchester Politician 1750-1912* (London: Sherratt and Hughes, 1912).

Kelly, Edith and Thomas, eds., *A Schoolmaster's Notebook* (Manchester: The Chetham Society, 1957).

McCord, Norman, *The Anti-Corn Law League 1838-1846* (London: Allen and Unwin, 1958).

Maltby, S. E., *Manchester and the Movement for National Elementary Education, 1800-1870* (Manchester: Manchester University Press, 1918).

Pearson, Karl, *The Life, Letters and Labours of Francis Galton*, Vol. 2 (London: Cambridge University Press, 1924).

Redford, Arthur, *The History of Local Government in Manchester*, Vols. 1 and 2 (London: Longmans, 1959).

Smith, Frank, *The Life and Work of Sir James Kay-Shuttleworth* (London: John Murray, 1923).

Woodward, Sir Llewellyn, *The Age of Reform 1815-1870* (2d ed.; Oxford: Clarendon, 1962).

2. periodicals

Journal of the Statistical Society of London, 1-16 (1838-1853).

Manchester *Guardian*, various numbers from 1836-1839.

Transactions of the British Association for the Advancement of Science, 2-30 (1834-1863).

Transactions of the Manchester Literary and Philosophical Society (1829-1863).

Transactions of the Manchester Statistical Society (1858-1876).

3. reports and pamphlets

Adshead, Joseph, *Distress in Manchester* (London: Henry Hooper, 1842).

Anti-Corn Law Conference, *Report of the Statistical Committee of the Anti-Corn Law Conference* (London: C. Fox, 1842).

Greg, Samuel, and William Rathbone, *Analysis of the Evidence Taken Before the Factory Commissioners as far as it Relates to the Population of Manchester and the Vicinity Engaged in the Cotton Trade* (Manchester: Bancks, 1834).

Kay-Shuttleworth, Sir James, *A Letter to the people of Lancashire, concerning the future representation of the commercial interest, by the return of members for its new boroughs for its reformed parliament* (London: James Ridgeway, 1831).

_____, *The Moral and Physical Condition of the Working Classes Employed in the Cotton Industry in Manchester* (London: James Ridgeway, 1832).

Report of the Commission on the Condition and Treatment of the Children Employed in the Mines and Colleries of the United Kingdom (London: William Strange, 1842).

Report of the Commission on the Physical and Moral Conditions of the Children and Young Persons Employed in Mines and Manufactures (London: John Parker, 1843).

Report of a Committee of the Manchester Statistical Society on the State of Education in Bury (London: James Ridgeway and R. H. Moore; Manchester: Bancks, 1835).

Report of a Committee of the Manchester Statistical Society on the State of Education in Liverpool (London: James Ridgeway and R. H. Moore; Manchester: Bancks, 1836).

Report of a Committee of the Manchester Statistical Society on the State of Education in Manchester (London: James Ridgeway and R. H. Moore; Manchester: Bancks, 1835).

Report of a Committee of the Manchester Statistical Society on the State of Education in Salford (London: James Ridgeway and R. H. Moore; Manchester: Bancks, 1836).

Report of a Committee of the Manchester Statistical Society on the State of Educa-tion in York 1836-37 (London: James Ridgeway and R. H. Moore; Man-chester: Bancks, 1837).

Report of a Committee of the Manchester Statistical Society on the Condition of the Working Classes in an Extensive Manufacturing District in 1834, 1835, and 1836 (London: James Ridgeway and R. H. Moore; Manchester: Bancks, 1838).

4. articles and abstracts

A Committee of the Manchester Statistical Society, "Report on the Condition of the Working Classes in the Town of Kingston-Upon-Hull," *Journal of Statis-tical Society of London*, 5 (1842), 212-221.

Ashworth, Henry, "Statistics of the Present Trade at Bolton; showing the modes in which it affects the different Classes of a Manufacturing Population," *Journal of the Statistical Society of London*, 5 (1842), 74-81.

Aspland, Alfred, "Inaugural Address," *Transactions of the Manchester Statistical Society*, 1863-1864 (1864), i-xxvi.

Cole, Stephen, "Notes on Nineteenth-Century English Empirical Social Research," 1964, unpublished paper.

Greg, W. R., "On the Social Statistics of the Netherlands," *Transactions of the British Association for the Advancement of Science*, 6 (1836), 151, abstract.

⸻ , "Outlines of a Memoir on Statistical Desiderata," *Transactions of the British Association for the Advancement of Science*, 5 (1835), 125, abstract.

Read, Donald, "Chartism in Manchester," in Asa Briggs, ed., *Chartist Studies* (Lon-don: Macmillan, 1959), pp. 29-64.

Wilkinson, Thomas Read, "On the Origin and History of the Manchester Statistical Society," *Transactions of the Manchester Statistical Society*, 1875-1876 (1876), 9-24.

continuity
and
institutionalization
in science:
a case study
of failure
•
stephen cole

Scientific progress is to a great extent dependent upon intellectual continuity. If we are to produce science more capable of explaining empirical phenomena than the science of our predecessors, we must build upon their contributions. Without intellectual continuity we would be constantly beginning anew; each generation would have to rediscover the answers to simple problems, develop their own methodologies and their own theories. Given the crucial importance of intellectual continuity for scientific progress, sociologists of science should be concerned with conditions making for varying degrees of continuity. In this paper, I shall present a case study of a science in which there was little or no continuity. In studying the reasons behind failure, we may learn some of the conditions necessary for success. The science I shall analyze is empirical social research as it existed in nineteenth-century England. Here is a field that in the middle of the century showed signs of takeoff and by the end of the century was basically nonexistent. I shall try to show why continuity failed and progress was halted.

Stephen Cole is Associate Professor of Sociology at the State University of New York at Stonybrook where he is doing research in the sociology of science. Born in New York City in 1941, he received his Ph.D. in Sociology from Columbia University in 1967. Cole is the author of *The Unionization of Teachers: A Case Study of the UFT* (1969) and coauthor of *Social Stratification in Science* to be published in 1972 by the University of Chicago Press. This paper was originally written for a graduate seminar at Columbia University taught by Paul Lazarsfeld and Robert K. Merton. The research was supported by a National Science Foundation grant.

73

Social philosophers have speculated on the causes of human behavior throughout recorded history; yet it is only in the very recent past that men have tried to study their own behavior scientifically, as they have studied the behavior of physical, chemical, and biological phenomena. A historian writing the history of empirical sociology might begin with Durkheim and Weber. He would certainly have little to say about research done before the 1920s. Such a historian would be right in neglecting the large body of empirical social research produced by Victorian Englishmen as there was no continuity between this research tradition and our own. Almost everything that occurred in this research tradition would be irrelevant to the history of ours. This paper is concerned with the reasons for this discontinuity. First, however, we must describe what kind of social research was done in nineteenth-century England.

Very little empirical social research was conducted in the eighteenth century; but even then a pattern had appeared that was to be developed in the next century. A philanthropist or reformer who was deeply disturbed by some social problem would gather data on the problem in order to make others aware of it. Typical was John Howard (1726?-1790) who assembled a large body of data on prison conditions and presented his data before the House of Commons. His testimony was said to have been instrumental in the passage of a prison reform bill in 1774.[1] In the first decades of the nineteenth century much research was done on the workings of the Poor Law. The basic concern of Sir F. M. Eden's three-volume work, *The State of the Poor*, was the method by which the destitute were being cared for. Eden's work contains a county-by-county report with detailed information on baptisms, burials, marriages, poor rates, occupations, religion, the cost of land, wages, and prices.[2] In 1796 the Society for Bettering the Conditions of the Poor sponsored an inquiry by Matthew Mortin on the misery of the poor in the metropolis; in 1806 Patrick Colquhoun examined the cost to the country of widespread poverty.

At first research was conducted primarily by individuals. However, as more and more people became interested in collecting empirical data on social conditions, a number of societies were set up for this purpose. The first of these societies was founded in 1834 in Manchester.[3] Within a few years statistical societies were set up in London, Bristol, and other cities. Later, in 1857, the National Association for the Promotion of Social Science (SSA) was founded and published its *Transactions*. In 1861 a group of "social scientists" began to publish the *Social Science Review*.

What were the attitudes of these researchers toward their work? If one were to read only introductions and prospectuses, one would come away with the belief that these empirical re-searchers were greatly concerned with being "scientific." Like the physical sciences, social science had as its goal the discovery of quantifi-able laws. Social science was to be free of value judgments. The pro-spectus of the Statistical Society of London announces: "The Statistical Society will consider it to be the first and most essential rule of its conduct to exclude carefully all *opinions* from its transactions and publications—to confine its attention rigorously to facts—and, as far as it may be found possible, to facts which can be stated numerically and arranged in tables."[4]

Not only was social science to exclude opin-ions not based upon fact, but it was to strive to meet the methodological standards of the physical sciences. Professor Henry Fawcett begins an article on "The Theory and Tendency of Strikes" by saying: "Social science requires the same mode of investigation as physical science. Deductive principles are necessary to explain the observations of physi-cal science, to connect them one with another, and to bring out their relative importance. Similarly, unless some theory of strikes is applied to our facts, our conclusions must be vague and empirical."[5]

Many articles may be found with titles similar to that of J. T. Danson's "On the Method, and the Range of Statistical Inquiry as applied to the Promotion of Social Science," read before the SSA. Danson began by telling his listeners: "Our presence here assumes the existence of, or at the very least, the admitted possibility, of a Science of Society."[6] He went on to say that social science was still destitute of scientific method and would not become a science unless it acquired a scientific methodology. This methodology would be built upon that of the physical sciences. If the "laws" of social science are to be valid, they must be capable of being expressed in quantitative terms. Therefore, statistics should be defined as the art of "bringing facts within the range of mathematical computation."[7] Seeming to preview the Austrian and American social scientists of the 1920s and 1930s, Danson felt that the statistician should be able to "bring all the facts presented to him whatever they may be, touching any given topic, properly within the category of number, or of quantity."[8]

Talk of "laws" and of "quantification" is scattered throughout the literature of the social sciences during the nineteenth century. Thus we are not surprised to see the very honorable Lord Brougham speak to the SSA of "the laws which govern men's habits and the principles of human nature, upon which the structure of society and its movement depends."[9] Rawson W. Rawson defends social science in the *Journal of the Royal Statistical Society:* "Undeserved ridi-cule has been cast upon some attempts which have been made to show that moral phenomena are subject to established and general laws; for surely there can be no reason for denying that moral, no less than physical, phenomena may be found to be controlled and determined by peculiar laws. . . . Mankind is not exempt from these laws."[10]

Beatrice Webb, who served her apprenticeship as the research assistant to Charles Booth, tells us of the effort of Booth and herself to quantify all observations. "I am indeed embarrassed by its mass, and by my resolution to make use of no fact to which I cannot give a quantitative value. . . . There is struggling poverty, there is destitution, there is hunger, drunkenness, brutality, and crime; no one doubts that it is so. My object has been to attempt to show the numerical relation which poverty, misery and depravity bear to regular earnings and comparative comfort, and to describe the general conditions under which each class lives."[11]

Despite these high ideals, there was often little correspondence between the prospectus of a statistical society and the work of its members. It is not my aim to echo the *Times* of the nineteenth century and ridicule Victorians who called themselves social scientists. It would be of little value to demonstrate the unscientific nature of social science or the many methodological errors made by these investigators. Rather, I will show exactly how far empirical social research had advanced, and it did advance quite far.

overview: the type of research done

monographs

During the nineteenth century many monographs were published that made use of quantitative data. I have examined in detail only those monographs dealing with the subject of crime. Of the ten monographs on crime I have examined, only four were predominantly quantitative. The other six consisted of qualitative analyses of crime causation, introducing only occasionally descriptive tables, that is, marginals. The four quantitative monographs (to be examined in detail below) made use of elaborate statistical tables prepared by the government. All four analyses were quite similar. Each one was basically ecological, comparing crime rates in counties with other statistics such as extent of pauperism, education, or chief industry.

journals

JRSS / The *Journal of the Royal Statistical Society* began publication in 1839 and is still being published today. Table 1 presents a breakdown by subject matter and form of all the signed articles in Volumes 2, 4, 6, 8, and 18 of the *JRSS*.

table 1 · subject matter and form of articles appearing in the *JRSS*[a]

	form						
subject matter	descrip- tive	explana- tory	program- atic	methodo- logical	theore- tical	histor- ical	total
Agriculture	5	–	2	1	–	–	8
Public health	8	7	2	1	–	2	20
Population and census	13	1	1	1	–	2	18
Crime	5	6	–	1	1	–	13
Economic	13	1	–	1	1	3	19
Education	9	–	1	–	–	–	10
India	5	–	–	–	–	–	5
Army	5	1	–	–	–	–	6
Government	4	1	1	–	–	4	10
Condition of the poor	8	–	2	–	–	–	10
Statistics as a science	–	–	–	1	1	–	2
Total	75	17	9	6	3	11	121

a Articles falling into more than one category were so classified.

"Descriptive" articles are those that present data of either a quantitative or qualitative nature without making any attempt to interpret the data or to fit them in with any theoretical notions. A good example is Richard Edmonds' "A Statistical Account of the Parish of Madron, containing the Borough of Penzance, in Cornwall. Digested from the Replies to the First Series of Questions Circulated by the Statistical Society of London."[12] Mr. Edmonds was a solicitor in the town of Penzance, and this article is the reply to a series of questions sent out by the Statistical Society. The author describes the climate, industry, population, and charitable institutions of the Parish of Madron. There are descriptive tables, such as one showing average rainfall in Cornwall over a period of 25 years. The paper presents much data but no inferences are drawn.

"Explanatory" articles are those that present data, usually but not always quantitative, and then try to explain or interpret the data. The best examples were contributed by the physician William Augustus Guy. In his article "Contributions to a Knowledge of the Influence of Employments Upon Health," Guy presents data on health and occupation collected from the registers of King's College

Hospital where he worked.[13] He breaks down his data by sex, whether the occupation is an in- or outdoor one, whether the occupation is strenuous, and he even considers the biasing effect of social class. He finds that outdoor occupations are more favorable to the preservation of health. He then goes on:

It seemed highly probable that those occupations which were most injurious to health would evince their deleterious effects not only by raising the ratio of consumptive cases, but by claiming their victims at an earlier age.

He then presents a table showing tuberculosis rates by age, by whether the occupation is an in- or outdoor one.

Another explanatory article was contributed by the chaplain to the Preston House of Correction, the Rev. John Clay. "Criminal Statistics of Preston" is concerned with the causes of crime.[14] Clay interviewed the prisoners and presents a table showing age and sex by cause of crime. The "causes" of crime are drinking, idleness and bad company, weak intellects, temptation, and the like. Clay tries to show from his table the importance of each one of these "causes" of crime. Later he tries to account for the variation in crime rate from year to year. The very high crime rate in one year he says is due to a "strike." A third explanatory article, "Progress of Crime in the United Kingdom," was contributed by the actuary Joseph Fletcher who attempts to show the effect on crime of education.[15] He compares the education of criminals with the education of the general population and concludes:

The [data] . . . lead us to the melancholy conclusion that there were among the persons accused of crime in 1842, only 31.7 in 100 of the men, and no more than 35.2 in 100 of the women who could not, at least, "write imperfectly," and therefore sign their own names; which is an excess of instruction greatly on the side of crime, especially in the case of criminals.[16]

"Programmatic" articles are those that are predominantly devoted to putting forth suggestions for social reform. An example is the Rev. Theodore Dury's "Hints for improving the Condition of Agricultural Labourers."[17] The author presents suggestions for alleviating the plight of the poor agricultural laborers so as to prevent the occurrence of "sanguinary jacqueries" as in France.

"Methodological" articles deal with the methods of statistics in general or particular aspects of data collection and analysis. In Guy's "On the Value of the Numerical Method as Applied to Science, but especially to Physiology and Medicine," one point discussed is the effect of increasing the number of observations made on the validity of conclusions.[18] "The more we increase the number of our observations, the more do individual penchants and exceptions to the general rule disappear."[19]

Of the three "theoretical" papers, two are essays, for example, G. P. R. James's "Some Observations on the Book Trade, as connected with Literature in England."[20] The third paper, Rawson W. Rawson's "An Inquiry into the Statistics of Crime in England and Wales," briefly discusses the "theory of cultural determination":

Some indeed have gone further, and have even asserted that the passions are wholly subject to outward impressions; that if a child were so brought up, that it should never see a person weep except from pleasure, nor smile except in grief or anger, it would adopt weeping as the symbol of joy, and mirth as the token of sorrow, and would express its own feelings in that contrary manner.[21]

"Historical" articles deal with a topic over an extended period of time. Such papers are always descriptive. They differ from the "descriptive" articles only in that they deal with either subject matter of the past or with the development of a particular subject. One example will suffice: William Newmarch's "On the Loan's Raised by Mr. Pitt during the First French War, 1793-1801; with some statements in defense of the methods of Funding Employed."[22] The paper contains tables showing such things as the amount of annual interest on each loan, market prices of stock at the time of the loan, and the like.

Transactions of the National Association for the Promotion of Social Science / The main difference between the work appearing in *Transactions* and in the *JRSS* is that the former had very few quantitative papers. Of the 110 papers appearing in the first volume of the *Transactions*, only 3 were in any sense quantitative. Using the same criteria for classifying articles as quantitative or qualitative, more than 65 percent of the articles in the *JRSS* were quantitative. Also, *Transactions* had many more "programmatic" articles than the *JRSS*.

The Social Science Review / This weekly journal was published for two years beginning in 1861. The following is an excerpt from an advertisement for the journal:

Social science means the introduction of a method by which social problems may be investigated on a rational and scientific basis; a method which accepts that social like organic life is governed by fixed laws; that all policy is empiricism which is not based on these laws; and that the laws themselves are discoverable and susceptible of arrangement as the laws of a fixed science.[23]

Despite such admirable intentions, most of the articles were meant to be entertaining and might be described as a Victorian version of a combination of *Time* and *Life* magazines. However, *Social Science Review* occasionally published articles that more closely resembled those appearing in the *JRSS*. Typical of these is an article by J. N. Radcliffe in which the author presents suicide statistics and examines the effect of age, sex, and method of killing oneself, on rates of suicide. This article would be classified as explanatory because, an effort is made to interpret the data presented. Radcliffe notes that suicide increases sharply with age. Then, unlike Durkheim, Radcliffe resorts to ad hoc explanations to interpret this finding. "Suicide is not chiefly the resort of the thoughtless, the weak-minded, the impulsive, or the lunatic, but it is the refuge mainly of those who are worn out in a bitter and hopeless struggle against accumulated ills. Disease, suffering, and misery are, indeed, the chief factors in the causation of suicide."[24]

the methodology utilized in empirical research
strategic research sites

Often the factor distinguishing the famous and successful scientist from the merely competent one is the ability to find research sites suitable for testing his hypothesis. A few of the empirical researchers state that they have chosen a specific research site because it is strategic. G. W. Hastings saw that studying a reformatory could yield results significant in fields other than crime prevention. A reformatory indeed could be thought of as a replica of the larger society.

Take for instance, reformatory work. Viewed in its real aspect, as a special movement organized to remedy the defective condition of our criminal law, and to check the disastrous flow of young casual offenders into the ranks of regular crime, *it is not only important and interesting in its own facts and results, but highly illustrative of other social subjects.* In a well-regulated reformatory school may be seen the effect of moral and religious discipline, combined with good sanitary conditions, and a proper union of industrial and intellectual education, upon wayward, ignorant, and hardened natures. Such an institution is a type of the great work before us, for there is nothing done in a reformatory school which might not with proper appliances, be effected for society at large.[25]

The Rev. Robert Everest was interested in the effects of "social degradation" in producing crime and pauperism. He took as his research site the condition of the free blacks in the United States. "The United States, then, appeared to afford a good example in its free colored citizens, of a distinct class, socially degraded, and the object was to ascertain in what numbers, relative to the total population of each, they and the white race were held in confinement."[26]

sampling

Charles Booth is generally believed to be one of the first social scientists to make use of systematic sampling procedures. Booth realized that it would be impossible to do a survey of all of London if information on every individual had to be included, as was the practice in former surveys. He thus devised sampling techniques. In his study of the East End of London, using the family as the central unit, he acquired information from each of 66 school attendance officers in the East End. Booth started out with the knowledge that every fact he wanted was known to somebody. He then interviewed a large sample of informants. In his analysis Booth took into consideration the possible bias resulting from his sampling technique. "The calculations are based, as before, on the general assumption that as is the condition of the families with school children, so on the whole will be that of the entire population, or so far as there is any difference better rather than worse."[27]

Whereas Booth used techniques approximating sampling in the collection of data, William Augustus Guy had been using sampling techniques in the analysis of already existing data throughout the nineteenth century. In a paper on the influence of weather on sickness, Guy carefully describes his sampling procedure before proceeding with his analysis.[28] Robert Giffen also used sampling in his study of the changes in real wages of different occupations. Unable to get data on as many occupations as he would like, he chose occupations that were representative of a certain category of jobs, traced the rise in real wages in these occupations, and then abstracted his finding to the whole occupational category. If the changes were "in the same direction, or almost all in the same direction, then there would be sufficient reason for believing that similar changes had occurred throughout the entire mass."[29]

data collection

The majority of empirical social researchers based their research on already existing statistical data. Such data were institutionally generated, predominantly by the many branches of the government. When social science becomes institutionalized there is less dependence upon institutionally generated data which often are unsuited to answering factual and theoretical questions. If the necessary

data do not exist, they must be collected. Although the collection of
data never became institutionalized in England during the nineteenth
century, many researchers did collect their own data.

In the 1830s and 1840s, many surveys were
conducted with the aim of investigating the conditions of the working
classes. Such inquiries were usually undertaken and paid for by a statistical society. The simplest type of research sponsored by the Royal
Statistical Society in the 1830s and 1840s consisted of the preparation
of a series of questions which were then sent to the occupants of some
official status, such as county clerk. These questionnaires required only
factual information. The report by Richard Edmonds used earlier as an
example of a "descriptive" article was based upon replies to such a set
of questions. The editors commenting on Mr. Edmonds' article tell us
that "Mr. Edmonds had not given any speculative opinion upon the
social condition of the inhabitants. In the Queries put forth by the Statistical Society of London, the eliciting of such an opinion was studi-
ously avoided."[30] Thus, these "mail questionnaires" were far from being
the predecessors of our attitude surveys. Opinions were considered
damaging; what was needed were "facts." These surveys were basically
an extension of the census—with the purpose of collecting data that
the government had not yet gotten around to collecting. Perhaps one of
the reasons for the disappearance of such surveys sponsored by the
statistical societies is that the government statistical agencies expanded
their coverage. Edmonds' article was based upon replies to a questionnaire asking for general economic and demographic data. Some of the
questionnaires sent out by the Royal Statistical Society, however, requested information on a specific topic. One such questionnaire dealt
with strikes and their economic effects. The Society sent out a list of
questions requiring purely factual answers such as "How much money
has been lost as a result of the strike?"[31]

The questionnaires discussed thus far were all
distributed through the mail. The societies also sponsored surveys employing interviewers. Perhaps the first such survey was sponsored by
the Manchester Statistical Society. "When no reliable method of ascertaining the condition of hand-loom weavers could be thought of, a
survey was undertaken—a Mr. Henderson was hired to collect data—he
sampled (1 person in every other house) and produced a descriptive
survey which had such data as origin (e.g., Ireland), rent paid, education
of children, etc."[32] The hand-loom weavers were suffering due to their
replacement by steam-run machines. The social reform-oriented members of the Manchester Statistical Society, being good Victorians, wanted
to find some way of relieving their plight without impairing their independence. The resulting survey was deemed so successful that it was

extended. The total outlay of money was £175—not a small sum in those days.

The British Association for the Advancement of Science also supported surveys. In 1839 the Association gave out three grants: (1) £150 for studying the state of schools in England— "considered merely as a numerical analysis." (2)£100 for studying the state of the working classes "specified in the form of numerical tables." (3) £50 for enquiries into the statistics of collieries upon the Tyne and Wear. All these grants were administered by members of the statistical section of the Association.

One of the main worries of the sponsors of surveys was that the respondents would lie. Techniques were derived to check the accuracy of collected information. Booth compared different types of data to see if they led to the same conclusions. The Mayor of Manchester contributed a paper to the *JRSS* on the way in which working-class families spent their income. He tells us that personal knowledge of the respondents "gave a guarantee to the accuracy of their statements." The mayor goes into detail on how accuracy in his study was assured:

To insure to such statements as these as much accuracy as possible, some precautions are necessary in collecting the information. The husband can rarely furnish any statements in detail; it is better in nearly all cases to apply to the wife. She has her character, however, as an economical manager at stake, and requires cross-examining to elicit the exact expenditure. Without this, she is also liable to err, not from any wish to mislead, but from mere want of caution and sufficient thought. In such cases, the books of the shopkeeper were examined, and compared with the statements given by the parties themselves.[33]

The collection of data by the societies was not continued into the last part of the nineteenth century. These early social surveys did not aid the growth of empirical sociology because their potential was not realized. The surveys sponsored by the societies were never initiated to supply data that could be used in what we have called an "explanatory" fashion. These surveys were limited to the social reform interests of empirical social research. However, during the course of the century several individuals did collect data for more "sociological" purposes. Robert Everest, in his study of the effects of social degradation on crime referred to above, found that the institutionally generated crime statistics did not separate white convicts into native born and foreign. Such information was necessary to test his theory of the effects of "social degradation" in creating crime and he proceeded to collect it by visiting different jails and enquiring among the prisoners as to nation of origin.[34] When William Lucus Sargant found that the necessary data to evaluate the effects of public education did not exist, he collected his own data by correspondence with knowledgeable officials. As a last example, we may refer to Jelinger Symons who collected crime statistics in different-sized cities in order to prove his theory of the effect of population density on crime.[35]

problems of measurement

In empirical sociology many of our concepts cannot be directly measured; therefore, we must use indicators. Here I shall discuss those indicators used to measure the "moral character" of the population. Of such indicators, crime rates were the most important. Most of the researchers who dealt with crime did so because they believed crime to be an indicator of the morals of the population. Thus Jelinger Symons tells us that female crime, especially, is an indicator of demoralization.[36] Robert Everest tells us that the want of moral character "might be measured by the proportionate numbers of each class that were to be found in the various prisons, jails, and almshouses throughout a country."[37] And Thomas Plint prefaces his study of crime by telling us that the design of his study is to "show the real progress and character of crime since 1805; and its significance as a test of the moral condition of the people at large."[38] Plint later goes on to say that he does not think that crimes are really a very good indicator of the moral character of the people because they are committed by a "comparatively small class."[39] Later on, Plint sums up what he takes crime statistics to indicate.

The statistics of crime do not so much help to measure the morality of a nation, as they help to measure the degree of the morality of particular classes—the depth in the social strata to which religious influences have penetrated, and the counteracting force of the evil influences springing out of great luxury and wealth, in juxtaposition with a great preponderance of the very lowest classes; those classes being comparatively isolated from the more refined, educated, and moral sections of the community.[40]

There was considerable disagreement among the researchers over what type of crime statistics were the best indicators of the moral character of the people. Some maintained that "summary" convictions (i.e., those made by a judge without a trial) were not a good indicator of morality, as they represented only "minor" violations of the law. Thus the Rev. John Clay's paper on the effect of economic conditions on crime was criticized by the *Economist*, one of the leading liberal journals of the time, because Clay's analysis was based on summary convictions. Clay's answer to this criticism is to deny that summary convictions are only, or primarily, made for petty offences.[41] According to him, summary convictions include those made for such crimes as stabbing, housebreaking, and horse stealing. The use of summary statistics to measure immorality was also criticized by a professor of political economy at the University of Dublin, Richard Hussey Walsh. "It is not fair to estimate the morality of a nation by the number of petty offences committed in one or two districts, or even throughout the entire country."[42] Walsh suggests that a more accurate measure of morality is to be found in the "returns offences sent for trial to assizes and quarter sessions. . . . These are the returns to be employed in measuring the morality of a nation, and they should not be mixed up with the summary convictions."[43]

Perhaps the worst problem plaguing criminologists today is the inadequacy of crime statistics. We know that crime is differentially detected in different social classes and that crime statistics are often not comparable in that judicial procedures differ. This knowledge was also common to many nineteenth-century researchers. Thus Mary Carpenter, the author of books and articles on juvenile delinquency, tells us that the crimes of the upper classes do not come to the attention of the authorities because they are hidden and not reported; and that crime statistics are only an indicator of the amount of actual crime committed, as a large number of crimes are never reported.[44]

In discussing the increase or decrease in crime, most writers were aware of the effect of changes in judicial practices on raising and lowering crime statistics.

A still more satisfactory conclusion, however, may be drawn from these data. The tables cannot show the amount of actual crime, but only of such as has been detected, and become the subject of legal cognizance. Several causes have been in operation which must necessarily have increased the proportion of detected crime to that actually committed. Amongst these the following may be enumerated: a better organized, more numerous, and more active police; the mitigation of the criminal law, and the consequent increase of prosecutions; and improved prison discipline, and therefore a greater willingness on the part of the public to prefer charges; vast facilities for rapid communication, inevitably leading to a greater amount of detection. These causes must occasion a greater proportion of the committed crime to be detected; and if even detected crime decreases, then it necessarily follows that actual crime must, to a still greater extent, have diminished.[45]

Plint recognizes much the same point.

It is essential to note, preliminarily, that the increase of crime, as indicated by the records of the sessions and the assizes, may not correctly measure the degree of crime at the more recent epochs, as compared with its degree at the earlier. Changes in the law, greater activity of the police, may have had much to do with the increased ratios of *detected crime.*[46]

Because crime was used as an indicator of the morality of the nation, nineteenth-century researchers thought that if the causes of crime could be discovered, these would also be the causes of "immorality." It was frequently hypothesized that crime was caused by a lack of proper education. To test this hypothesis the researchers tried to show that where education was weak, crime rates were high. Crime statistics existed, but a measure of the extent of education was not directly available. The indicator most often used was the percentage of people who signed the parish marriage registry with a "mark" (i.e., could not write). Joseph Fletcher's use of this indicator is typical. "The numbers unable to write at the age of marriage, therefore, represent those who yet remain in a state of primitive ignorance."[47]

There were two criticisms put forth of the type of use that Fletcher and others made of marriage marks as indicators of education. It was often claimed that such marks were not a good indicator of education as it was possible to know how to write one's own name and still be virtually uneducated. Also, it was claimed that often the parish minister would sign a name for the party getting married. Others claimed that sometimes, even if a man knew how to write, he would often refuse to sign the register.[48] Several researchers pointed out that even if marriage marks were correlated with crime rates, this did not mean that lack of education was the cause of crime. Marriage marks were correlated with other social and industrial conditions of the county, which in turn might have influenced crime.

The simple solution of these apparent anomalies is, that the marriage marks indicate the comparative ratio of the merely operative classes to all other classes; and that the wide difference betwixt the ratios of crime in counties which exhibit the same marriage marks; or equal ratios of crime, with widely different proportions of marriage marks, indicate variations in social and industrial condition, which have far more to do with the prevalence of crime, than either the one or the other.[49]

rates

One of the first requisites of methodological sophistication is the use of rates rather than absolute numbers. If only the latter are considered, the findings are influenced by the marginal distribution and we learn nothing of the effect of the variable we are interested in. The failure to convert into rates weakened many analyses of crime before they began. Often, in analyses of the effects of education on crime, the *number* of educated criminals is compared with the *number* of uneducated criminals, and the conclusion is drawn that it is lack of education that causes crime.[50] Joseph Fletcher, however, pointed out that in order for such conclusions to be valid, the rate of uneducated in the criminal population must be compared with the rate of uneducated in the noncriminal population.

In making use of the education statistics contained in the criminal and gaol returns, it is important to guard against the common assumption that the mere positive excess of the ignorant over the instructed is any evidence that the want of instruction in the common arts of reading and writing, and arithmetic, to which the name of education is popularly applied, is the direct cause of crime, or that their general communication would be a direct remedy against its extension. No proof whatever is afforded by these data of the greater association of crime with ignorance than with instruction, *unless it be shown that the ignorance which prevails among those commited to prison is greater than that which prevails throughout society generally*; a position which is always tacitly taken for granted.[51]

reliability

Very few empirical social researchers were concerned with the reliability of the conclusions they drew from their statistics. A happy exception is again the physician William Augustus Guy. Guy is one of the only empirical researchers who was familiar with and made use of mathematical statistics and specifically probability theory. Guy addresses himself to the question of how many observations are necessary to get a "true" average. His procedure appears to be basically sound. He suggests that two separate samples be taken and the averages compared. When the difference between the two averages approaches zero, we have obtained the true average. He concludes that "Though the *possible* error to which a given small number of facts is liable is very large, there is always a fair probability in favor of any particular average coinciding, or approaching very closely to, the true average."[52]

random distribution of error

Connected with the problem of reliability is that of the distribution of error. A few of the researchers addressed themselves to this problem. They decided that if no reason could be thought of why there should be more errors in one section of the data than in others, it could be assumed that the errors would cancel each other and reliable results could be obtained despite the existence of error. Although the results may not tell us the exact truth about each respondent, in comparing groups of respondents there is no reason to believe there is more error in one group than in another. This truth was recognized by William Lucus Sargant: "Some, I know, can read with pleasure, who cannot write; it is said that a few can sign their names, but are unable to read print. But for the purposes of comparison we may disregard these exceptions, because where considerable numbers are taken, there will be about as many exceptions in one place as in another."[53]

methods of data analysis

I shall conclude the analysis of work done by nineteenth-century British social researchers by describing the basic modes of analyzing data. I shall then proceed to a more detailed discussion of the attempts to discover the causes of crime. The discussion below applies only to the small group of researchers who attempted to analyze their data.

The predominant mode of analysis was "ecological." The association between two or more variables would be compared within geographic areas—usually counties. Sometimes the association between variables would be compared over time in a single geographic area— such as England. Ecological analysis was used with varying degrees of sophistication and it must not be assumed that because this type of analysis is "no longer in style" that it is not a legitimate sociological method. To dispel any such suggestions we need only point out that Durkheim's analysis in *Suicide* was ecological, very similar in form to the type of analysis carried out by Englishmen such as Fletcher, Plint, Symons, and Rawson.

A typical ecological analysis was one in which population density was compared with crime rates in the forty English counties. Such analyses were carried out by Jelinger Symons and Leone Levi. The counties are arranged in one column, with the county having the greatest density of population at the head of the column and the county with the sparsest density of population at the foot of the column. In an adjacent column the counties are arranged with the county having the highest crime rate at the head of the column and the county with the lowest crime rate at the foot of the column. Because the researchers did not possess a tool such as the Spearman rank correlation coefficient, they drew their conclusions on the basis of inspection. Both Symons and Levi reached the same conclusion: "The relation of crime and offences to density of population is very intimate, closer probably than to any other cause whatever."[54] The authors, however, usually fail to explain why density of population causes crime. Where they do so, they revert to ad hoc explanations and abandon proof by data.

Another mode of analysis, less commonly employed, is what might be called "demonstration by comparison." This type of analysis was carried out by Robert Giffen in his monograph *The*

Progress of the Working Classes in the Last Half Century. It is Giffen's
aim to demonstrate that the standard of living of the working classes has
gone up. After carefully deciding what occupations to compare,[55] he
presents a table showing the wages of different occupations in different
towns in 1835 and 1885. He then computes the percentage of increase
or decrease. All have increased, and therefore after demonstrating that
the cost of living had not gone up as much as wages, Giffen concludes
that the standard of living of the English working man improved during
that period.

An analysis similar in form to that of Giffen's
was carried out by David Chadwick who was interested in demonstrating
that free libraries will be used more if they have longer hours so that the
working classes could use them after work.[56] He divides libraries into
two classes—those that are open in the evening and those that are not—
and compares the circulation statistics.

Perhaps the mode of analysis that most closely
corresponds to the predominant one employed by sociologists today is
the one I have called the "testing of hypotheses." An empirical relationship is identified and then various explanations of the relationship are
tested by examining the necessary data. Thus Robert Everest found that
there was a higher percentage of blacks than whites in the jails of the
United States (i.e., the ratio of black inmates to noninmates was higher).
He then tests a series of hypotheses to explain this phenomenon. Do
blacks receive longer sentences than whites? Everest presents tables to
show that although it is true that for similar charges blacks do receive a
slightly longer sentence than whites, the difference is not enough to
account for the great divergencies in crime rates. He reaches the same
conclusion in regard to the possible role of education as an influence on
crime rates. The effect of religion is examined and found to have no
influence. When Everest is unable to find any data to account for the
phenomenon he has identified, he reverts to an ad hoc explanation.

The testing of hypotheses was the predomi-
nant mode of analysis used by William Augustus Guy. We have shown
above how Guy collected data to test the hypothesis that the relationship between types of occupations and health was spurious. This was
perhaps Guy's favorite topic. Let us briefly review the way in which he
approached it. Guy was aware of the difficulties involved in determining
the influence of employment—isolated from other variables—on health.

It is extremely difficult to determine the real influence of employments upon
health; for, on the one hand, employments closely resembling each other in character may be associated with very dissimilar habits of life; and, on the other, employments having nothing in common may be combined with some one bad habit
which may be sufficiently powerful to render all of them unhealthy.[57]

But Guy proceeds confidently. He notices that outdoor occupations are favorable to women (in respect to tuberculosis rates) but that indoor occupations are favorable to men. He closely inspects the occupations he has been dealing with and finds that some indoor and outdoor occupations exert an injurious influence upon health independently of their being carried on indoors or outside. He withdraws patients with these occupations from his sample and finds that whether an occupation is outdoors makes very little difference in tuberculosis rates. He then goes on to examine other factors such as high temperature. After an extended analysis he develops a "theory" of the effect of different types of occupations on health. "Sedentary employments are unfavorable to health in the many, but favorable to longevity in the few. On the other hand, employments requiring greater exertion, are favorable to youth and manhood, but unfavorable to old age."[58]

        A similar approach to Guy's was that in which the researcher listed all the existing explanations of a phenomenon and then examined data to see which one was most adequate. This is the procedure followed by Edward Shepherd, the governor of the house of correction at Wakefield, in an article on the factors affecting recidivism. Under the "silent system" the rate of recidivism is 28.6 percent, under the "separate system," 26.6 percent. From these statistics he concludes that the system of incarceration employed has little effect on recidivism. He then proceeds to examine the effect of age at first committal, age at time of last committal, the nature of offense leading to recommittal, the length of the sentence (he finds "moderate" sentences the least effective), and education. He makes no statements on the effect that education may have on the first committal, but he concludes that education exerts a strong effect on recidivism.[59]

a case study: plint's crime in england

It is the design of the following pages to show the real progress and character of crime, since 1805; and its significance as a test of the moral condition of the people at large—its connection, or not, with new industrial organizations; and directly to combat the prevailing theory that ignorance and immorality are greatly on the increase.[60]

        These are the stated reasons for the existence of Thomas Plint's monograph. Yet the discerning reader may see quite another reason motivating the author. Plint is using the new "social science" in defense of the industrial system and its accompanying social conditions. Social science was not to be left in the hands of the critics of industrial society. Why is it that the obvious ideological motivation of the author of this book does not bother us? It is because the value of

nineteenth-century English "sociology" cannot be judged in terms of
how closely it approximates "truth." The explanations of social phenomena offered by nineteenth-century social researchers are so questionable to the contemporary sociologist that their approximation to
"truth" is not the most significant criterion for their evaluation. Practically everything Plint said is no doubt questionable; yet this detracts
not in the least from the brilliant quality of the book. Considering the
structure of the institution of social science in England at the middle
of the nineteenth century, it is surprising that such a fine piece of research was done at all.

Plint's book is magnificently polemical. He
systematically destroys the arguments of his predecessors—Joseph
Fletcher, Jelinger Symons, and F. G. P. Neison. The basic mode of
analysis of these three writers was to classify counties as being predominantly agricultural, mining, or manufacturing, rich or poor, densely
populated or sparsely populated, and so forth, and then to compare
crime rates in different groups of counties. Plint begins by saying that
he will not employ this system because "The grouping is absurd, so as
to be ridiculous, has obviously been adopted to serve a theory, and will
not bear a moment's examination."[61] If it is true, as Fletcher maintains,
that the industrial organization of the manufacturing districts engenders
crime, then the counties that Fletcher calls industrial should have "uni-
formity in the ratios of crime and ignorance."[62] Plint presents a table
to prove that this is not the case. The table shows crime and ignorance
rates for the counties which his predecessors called "manufacturing."
The variation in the crime rates is great as is the variation in ignorance
rates. Also, some of the counties with the least amount of ignorance,
have the highest crime rates.[63]

Plint presents a table showing crime rates in
each county from 1801 to 1845. Crime rates increased in this period
in every county. From this piece of evidence one might expect pessi-
mistic conclusions to be drawn; but Plint desires to draw optimistic
conclusions and designs an analysis that is quite convincing. The increase
in crime rates may be explained in one of two ways: (1) Either crime
among the general population has gone up, indicating a degeneration
of morals, or, (2) the "criminal class" has increased and the general
population is in fact more "moral" than in the past. Before choosing
between these two alternatives, Plint points out that because judicial
procedures have changed in the course of the century, the crime statistics may be meaningless as far as indicating moral conditions. He then
arranges counties in groups according to the amount of increase of
crime, that is, he places in one group counties where the increase in
crime has been under 100 percent, and in another group counties where

the increase has been between 100 and 150 percent, and so forth. He concludes that the increase in crime has been greatest in those counties having relatively the smallest amount of crime. In fact, the ratio of increase in crime to increase in population has even decreased. To prove this he presents the data reproduced below (table 2).

table 2 · increase of crime relative to population

period	percent increase
1801-1821	112.0
1821-1831	26.9
1821-1836	32.1
1821-1845	35.6
1831-1845	6.9
1836-1845	2.7

On the basis of the table, Plint is able to conclude: "either that some powerful causes are in operation retarding crime, or that crime—that is, the offences which the national tribunal recognizes as such—has its limits—and that in particular localities it is approaching such limits."[64] It is of course quite obvious to the sophisticated reader that crime increased. But presenting the data in this fashion enables a more "optimistic" conclusion to be drawn, than if simple increase had been shown. Why has crime been increasing? It is because with an increase in wealth and luxury there have been greater opportunities to commit the crime that makes up the great bulk of the crime rates—larceny:

In 1841, 73 percent of all crime consisted of simple larcenies and embezzlements; and in 1845, 76 percent. What chance has the perpetrator of petty larcenies in such counties as Cumberland and Westmoreland, or even Durham, compared with counties like Lancashire, Yorkshire, Middlesex, and Warwick, with their densely populated capitals and chief towns? It is rather a vague evidence of the morality of a county, that offences are *not* committed, which, from their very nature, must be few in it. The pickpocket and the thief can find no nestling place amongst the statesmen of Cumberland and Westmoreland, or the miners of Durham and Cornwall. They fly to Birmingham, London, Manchester, Liverpool, Leeds. They congregate where there is plenty of plunder, and verge enough to hide in.[65]

The fact that the members of the criminal classes congregate in densely populated areas does not mean that we can attribute to the factory system the production of anything more than cotton goods. In fact, Plint shows that the rate of decrease in the increase of crime has been least in the *agricultural* counties.

What does Plint say about the hypothesis that it is lack of education that is the cause of crime? It is obviously absurd. Crime has been increasing and it is obvious to everyone that education has also been increasing. Therefore, if any relation exists between the two variables, it must be a negative one. Furthermore, to measure the extent of education by the percentage of marriage marks is wrong because different rates of marriage marks merely indicate the existence in different proportions of the different social classes.

The simple fact indicated by the fewer marriage marks, or the greater proportion of persons of independent means, in particular counties, is, that the middle and upper classes preponderate in such counties; and to draw from such proportions the inferences: (1) That the *people*, meaning thereby the mass, are more ignorant; and (2) That the presence of a higher proportion of persons of independent means, promotes the general intelligence and morality of the operative population—is a *non sequitur*—is absurd. It is obvious that if the relative proportions of the middle and upper classes, to the *so-called* operative or working class, were alike in all counties, the marriage marks, and the amount of crime, would indicate the comparative degree of instruction, and also the morality of the operative class; because it is obvious, that in the middle and wealthy classes, few, if any instances occur, of inability to write, and it is also clear, from the nature of the crimes which come before the sessions and the assizes, that the great mass are committed by a class among the operatives; or rather, as will be shown in the sequel, by a criminal class, distinct from the indigenous working population.[66]

Later on Plint futher criticizes the theory that lack of education is the cause of crime. Crime rates oscillate greatly. Education is a rather stable phenomenon and does not vary from year to year.

Violent oscillation is on the supposition impossible; and it is proof positive of the blinding influence of theory, that men, accustomed to a minute examination of our criminal records, should never have had any misgivings as to the soundness of their theory, when the phenomena before them were so clearly and unequivocally unconformable to the cause assigned.[67]

The oscillations in crime rates from year to year suggest to Plint that crime should be related to other variables that oscillate—such as economic conditions. Plint presents a table showing the price of bread and the amount of crime. He finds the data offering partial support for his theory. He wisely does not propose a monocausal theory of crime and states that it is necessary to discover the conditions under which dear food brings about an increase in crime. Plint then presents a three-variable table to show that crime increases most in industrial counties when bread prices increase. He then further elaborates his analysis by introducing type of crime. He finds that the type of crimes that are committed by the "criminal classes"—for example burglaries, highway robberies, house and shop breaking—are those that increase the most in periods of economic distress as measured by bread prices. He concludes: "It is quite obvious that any comparison betwixt counties so differently affected by variations in the *price of food*, and the state of trade, which exclude, or disregard, the influence of these variations, can only lead to error."[68]

Plint goes on to an analysis of the effects of age on crime. After adjusting the population of each county, he finds that counties that have the same average criminality have crime distributed among age groups in quite different proportions.

It needs no deep philosophy to perceive that there must be some great difference in the social condition, at the several sections of ages. . . . It is mere empiricism to group counties, on account of similar general organization, or of equal absolute crime, to all the population. Averages are more deceptive. Science asks for *means*, all other things being alike![69]

Thus we must only compare counties when all relevant variables have been controlled. When population is split into age groups, there is no longer any relation between type of county (manufacturing-agricultural) and crime.

Next Plint considers the effect of occupational class on crime and here his procedure is, although ingenious, logically assailable, especially by those having the benefit of an advanced methodology course. Plint reasons that the greater part of crimes are committed by members of the operative class. He therefore controls for occupation and age, and then concludes that crime is *higher* in the agricultural than the manufacturing counties "vis., that the morality of the manufacturing population ranks above the agricultural."[70] This is equivalent to controlling for all social differences between blacks and whites and then concluding that there is no difference in unemployment rates or that whites in fact have higher unemployment than blacks.

Plint now leaves ecological analysis and carries out an analysis of crime in Manchester that is truly far ahead of its time. Manchester has a high crime rate. But who commits these crimes? (He has at least implicitly realized that more than ecological data is necessary to analyze crime.) Plint discovers a table giving the occupations of criminals. He then presents the summary table reproduced below (table 3).[71] From this table he draws the following conclusions:

table 3 · social class and crime

classes	percentage of population	percentage summary convictions	percentage committed for trial
Manufacturing classes	49.0	13.2	16.2
Laborers	6.7	13.1	12.3
Handicraftsmen, retail dealers, servants, clerks, etc.	43.0	37.7	37.3
No trade, prostitutes, etc.	1.3	36.0	33.2
Total	100.0	100.0	100.0

The conclusion demonstrated by this short Table, combined with the two immediately preceding, cannot be better expressed than in the words of the Rev. John Clay, chaplain of the Preston House of Correction:—"It is now sufficiently evident that it is not a manufacturing population, as such, which fosters crime. . . . It is not manufacturing Manchester, but multitudinous Manchester, which gives birth to whatever criminality may be imputable to it. It is the *large town*, to which both idle profligates and practiced villains resort, as a likely field for the indulgence of sensuality, or the prosecution of schemes of *plunder.*[72]

If 40 or even 30 percent of the crime of the metropolis be committed by the criminal class, then, in whatever degree the crime so committed exceeds the crime perpetrated by the same class in other counties, the crime of the metropolis will require correction, in order to a fair comparison of the relative morality of the indigenous and industrious classes.[73]

The broad general conclusion from the preceding analysis is this: that there is a far larger proportion of all offences committed by the vagrant and predatory classes in the manufacturing than the agricultural counties, because of the greater number and populousness of the towns—to which, for reasons sufficiently stated before, these dangerous and vicious classes resort."[74]

I have not found a more convincing explanatory analysis in all the literature of nineteenth-century English empirical sociology that I have read.

why was empirical research undertaken?

In nineteenth-century Britain people who did empirical social research did not do so as occupants of specialized statuses. Why then was research done at all? I shall discuss the three factors motivating empirical researchers: the empiricist milieu, the need for efficiency, and the need for reform.

the empiricist milieu[75]

The nineteenth century in England was a period in which people became increasingly interested in the facts of their existence. Empiricism became important in philosophy and the sciences. Geology, for example, became increasingly an empirical descriptive science based upon minute observations of fossils and rock formations.[76] The interest in social facts probably received its greatest impetus from the far-reaching changes brought about by the industrial revolution.

The importance of the social milieu in stimulating research was recognized by contemporaries. Frederick J. Mouat, writing on the history of the Statistical Society of London, commented that

It will thus be seen that young as we are in the history of the world, we made our appearance with kindred institutions of similar character, only when the age was ripe for the more exact observation of phenomena and facts of all kinds and classes in physical science, as well as in the moral and social relations of man, in the mixed and complex conditions of modern civilization and progress.[77]

In the prospectus for the *JRSS* it is said "that the *spirit of the present age* has an evident tendency to confront the figures of speech with the figures of arithmetic; it being imposssible not to observe a growing distrust of mere hypothetical theory and *a priori* assumption. . . ."[78]

Nathan Glaser, in his paper "The Rise of Social Research in Europe," goes so far as to maintain that curiosity stimulated by the changes of the industrial revolution was the *primary* motive behind empirical research: "Curiosity alone, the same curiosity that led travelers to new lands and the study of new peoples, made the poor an important subject of study."[79] As Glaser points out, the growth of a large and isolated factory working class created as much curiosity as it did fear. The life of the working class seemed to Victorian Englishmen to be romantic and exotic.

We read in English parliamentary reports of children who had not heard of Jesus Christ at the age of fourteen, of the almost complete disappearance of any traditional religion among the new working-classes, of an almost complete breakdown of traditional patterns of sexual control.[80]

That curiosity was an important motivating force is undeniable. But that research was done mainly to satisfy curiosity, as is maintained by Glaser, would be a misstatement of fact. People wanted to know what the conditions of the poor were; but in an overwhelming majority of cases, they wanted to know for one of two specific reasons: to increase administrative efficiency and to bring about social reform.

Before discussing research for administrative
and social reform purposes, we shall briefly discuss another aspect of
the empiricist milieu. A definite product of the nineteenth century
was the belief that views of society not based upon hard data were un-
trustworthy. Many of the researchers took pleasure in proving great
men such as John Stuart Mill to be wrong. Thus Jelinger Symons tells
us that despite Mr. Mill's reputation as a

profound thinker and a masterly writer, it is needful, in defence of the true interests
of the working classes, to protest against such views and statements as he has conceived and put forth in the above and similar passages, *without any adequate experience or knowledge of the facts to warrant them.*[81]

Symons goes on to say that Mill has no conception of what the actual
conditions of the lower classes are, and that, furthermore, he will never
learn them from the study of political economy.

In an article in the *JRSS*, William Sargant
criticizes a Professor Fawcett because the latter has proposed a theory
in direct contradiction to reality as revealed by facts. "Professor Fawcett seems to me guilty of this error: he pronounces the agricultural
laborers (who are in truth, as well instructed as the town population)
entirely illiterate: he says that 'their ignorance is as complete as it is
distressing.'"[82] F. G. P. Neison, an actuary for an insurance company,
in an article with a title as long as it is informative, tells us that the
commonly held belief that the living conditions of the working classes
are unfavorable to long life is wrong. Life tables, he says, prove that the
rich have no longer life expectancy than the poor.[83] Joseph Fletcher,
who like Neison was one of the most original researchers of the century,
takes pleasure in relating how his empirical research has proven economic
theory to be mistaken.

The second table is the result of careful inquiries of my own in the winter of 1838.
It shows that the preceding deficient harvest, and the consequent rise of prices,
caused at least a temporary increase in the money wages of the agricultural laborers
of this part of the kingdom, *contrary to what would have been anticipated by any
one placing a reliance upon the principles of the best economists,* unqualified by
any allowance for disturbing causes or unreduced phenomena.[84]

In an address before the statistics section of
the British Association for the Advancement of Science on the "connection" between statistics and political economy, T. C. D. Lawson
optimistically announced that "statistics offered at once the materials
and the text of political economy." Lawson goes on to analyze the
proportion of marriages in cities of differing degrees of wealth:

In Edinburgh the proportion of marriages to the whole population is 1 in 136. In

Leith, however, where the population is of much humbler grade, the proportion is 1 in 110. Again, in Perth, there is 1 marriage in 159 inhabitants; while in Dundee, which is a much poorer place, there is 1 in 111 inhabitants. *Thus statistics prove that poverty is not a check on marriage, though political economists have always assumed that it is.*[85]

The researchers believed not only that "economic theory" could be tested by the collection of empirical data but also that problems that had for a long time remained unsolved could now be attacked with the aid of empirical data. This is not to say that research was actually carried out to test ideas, but only that it was felt it was *possible* so to test ideas. The belief that theories must depend upon fact, and even follow facts, is an indicator of the growth of empiricist notions. However, when it came to actual research the testing or developing of hypotheses was of less than secondary importance. Research was conducted as a means to more efficient administration and to bringing about social reform.

desire for efficient administration

One of the motivations behind empirical social research was the belief that the efficient administration of bureaucratic organization depended upon the possession of relevant empirical information. In this respect social research was influenced by the practices of businessmen. Social research is sometimes revealingly referred to as "the business of social science"[86] Charles Booth first did empirical research in connection with his shipping business. He believed that the key to business success was in the collecting of relevant empirical information. When Booth later did his social research he applied the methods he had used successfully in his business. "As a businessman, his practical decisions were invariably founded on a careful and comprehensive review of the facts under consideration. What more natural than that he should apply the same method in the problem of poverty?"[87]

Many articles appear in the *JRSS* that present table after table of descriptive statistics. The authors believed the statistics they had collected and presented had a functional administrative purpose. Typical is an article by Charles Fripp, Esq., on the statistics of the City of New York. Mr. Fripp tells us what the "purpose of his inquiry" is:

At the present period, when the intercourse between this country and the United States is receiving a new stimulus from the establishment of transatlantic steam navigation, it becomes doubly interesting to obtain an accurate knowledge of their internal economy, as well as of our mutual relations . . . . It is with the hope of contributing to this important end, by the evidence of *facts*, that I lay before the society the following paper.[88]

It was fell that commerce between England and her former colonies would be more efficiently conducted if a knowledge based upon data was possessed. W. A. Graham published a series of descriptive statistical tables on railway traffic with the expressed belief that in so doing he was rendering an "important service to the public by throwing light upon the condition and employment of the population of different places, and upon the state and variation of local trade.[89]

social reform

Curiosity, the empiricist milieu, and the need for statistics to aid in efficient administration were all important in motivating empirical research. However, the overwhelmingly dominant motive was the need to collect information that would be useful in bringing about social reform. Even if some articles did not explicitly mention a particular desired reform, all research was carried on in an environment dominated by reform interests. The self-image of the members of the Royal Statistical Society and the Social Science Association was that of social reformer. They thought of social research as a tool for bringing about social reform.

In my paper, "The Charitable Impulse in Victorian England," I argue that empirical social research was made necessary by ambivalence in the value system of Victorian Englishmen.[90] The ideological child of the industrial revolution was the laissez-faire value system—dominated by the two pillars of individualism and independence. This value system stressed the idea that charity and social reform must not impair the independence of the working classes. Another set of values, however, a holdover from preindustrial England, one that emphasized communal social ties, competed with the dominant laissez faire. When industrialization caused the separation of the classes (the poor living in the city slums, the well-to-do in the new suburbs) many wealthy Victorians felt the need to relieve the plight of the poor.[91] The doctrine of individualism had not completely destroyed the Victorian sense of communal responsibility. Motivated by religious beliefs and compunctions of guilt as well as by a sense of duty, Victorians felt that they had to look after the poor. But how was the need for reform to be reconciled with the ideology of individualism? How was reform to prevent the lower classes from losing the independence necessary for human life? Empirical social research was the means of reconciling two incompatible goals. By investigating the actual conditions of the poor, reformers could determine what the most efficient means were of helping the poor without impairing their independence. We are here only able to mention this hypothesis. Our basic concern in this paper is not to explain why people felt that empirical research was necessary for social reform, but rather to show that social research *was* carried out for reform purposes.

So closely was the study of statistics and social research connected with social reform that they were often defined as equivalent to each other. William Deverell, writing in the *JRSS*, carried such a definition to an extreme when he said that

facts *are* statistical only as much as they can be shown to have a direct relation to the ostensible end for which social union is established—the greatest happiness of the greatest number; and that, all national and even local legislation can be just and equitable only as it proceeds upon the general average principles obtained from statistical documents.[92]

Other researchers emphasized emphatically that facts were *not* collected merely for the sake of curiosity.

The statist is not animated by a mere spirit of curiosity, nor does he content himself with the simple documentation of facts. His objects are at once nobler and more practical. He aims at discovering the actual condition of his country and the causes of that condition, with a view to discover also the methods of improving it. Now, even the true condition of the country is not immediately obvious to the superficial observer; while the causes of the several phenomena which it exhibits lie very deep, and can only be discovered by the aid of patient and extensive inquiries.[93]

Social reformers often believed that all that had to be done to bring about reform was to publicize the shocking living conditions of the working classes.[94] A good portion of the rich knew absolutely nothing of the havoc industrialization was playing among the poor. "When Sir Robert Peel in 1802 brought up the matter of apprentice children in the new cotton factories, he confessed that he had not until lately known about them even in his own mills."[95] When the members of the SSA said that only publicity was necessary to cure social evils, they were in part right.[96] Charles Booth also believed that publicity would aid reform. He wanted a means of "influencing public opinion for good, which would be based upon a knowledge of science and the natural laws governing human behavior."[97]

Thus research would alleviate ignorance and aid reform. But research was needed not only to publicize evils, but also to discover the best means of curing social evils. It was constantly stressed that "the Samaritan's heart must be accompanied by knowledge, or he may injure the object of his care. The actions of good men must be wise to insure success, and bring an appropriate reward."[98] Thomas Beggs, the source of the above advice goes on to maintain that social research will "lead to the substitution of preventative measures for the palliative policy, which has hitherto obtained."[99]

Social reform was the predominant reason for the founding of all the societies whose members carried out empirical research.[100] The first such society to be established was the Manchester Statistical Society, founded in 1834. T. S. Ashton, the English economic historian, tells us that the society was founded because "corporate maladies on a scale hitherto unknown made it imperative that Manchester men should turn to social inquiry."[101] The founders of the society were professionals and businessmen who had been concerned with social reform for a long time. William Langton, the man who took the lead in organizing the society, had had experience with the Provident Society. He had set up in March 1833 the Manchester and Salford District Provident Society—"for the encouragement of frugality and forethought, the suppression of mendicity and imposture, and the occasional relief of sickness and unavoidable misfortune amongst the poor."[102] It was through his work in this Provident Society that Langton came to believe in the need for a society to collect social data. The Manchester Statistical Society was set up as a companion organization to the Provident Society. Its members specifically disavowed an interest in statistics for their own sake:

It will be evident that few, if any, of the founders of the Society were statisticians in the modern sense of the term. They were less interested in enumeration and computation than in effecting improvement in the state of the people among whom they lived. Like its contemporary the District Provident Society, the Statistical Society was the means to an end. The one stood to the other in the relation of theory to practice, of science to art; and the membership of both bodies is largely identical.[103]

The Statistical Society of London, known later as the Royal Statistical Society (RSS), was set up for the same reasons as was the Manchester Society. In an unsigned article, presumably by the editor, in the first volume of the *JRSS* the society is classified along with other "reform" societies as having the purpose of improving the conditions of the laboring classes.

One of the distinguishing characteristics of the present era in this country is the increasing desire which exists on the part of the higher classes of society to improve the condition and to raise the character of the poor and laboring classes. The legislature is occupied in discovering and removing errors and defects which a faulty constitution or the progress of time has introduced into the operation of the laws. Benevolent individuals are united in numerous societies for the purpose of enquiring accurately into the state of the poor; of searching out the true character of their wants; of considering and discussing the best method of supplying those wants; and, lastly, of pointing out and endeavoring to remove the obstacles which at present hinder national improvement. Such, for instance, are the various Statistical Societies, and the Central Society of Education, for the purposes of enquiry; the Laborers' Friend Society, the Children's Friend Society, the Small Loan Fund, and the Friendly Loan Societies, with many others, to which men of opulence have given their time and money, for the purpose of improving the character of the laboring classes, and or raising them from a state of pauperism, by their own exertions, to that of honest independence, and useful industrious employment.[104]

There was one important aspect in which large societies such as the RSS and the SSA differed from the provincial societies such as those of Manchester and Bristol. The former societies considered themselves to be branches of the government and thought that one of their primary responsibilities was to provide the two Houses of Parliament and their many commissions with the data necessary to carry out rational and efficient social reform. In 1855 the council of the RSS reported that

The importance of the Society was increasing every day. It was clear that Parliament was becoming more and more unfitted for the complete discussion of great questions, which required calm and lengthened consideration. Parliament was overwhelmed with business, and it was not to be expected that, under such circumstances, 500 or 600 men could meet and discuss philosophically those great and abstruse subjects with which it was the duty of the Society to deal. One of the functions of the Society was to prepare matters for that great assembly, and that duty it appeared to be performing well.[105]

The council went on to say that legislation founded upon assumptions and not hard data could only be speculative and might even be "injurious to the community." But legislation based upon statistics would be sure to solve the social problems it was aimed at alleviating.[106] When Parliament had either passed a specific reform or else undertook an investigation itself, the members of the Statistical Society could see no reason in pursuing the topic any further. Thus William Lucus Sargant, commenting on the lag in interest in education, attributes this decline in interest to the fact that Parliament had taken up the problem.

The Government, through the Educational Committee of the Privy Council, distribute the considerable funds voted by Parliament; and the late Royal Commission by means of able and paid assistants, have carried out inquiries far more costly and elaborate than were possible for private persons; it would therefore have been useless for the Statistical Society to continue its earlier efforts.[107]

If we are to believe Sargant, and I am inclined to do so, we have conclusive evidence that the social researchers were primarily interested in social reform, thought of themselves as reformers, and abandoned a problem when it was no longer significant for reform. Social research was not done for its own sake.

Up to this point we have demonstrated that the "institution of social science," such as it was, was more concerned with social reform than with social science. But we might still be accused of committing the "ecological fallacy," that is, it would be possible for the statistics and social science societies, as units, to be highly concerned and involved with social reform and for there still to be a substantial number of individuals who were interested in social science for its own sake. We must show that the individuals who were the most original and made the greatest advances also conceived of themselves as social researchers-reformers.

We have already pointed out that Charles Booth, considered by many to be the most important English social researcher of the nineteenth century, was strongly motivated by the desire for social reform. Booth, in many respects, was, in values and attitudes, very much like the average Englishman who did social research. Not only did Booth begin his research with the hope of bringing about social reform, but also his books are permeated with moral judgments and programmatic statements.

It is my opinion that Booth is not as advanced as some authors whose work appeared in the *JRSS* throughout the century. What was the attitude of these men toward social reform? William Augustus Guy contributed more papers to the *JRSS* during the nineteenth century than did any other author. The majority of Guy's statistical papers were "explanatory" as opposed to "descriptive." He was familiar with, and made use of, probability theory in his work. Yet he believed that the proper function of the society to which he belonged was social reform. In an article entitled "On the Claims of Science to Public Recognition and Support; with special reference to the so-called 'Social Sciences,'" Guy says in referring to the RSS and the SSA:

Our two societies have a common aim—the improvement of man's condition physical, intellectual, and moral, through the patient heaping up, intellectual sorting, and critical examination of the elements of knowledge which, properly applied, is power indeed.[108]

Even the title of Jelinger Symons' book, *Tactics for the Times: As Regards the Condition and Treatment of the Dangerous Classes*, is indicative of the author's value system. Yet, as we saw above, this work is one of the finest examples of empirical research of the century. Symons prefaces his book with a statement on the duty of the upper classes toward the poor:

To bind the various elements of society as far as possible in the bonds of charity and mutual good will, enlisting the superior intelligence of the higher classes in behalf of the improvement of the lower, is one mode of advancing the true interests of England:—to dissever these relations and widen existing schisms, substituting fear for love, and self-defence for philanthropy among the higher classes, and a premature and suicidal independence of moral discipline among the lower—is another, but in my humble judgment a very mistaken, means of furthering the common weal. . . . One of the happiest symptoms of the times is a diminution of that godless apathy in high places towards the poor, which has done so much to place classes in conflict whose interests are common. From these negligences of the rich the sins and the ignorance of the poor have mainly sprung.[109]

Later, Symons goes on to say explicitly that the purpose of his research on crime is to find some way of preventing it.

By first ascertaining as far as we can the exact facts about crime, and in the next place the relation in which it stands to surrounding circumstances and localities, I think *we may arrive at definite conclusions as to its chief causes, and thence may we hope to arrive at the cure best adapted to the case.*[110]

Similar quotations could be made from the work of the frequent contributors to the *JRSS*. To do the painstaking and detailed work of a Booth, a Guy, or a Symons took a great amount of time and energy. It is unlikely that a Guy or a Symons would have given so much care to the preparation of complicated statistical tables unless they had a good deal of interest in the work for its own sake. In our time a Booth, Guy, or Symons would certainly have been a sociologist. It is the institutional structure of empirical social science that prevented men like these from dropping the "reformer" from the "social researcher-reformer" that I have called them.

Social research was very rarely thought to be of value for its own sake. It was always thought of as a utilitarian device for improving society. Social research was predominantly a tool of social reformers. This being the case, research was usually permeated by ideological beliefs. This became particularly evident in the analysis of criminology. Plint's motives were to defend the factory system and to show that it created conditions more conducive to morality than other types of "social organization." Fletcher and Symons were both school inspectors and wanted desperately to prove that crime was caused by lack of education, so that Parliament would pass legislation providing for publicly supported elementary schools. The adherents of "temperance" and prohibition such as the Reverend Clay desired to show that crime was due to the demoralizing influence of alcohol. All the researchers were members of a middle class that was earnestly trying to reconstruct society just enough to insure the preservation of its bourgeois institutions. As long as "truth" was secondary to ideological

causes it was impossible for social science to become institutionalized.
Let us take the example of Charles Booth.
Booth originally decided to do his research on the life and labor of the
London people because he became involved in a controversy with
Henry Hyndman, a socialist and one-time associate of Karl Marx, over
the exact extent of poverty. Booth believed that Hyndman's estimate
was greatly exaggerated. He spent years of arduous work in finding out
exactly what the extent of poverty was. He found out that not only
was poverty greater than he had thought it to be but it was even greater
than Hyndman's estimate. What do the biographers of Booth tell us
about his reaction?

Having regard to the fact that his survey had thus justified Hyndman's estimate
rather than his own expectations, one might have supposed that the situation thus
created called for comment and appraisal, to put it mildly. However, he refused to
be drawn into controversy and took refuge in reasurrances addressed perhaps as
much to himself as to his middle-class audience.[111]

Booth was honest enough with himself to admit, at least to his close
friends, that he had been wrong. Many nineteenth-century researchers
would have manipulated the data to make them appear to support their
own ideological positions. Booth, from this point on, withdrew into
pure empiricism and hardly ever speculated on the significance of his
research. Booth, the Victorian, could only be a social investigator—but
not an empirical sociologist.

continuity in nineteenth-century english social research

I began this paper by discussing the necessity
for continuity in science. How much continuity was there in nineteenth-
century English social research?
It is true that research done at the close of
the nineteenth century differed from that done at the beginning and
the middle of the century. But, although this work was different, it
would be difficult to show that there was any advance in sophistication.
It is my opinion that the work done by men like Plint at the middle of
the nineteenth century was at least equal to and perhaps superior to
most done at the end of that century. Advance in quality aside, we can
show that the century is riddled with discontinuities. Whether or not
late nineteenth-century research was better or worse than early nineteenth-century research there were few links between the periods. Each
generation did not grow to maturity learning the work of their predecessors and then continuing on their own. Rather, each generation

began all over again, ignoring the work of their ancestors. It is always easier to show the presence of continuity than the absence of continuity. To demonstrate the former one need only show that a writer at time "2" quoted or made use of in some other way the work of a writer at time "1." To show discontinuity is more difficult: The mere absence of "footnotes" does not necessarily indicate the absence of continuity. To show the absence of continuity a more extensive analysis must be carried out.

Let us first examine continuity in nineteenth-century English criminology. I have been unable to find any empirical social research dealing with crime prior to the 1830s. If such work does exist, and it probably does, there were no references to it in the literature I have examined. Therefore, this discussion of continuity treats the period c.1835-1885. In 1836 an event occurred that proved to be a great stimulus to criminology—the government published an extensive statistical report on crime. From this year on, the government was to issue crime returns every year. The fact that empirical research on crime was not done before the government published these statistics tells us a lot about the organization of English social science. Research topics were largely determined by the availability of data.[112]

The first analysis of the government crime data was presented to the Royal Statistical Society in 1836 by Samuel Redgrave, the civil servant who prepared the government statistics.[113] The first "explanatory" paper making use of the government statistics was written by Rawson W. Rawson in 1837, but did not appear in print until the first volume of the *JRSS* was published in 1839. I have been able to find six monographs making use of the government statistics and approximately twenty articles published between 1839 and 1857.

The continuity in criminology between 1839 and 1857 is rather impressive. In table 4 are listed five of the chief criminologists of the period in order of the appearance of their first work on crime. Thus, because Rawson published first it was impossible for him to refer to any of the other authors. Of the ten possible references that could have been made, eight were made. We may conclude that the criminologists of 1839 through 1857 were highly aware of the other work that was being done in the field. Practically every author both criticizes the work of other criminologists and uses such work where applicable as support for his own. We have seen that Plint's book was a systematic critique of the work of Neison, Fletcher, and Symons, especially the latter two.

One scientist can be aware of the contributions of his predecessors and yet not make advances on them. In mid-nineteenth-century criminology, significant progress was made. Neison's

table 4 · references between criminologists

reference made to	reference made by			
	Neison	Fletcher	Symons	Plint
Rawson	√	√		
Neison	–	√	√	√
Fletcher	–	–	√	√
Symons	–	–	–	√

innovation of considering age specific rates was accepted and became common practice. (Priority on this innovation is claimed by Fletcher for Rawson.) Neison's technique was even improved upon by Plint. The analyses of Fletcher and Symons were improvements over that of Rawson, and as was stated above, Plint's book is, in my opinion, the finest empirical sociological monograph of the century.

Thus far we have reason to be optimistic. But good things come to an end, and it is with Plint that the progress of criminology comes to an abrupt halt. Gradually even interest in criminology lagged, and between 1855 and the end of the century it is difficult to find papers written on crime. I have been unable to find any empirical criminological monographs and only an occasional article after this date. The articles that do appear do not refer to the work done in the middle of the century, and we can tell by examining them that Fletcher, Symons, and Plint did not exist for these later writers.

An example of one of these later criminological pieces is that by Leone Levi appearing in the *JRSS* in 1880. Levi does not make a single reference to another English criminologist. He makes assumptions, by-passing the problems of some earlier researchers. "Crimes against property usually diminish as trade is good and the rates of wages are high; but in proportion as these increase, so the offence of drunkenness usually increases."[114] No data are offered to support this assumption. This type of analysis is a long distance from the arguments of even the moralistic Rev. John Clay, who at least tried to support his conclusions with data.

When Levi discusses the "causes of crime" he introduces a table published by the French government.

The French judicial statistics give the causes of crime in all cases of murder, arson, and poisoning; and it would be a great advantage if an attempt was made, in as many cases as possible, to arrive at the relative influence on crime of violence, vindictiveness, want, greed, intemperance, and insubordination.[115]

This "psychologistic" analysis is in no sense an extension of the work of Plint and his peers. When Levi finally gets around to considering the effect of social factors, his analysis closely resembles that of some of his predecessors. But he has learned nothing from them, probably because he never read them. Because Levi's article is typical of later work on crime we can say that although there was a midcentury naissance of British criminology, there was very little continuity in ideas or techniques of research during the nineteenth century.

Many nineteenth-century empirical researchers were aware of the history (i.e., of the eminent figures of the past) of their discipline. The first volume of the *JRSS* contains a brief history of statistics in which Reynolds, Child, Petty, Price, Arthur Young, Chalmers, and Playfair are mentioned. Achenwall is often mentioned and perhaps the name appearing most often is that of Adolphe Quételet.[116] Practically every researcher of note paid homage to the venerable Quételet—Rawson calling him the "Nestor" of statistical science. Florence Nightingale treasured her copies of *Physique Sociale* and *Anthropometrie*, which Quételet had given her and which she had carefully annotated on every page. The "passionate statistician" wrote Francis Galton on a conversation she had had with Quételet. "He said almost like Sir Isaac Newton: 'These are only a few pebbles picked up on the vast seashore of the ocean to be explored. Let the explorations be carried out.'"[117]

Although empirical researchers often praised great men, they very rarely paid any attention to their work. It is very rare that any one of the researchers would pay enough attention to past work to either criticize it, as Guy does Quételet, or to make advances on it. An intellectual history of British social research in the nineteenth century would not be very interesting reading. The end would be no different than the beginning and the middle no different than either end.

indicators of institutionalization

Thus far we have seen how there was a great deal of empirical research done in England in the nineteenth century. Some of this work, particularly that of the midcentury criminologists, was relatively sophisticated. Yet this tradition never led to the development of an empirical sociology—it was a dead end. The question we must answer is why did continuity fail? It is my hypothesis that continuity is difficult to maintain when science is conducted in a noninstitutionalized setting. It is the social organization of science that provides the mechanisms for intellectual continuity.

What does it mean to say that a science is institutionalized?[118] Institutionalization may be generally defined as the existence of commonly held and usually binding norms governing the behavior of particular status occupants. To say that a particular science is institutionalized would mean that a status or set of statuses existed whose occupants' *primary* task is carrying out scientific activities and that this task was carried out in accordance with commonly held norms and values. Institutionalization is, of course, a matter of degree. A science may be highly institutionalized as physics, for example, is today or only slightly institutionalized as chemistry was in the sixteenth century. Below I shall outline several indicators which might be used to measure the degree to which a particular science has been institutionalized and apply each indicator to nineteenth-century English social research.

nonscientific concerns are dropped

Sciences have not always existed. Originally each science that we study today developed either as an aspect of another science and/or out of some concern of an institution other than science. The extent to which a science has autonomy—has dropped the interests of other institutional realms and of other sciences—is an important indicator of institutionalization.

In a paper entitled "Institutionalization of Scientific Investigation," Talcott Parsons comments that

unless investigation becomes the primary technical function of specialized roles, the advancement of knowledge is often very slow and halting. Perhaps the most fundamental reason is that for the "practical man" the primary focus is on the attainment of the immediate goal itself, and knowledge constitutes simply one of the available resources for achieving it.[119]

To what extent was empirical social research in nineteenth-century England the "primary technical function of specialized roles"? There was nobody who did empirical social research professionally. It was conducted by amateurs, ministers, physicians, civil servants, and businessmen who, as we have pointed out, were primarily interested in social reform. In nineteenth-century England empirical research was a leisure-time activity. The 110 papers contributed to the first volume of the *Transactions* of the National Association for the Promotion of Social Science were contributed by merchants, industrialists, barristers, magistrates, doctors, clergymen, M.P.'s, social workers, educators, engineers, professors, and civil servants. Only a small amount of time and energy of these contributors could have been devoted to empirical research. Even such a well-known researcher as Charles Booth was an amateur, as his biographers tell us: "To this heavily burdened businessman, research, even on so ambitious a scale, was simply a leisure-time interest which had to be filled into spare moments mainly in the evenings and at the week end."[120]

Did the type of person doing empirical social research change in the course of the nineteenth century? I have attempted to answer this question by analyzing a sample of contributors to the *Journal of the Royal Statistical Society* between 1839 and 1900 (see table 5). My procedure was to take all the contributors to 26 of the volumes of the journal and see if they were listed in the *Dictionary of National Biography (DNB)*.[121] Approximately 40 percent of the contributors were listed in the *DNB*. A comparison of the substance of the articles written by men listed in the *DNB* with those written by men not listed in the *DNB* brought out no differences. It is therefore assumed that any differences in the occupations of contributors whose occupations have been identified and those not identified did not affect the type of research done.

table 5 · percent of contributors to the *JRSS* in varying occupations

Occupation	1834-1854 (N = 66)	1855-1874 (N = 65)	1875-1900 (N = 70)
Actuary	3%	9%	6%
Army	14	8	7
Business	9	12	7
Civil service	28	27	24
Clergy	11	4	3
Physicians	21	14	16
Professors	2	14	24
Others	14	12	13
Total	100%	100%	100%

Perhaps the most significant generalization that might be made about the occupations of the contributors to the *JRSS* is that a majority of them had access to institutionally generated statistics.[122] This is obvious for the actuaries, army officers, and civil servants. Also, a large number of the physicians made use of hospital statistics and the clergymen were usually attached to institutions, such as reformatories, that collected statistics.

Table 5 also gives us information on the change that occurred in the course of the nineteenth century in the

occupations of contributors to the *JRSS*. If the first and last columns
are compared, it can be seen that there were decreases in the proportion
of army officers, clergymen, and physicians contributing, and a large
increase in the number of professors. The increase in the proportion of
professors might be taken as evidence that empirical research was becoming the "primary technical function of specialized roles." An impres-
sionistic analysis does not confirm this belief, at least as it applies to
specialized roles carrying out empirical sociological research. Some of
the professors who contributed to the journal were natural scientists.
Typical of these is Sir Joseph Henry Gilbert, an agricultural chemist and
professor of rural economy at Oxford, who contributed a paper on
agricultural statistics. Another such contributor was Sir John Williams
Lubbock, an astronomer and mathematician of whom the *DNB* says
that he was foremost among English mathematicians in adopting La-
place's doctrine of probability. Also, in the last quarter of the nineteenth century, the work appearing in the journal began increasingly
to stray from what we would call sociological subjects. Mathematical
statistics began to develop in this period and some of the professors
contributing to the journal were mathematical statisticians, such as G.
Udny Yule. The majority of the professor contributors, however, occupied chairs of "political economy." Today we would call these professors teachers of either economics or business administration. These men
tended to be professors for only limited periods of time—that is, being
basically businessmen or politicians, they would take a job as a professor of political economy for about five years. Typical of such contributors was Richard Hussey Walsh (1825-1862) who served as a lecturer in
political economy from 1850 to 1856 at Dublin. He then became a
government official in India. Another is Jacob Welley (1818-1873) who
was at times a legal writer, a barrister, and a professor of political economy. He lectured at the University College from 1854-1866. Such a
man probably would continue to carry on his law practice while teaching and probably never did any extensive social research. Thus we may
conclude that although men with academic connections became more
frequent contributors to the journal, it was not true that such contributors occupied statuses whose primary technical function was that of
carrying on empirical sociological research.

One of the striking aspects of the analysis of
journal contributors is the high percentage of contributors listed in the
DNB. This might lead us to suspect that the work of eminent members
of the statistical society was published in preference to the work of less
eminent members. If this was in fact so, it would be a good index of the
lack of institutionalization of social science. It would indicate that func-
tionally irrelevant statuses were being considered in organizations nomi-

nally devoted to social science. However, I would guess that this was not the case and that the editors of the journal were glad to get contributions from any source.

Another fact, not visible in Table 5, but brought to light by the analysis of the journal contributors, is the relatively small percentage of the society's members who did research or even took an interest in research. The same small group of people contributed to volume after volume; the same group attended the society's meetings and served as its officers. When we consider the number of nonempirical articles that appeared, and add to these the empirical articles written by authors who contributed only one or perhaps two such articles, *we are left with about ten people who consistently did empirical research.* The same is true of the contributors to the *Transactions* of the SSA. In the first volumes of *Transactions* there are only three papers that we might call quantitative research. Of these, one is purely descriptive. Thus out of 110 articles there are only 2 that could be classified as quantitative empirical social science. We may conclude that although there were many members of the "social science" organizations, there were very few people who actually did quantitative social research.

common problems and tools

In highly institutionalized sciences there will be much consensus among the practitioners as to what the significant problems are and the proper methods of solving them. Thus Harriet Zuckerman has found that Nobel prize physicists deny the existence of "schools" in physics.[123] Physicists believe that the problems and techniques of their discipline have been so clearly defined that there can not possibly be differences in approach great enough to justify the use of the word "school."[124] In less highly institutionalized sciences such as sociology, there is much less consensus on what the relevant theoretical problems, substantive areas of research, and methodological tools are. In such sciences a multiplicity of "schools" may exist.

The only sense in which nineteenth-century empirical researchers could be said to have pursued common problems is that they were concerned with similar subject matter—basically social reform problems. Perhaps the greatest failure of empirical research lies in the fact that it was never connected to any systematic body of theory. There was no nineteenth-century English empirical researcher whose work was conducted within a "theoretical framework." This was one of the great differences between the work of Durkheim and that of men like Plint and Fletcher. Because Durkheim was predominantly interested in testing theory, he was forced to discover ways of using available data to measure his abstract theoretical variables.

The best of the nineteenth-century British researchers attempted to demonstrate the existence of such relationships as that between crime and education. All these analyses were aimed at proving the validity of what were essentially isolated empirical generalizations. To demonstrate that crime is correlated with education is only to demonstrate the validity of an empirical generalization and is not the proof of a theory. If Durkheim would have attempted only to demonstrate that suicide varied with marital status, or religion, or sex, or age, and so forth, and stopped at that, his analysis would have been no different from Fletcher's, for example.

Thus we may conclude that the researchers had "common problems" only in the nontheoretical sense of the phrase. For not only did they not have common theoretical problems but also they had no theory at all—common or individual. What about common tools? Here we can see greater institutionalization. Similar techniques of data collection and analysis were employed by many researchers. We can also see development in such techniques throughout the century. But such development was quite limited. The only factor I shall discuss here is the "faulty arithmetic" of the researchers.

At first thought, it might seem petty and insignificant to bring up such a topic as faulty arithmetic. I believe that it is not; for it is not the present writer who has discovered such faults, but rather it is the contemporaries of the perpetrators. That arithmetic was faulty was one of the primary criticisms that nineteenth-century empirical social researchers leveled at each other. Both Symons and Fletcher accuse Neison of making a mathematical error, and Plint accuses Symons of reaching a false conclusion due to an arithmetic error.

The alleged proportions of population and crime are not found here. The population is "a little above a quarter of the population of England"; but the crime is not *one third* instead of nearly *one half*! There is palpably a great mistake. Mr. Symons appears to have added the crime of London to the crime of the seven counties named, and to have forgotten to add the population! Yet on this gross arithmetical blunder, Mr. Symons gravely pronounces "That to the evils of crowded districts and the concomitant evil of crowded dwellings and vicious companionship, *without adequate moral* counteraction, the *vast* increase of crime in England must be *primarily attributed.*"[125]

Whether Symons and the others actually made mistakes is not important. It is important, however, that the procedures of research were so unstandardized that these criticisms could be made. Thus the researchers had common tools in that many used a similar method of ecological analysis; but their tools were limited in number and in complexity.

development of scientific statuses

Professionalization / In its early days, the practitioners of a science are usually not "professionals." As science develops, people whose primary status is "physicist," "chemist," or "sociologist" begin to practice it. Such statuses will usually be attached to organizations—universities being the most common. Thus an important indicator of the institutionalization of a particular science is how many chairs exist in how many universities. In the nineteenth century there were no chairs of sociology in England. Chairs of sociology were first established in America in the 1890s. Professional statuses may, however, be attached to other organizations, such as the Royal Institution of London, which gave jobs to such illustrious chemists as Sir Humphry Davy and Michael Faraday.

Specialization / The more highly institutionalized a particular science, the greater will be the division of labor and the multiplying of statuses. Thus the natural philosopher gave way to the icthyologist, entomologist, paleontologist, and so on. Today we can see research becoming increasingly separated from teaching and both research and teaching separated from administration. Comparing the great variety of statuses occupied by professional sociologists today with the number of statuses occupied by professional sociologists in the early part of the twentieth century, we can see that specialization is a good indicator of how far sociology has come down the path of institutionalization.

During the course of the nineteenth century no statuses existed whose occupants' primary task was the conducting of empirical research. Charles Booth, the foremost researcher of the last part of the century, was an amateur, just as were Symons, Fletcher, and the others. Whereas Durkheim was able to institutionalize the status of "sociologist" in France, this did not occur in England until the twentieth century.

complexity

Just as the first practitioners of a science are amateurs, early scientific work can be understood by the educated layman. With professionalization comes increasing complexity. Sir Humphry Davy could lecture at the Royal Institution to a lay audience on subjects he was currently working on. This would indeed be difficult today. It is even said that sciences such as physics, chemistry, and biology have become so complex that highly trained professionals have difficulty in understanding the work of their colleagues working in other areas.

A science that is well institutionalized will be difficult for the layman to understand because its explanations of social phenomena will be removed from "common sense." During the nineteenth century empirical sociology became more complex. The statistical tables of a Fletcher and the formulas of a Neison are more difficult to comprehend than were the descriptive surveys of the early part of the century. Thus we can say that the statistical techniques became more complex and eventually gave way to mathematical statistics. However, the sociological modes of explanation remained throughout the century on a "common sense" level that any educated layman might have understood even if he did not accept them.

socialization

Behavior in scientific statuses may be "improvised" or it may be formally taught. One indicator of institutionalization is the existence of training schools in which new recruits are socialized. A highly institutionalized science will have a large variety and a great number of organizations that serve the function of preparing students for a scientific career. Thus, physics has been taught in universities ever since the seventeenth century. Today training in physics has been extended to include postgraduate work either at an institute or a university. It is only recently that provisions have been made for training institutes in empirical sociology. The existence of such training institutes is a very important indicator of institutionalization because they are a means of perpetuating a common body of knowledge and common scientific practices.

Throughout the nineteenth century there was not a single organization that served the function of training people to do empirical social research. Especially damaging was the failure of empirical social research to be admitted to the universities.[126] Contemporaries were occasionally aware that the progress of their science was hindered by the unavailability of formal training. In an address delivered to the education section of the SSA, Professor H. Hennessey expressed this point of view:

Professor H. Hennessey read a paper "On the Necessity of Establishing Academical Chairs for the Encouragement of Social and Political Science." He contended that till the same systematic attention was given to this subject as was given to other sciences, the community generally, and even men in high position—as statesmen and lawyers—would not be able to possess themselves of that knowledge of it which its importance demands. The close attention which almost every one requires to bestow upon his business or profession is such that, unless the elements of social and political science are thoroughly acquired in our schools and universities, it would in all likelihood never be systematically studied at all; and men occupying the most elevated places in society would be obliged to trust for their information on the subject, and their guidance in many important matters connected therewith, to inferior minds.[127]

Twenty-five years later, in 1885, the historian of the Royal Statistical Society was still able to lament the fact that statistics were not formally taught.

The teaching of statistics does not enter at present into our educational arrangements as a special branch of instruction, either in our primary, secondary, or higher curricula, from which some useless subjects might be eliminated with advantage, to make way for it. Figures of arithmetic in their applications and uses, are more valuable than figures of speech as a mental training. The subject has been carefully considered at some of the statistical congresses, and is deserving of being examined by ourselves, to aim in ridding our science and literature, and our enterprises of all kinds, from much which now overloads them injuriously, by teaching in early life what to do, and what to avoid in dealing with social, economic, philanthropic, and similar questions. In this important work the Statistical Society may greatly aid in the future, for it is at the source that all steps of progress and improvement may be most safely and profitably taken.[128]

And in 1891 Florence Nightingale wrote to Galton asking him for a scheme from someone of high authority as to what would be the work and subjects in teaching social physics and their practical application in the event of our being able to obtain a statistical professorship or readership at the University of Oxford. Although Galton cooperated with Miss Nightingale, he probably did more to hinder her plan than help it. As his biographer Karl Pearson tells us, Galton "had no faith in a man simply because he was a professor; the men who in his day had made the most important contributions to science—Darwin, Wallace, Lubbock—and such personal friends as Spencer and Groves—were not professors."[129] Galton would have preferred to establish a lectureship at the Royal Institute or to offer cash prizes for statistical essays. Such a plan would have been of very little value because it would not have provided what was needed—formal training.

It is my belief that a place in the universities is more important for the advancement of social science than for the natural sciences. Because social research was so intimately connected with "practical" endeavors, it needed a place in the universities to give to its study a sense of justification for its own sake. Universities are more than other organizations the place where study is justified in and of its own right. It is my hypothesis that the universities eventually proved to be the sieve through which the interests of other institutional realms were sifted out of empirical social science. The nonexistence of any training schools, in or out of the universities, did not allow for continuity of ideas and the perpetuation of common tools and problems. The failure of such schools to develop also probably accounts for the failure of empirical research to become integrated with a body of systematic theory.

textbooks

An indicator of the development of common tools and problems and of complexity is the appearance of different types of textbooks. The first chemistry textbook was written in 1597 by the German Andreas Libavius.[130] The first American textbooks on quantitative methods in sociology appeared in the 1920s. Not only do textbooks indicate a modicum of institutionalization, but they also help create continuity by exposing a large number of students to the same problems. There were no textbooks written in nineteenth-century England on methods of empirical social research.

channels of communication

If a group of individuals carried out scientific work in complete isolation there would be no institution of science. To speak of "statuses" implies social interaction among a number of actors. It is possible for scientific work to be carried on without anyone occupying the *status* "scientist." The first and probably still the most important kind of communication among people doing scientific work is face to face. However, if communication was limited to such contact the institutionalization of science would be hindered. Impersonal means of communication, that is, scientific journals and other publications, serve to knit the scientific community together. Such channels of communication make a science *a* community rather than a group of isolated *communities*. At first written communication was carried on predominantly by letter. Other than the *Transactions* of the Royal Society, the first scientific journals appeared in the latter half of the eighteenth century.[131] Increasing institutionalization of a particular science will be accompanied by the appearance of a larger number of specialized journals. Empirical social research did not fail to develop due to a lack of channels of communication. As we have shown, numerous journals existed for the purpose of publishing "social science."

scientific societies

Another way in which the scientific community is integrated is through the existence of scientific societies. Scientific societies facilitate intercommunication and joint striving for professional goals. Such societies tend to be formed early in the institutionalization process, but their character often changes as the science grows older.

In nineteenth-century England many societies existed that were, at least on the surface, devoted to the pursuit of social science. The National Association for the Promotion of Social Science was, as we have seen, almost entirely devoted to social reform. This society died in the 1880s for two reasons. (1) Social reform, as opposed to social science, had become institutionalized. By the 1880s the government was assuming responsibility for problems that had formerly been the concern of individuals. When the government took charge of the most pressing reform needs, there was no longer any purpose for the existence of the SSA. (2) When such venerable founders of the SSA as Lord Brougham and Lord Shaftsbury were no longer on the scene, the yearly meetings of the SSA became less fashionable. As the century progressed, fashionable circles lost interest in social science.

The Royal Statistical Society is still today a flourishing organization. The character of this society, however, changed in the course of the nineteenth century. For the first fifteen or twenty years of its existence the members of the Society worked on research that we must certainly call "sociological" in subject matter. Later, however, this type of work declined in quantity and was replaced by work that could be classified as economics—descriptive and quantitative—business administration, and finally mathematical statistics. Thus the Royal Statistical Society gradually dropped the concerns of empirical sociology.

joining the scientific community

Another indicator of institutionalization is the admission of the "new" science into the community of sciences. There is often a good deal of hostility on the part of the older sciences to a new one. However, as an emerging science becomes increasingly institutionalized and its scientific nature more firmly established, it will usually be admitted to the scientific community. Such acceptance may be seen in admittance to universities and general scientific societies. Sociology is still in the process of being fully admitted to the scientific community. The willingness of scientific bodies such as the National

Science Foundation and the National Institutes of Health to finance sociological research is an indicator of the increasing acceptance of sociology as a legitimate institutionalized science.

The only sense in which empirical sociology may be said to have been part of the scientific community is in the existence of Section F, Economic Science and Statistics, of the British Association for the Advancement of Science. This section was in reality simply an adjunct of the Royal Statistical Society. However, there was concern within the British Association over the "unscientific" nature of the papers read before Section F, and the section was on the verge of being dropped. This fate was only avoided by the advances made in mathematical statistics at the end of the nineteenth century by such people as G. Udny Yule.

The general attitude toward "social science" of both the educated layman and the practitioners of other sciences seemed to be one of hostility. Even such theoretical sociologists as Herbert Spencer looked down with scorn on empirical social research. We may conclude that empirical social research had not even made the first short steps down the path to acceptance by the scientific community.

continuity

Finally, perhaps one of the most important indicators of institutionalization is continuity itself. A highly institutionalized science is one that is well aware of its history and in which the solutions of problems at one time gave rise to the problems at a later time. It would be possible to trace the history of such a science by looking at the footnotes of the current literature. The continuity of physics, for example, is highly visible. The theoretical work of today has a direct relation to that of the seventeenth century.[132] I am aware of the logical flaw in including continuity as an indicator of institutionalization if one wants to show that continuity can not exist without institutionalization. This is, of course, assuming what we should like to prove and is thus tautological. However, the degree of correlation among the indicators of institutionalization is an interesting question. Any one of the indicators might be looked upon as a dependent variable influenced by the other indicators.

If a sociologist, browsing in an old bookstore, were to pick up a copy of *Crime in England* by Thomas Plint and glance through it, he would be truly surprised. Here, more than a century old, is a systematic empirical analysis of social phenomena. The factual existence of Plint's book poses two interesting questions for the sociologist of science. We are amazed at the mere existence of the work. Where did Plint learn how to do such an analysis? One of our questions then is what factors enabled social science to develop to the point where a book such as *Crime in England* could be written. This question is a fascinating one, but it has not been the direct concern of this paper. The second question that the existence of Plint's book poses is why we have not known of it before now—or why the development of nineteenth-century social science came to a halt and disappeared from view, only to be rediscovered in mid-twentieth century. This is the question of discontinuity. We have shown that there was little continuity in the development of English empirical social research. We have also shown on nine indicators that the institutionalization of empirical social science was minimal. We must now show that our two conclusions are related to each other, that is, that continuity was limited because empirical social research was conducted in a noninstitutionalized setting. We shall transpose our question: "Why were there no successors to Plint who were able to make advances on *Crime in England*?" We shall show how one variable of scientific institutionalization, continuity, is dependent upon the other nine.

A reason why Plint had no successors is that connected with personnel. One of the aims of the study of scientific institutionalization is to discover the role of individual genius in scientific development. The staunchest supporters of what A. Rupert Hall has called the "externalist approach[133] do not claim that scientific discoveries appear through the medium of mediocre minds. Rather it is claimed that genius is a necessary condition for scientific discoveries, but that there is no reason to believe that there is significant variation in the "brain power" available in different time periods. Because genius is constant and scientific development is not, genius is only a necessary condition of scientific advance and not a sufficient one. Given such an assumption, we face two problems: (1) What are the necessary conditions for genius to flower? (2) What factors affect the recruitment into science or any one science of the available mental resources at any point in time?

This last question has often been disregarded. In nineteenth-century England so few men carried on empirical social research that the probability of recruiting talented men to this area of science was low. No status of empirical researcher existed. Empirical research was not taught at the universities. Nobody thought of himself as an empirical sociologist. In short, we have shown social research was carried on in a noninstitutionalized setting. We therefore contend that the element of change in the recruitment to social science was a significant one. There were no channels of recruitment into empirical research.

All the men who did serious research were engaged in occupations in which they came into contact with quantitative data. Thus the mere fact that so few men conducted social research limited the chances of its continuous advance. One reason why Plint had no successor was the absence of a large enough group of men from which a successor might have come.

However, even if intellectually gifted individuals had taken up criminology, it is unlikely that much progress could have been made. This is so because social research was done for practical and/or ideological reasons. What *would* have been the next step, if empirical research was to continue to advance? One would have been the development of standardized and commonly accepted procedures for determining the nature and extent of a relationship between two variables. Today there is not a solitary qualified sociologist who would not reach the same conclusion upon the nature of the relationship between county crime rates and county ignorance rates. We would all agree that for all of England there was a small and statistically insignificant positive correlation between these variables ($K = .26$—Spearman rank order coefficient). Such a conclusion was not reached by all the researchers examining the data in Plint's time. The standardized methods could only be developed if the social researcher were primarily interested in finding out the causes of human behavior regardless of what ideological position the results could support.

Another necessary innovation would have been the collection of original data to supply what the institutionally generated data could not. Thomas Plint saw this. At the end of his *Crime in England* he tells us what type of data would be needed to understand the factors affecting the "criminal class."

The existence and the numbers of the criminal class is a great evil, and, it may be, a great and grave error on the part of society at large. How it is engendered—what are its elements—must be of permanent importance to be known. The first step to the effectual correction, or the greatest possible mitigation of this great evil—and no less calamity—will be the recording with more accuracy and minuteness whatever information can be elicited respecting the criminals who pass through our courts of justice. More would be known, after five years of careful scrutiny into the previous history of our criminals, than will be got by fifty years of the superficial and desultory observation which is at present practised. The inquiry should extend to the place of birth, occupation, place of residence, and to education, and other moral influences; in one word, all that is comprehended in the phrase—the "Natural History" of the class. The philosophy or theory of a criminal class, will assume a tangible shape when that is accomplished, but not before.[134]

Plint is so good that we cannot resist further quotation. What is needed, he says is

a careful and most exact analysis of the crime committed by the population betwixt 20 and 30, or say 15 and 30, with an especial reference to the determination
of its peculiar character of turpitude or otherwise, its connection with new organizations of society, or with alterations in the law, and the precise social position and
moral status of the actual criminals. The inquiry, in fact, ought to comprise *all
crime*. Voluminous as are the present returns, as to criminal offences, they are
greatly difficient in the one important matter of moral data. The tests of the ability
to read and write are of small value as moral indices. What is wanted is a clue to the
conditions and circumstances which accompany crime, of whatever kind. The reading and writing test supplies one element—often a most deceptive one—where other,
and even more potent elements, have been at work. The test is utterly valueless,
indeed, on the assumption, *and it is only an assumption*, that it is a measure of other
things—social status—home influences—intellectual tastes, and moral principle.[135]

The type of analysis Plint suggested was never
carried out because (1) people did not want to and (2) support for it
was not present. People did not want to because there was no reason to
go to so much trouble as long as an ideological argument could be supported by the clever manipulation of ecological data. Support for such
a study was not present because it would have been nearly impossible
for an individual to do so on his own. Plint assumed that the government
would collect the data, but the government was not in the social research
business. What would have been required was a group of men working
together with an amount of financial support far larger than the grants
given out by the British Association to investigate the conditions of the
working classes in St. James Parish, Westminster.

If these two steps, the standardization of tools
and the collection of original data for "explanatory" purposes, were not
taken, there was no where further that criminology could go. Fletcher,
Neison, Symons, and Plint could only be copied but not improved.
Indeed they were copied, as we saw in the discussion of Leone Levi's
work on crime. They were not improved upon. The advance of criminology was to wait for the twentieth century.

notes

1   Mildred Parten, *Surveys, Polls, and Samples* (New York: Harper & Row,
    1950).
2   Sir F. M. Eden, *The State of the Poor,* Vol. 2 (London: J. Davies, 1797).
3   Cf. the chapter by Elesh in this book.
4   "Prospectus of the Objects and Plans of the Statistical Society of London,"
    in *Report of the Third Meeting of the British Association for the Advance-
    ment of Science,* 3 (1834).
5   *Transactions* of the SSA, 3 (1860), 635.

6   *Ibid.,* p. 623.

7   *Ibid.,* p. 624.

8   *Ibid.,* p. 625. Danson's address to the SSA continues in the same fashion. Statistics must be verifiable. They must present all relevant information. They must be properly coordinated.

9   Address of Lord Brougham to the SSA appearing in *Transactions,* 1 (1857), 10.

10 Rawson W. Rawson, "An Inquiry into the Statistics of Crime in England and Wales," *JRSS,* 2 (1839) 316-344, at p. 316.

11 Beatrice Webb quoting Charles Booth, *My Apprenticeship* (London: Longmans, 1926), p. 229.

12 *JRSS,* 2 (1839), 198-233.

13 *JRSS,* 6 (1843), 197-211.

14 *JRSS,* 2 (1839), 84-103.

15 *JRSS,* 6 (1843), 218-240.

16 *JRSS,* 6 (1843), 233.

17 *JRSS,* 8 (1845), 273-275.

18 *JRSS,* 2 (1839), 25-47.

19 *Ibid.,* p. 38.

20 *JRSS,* 6 (1843), 50-60.

21 *JRSS,* 2 (1839), 316-344. at p. 317.

22 *JRSS,* 18 (1855), 242-288.

23 *Social Science Review,* 1 (1861), unpaginated.

24 J. N. Radcliffe, "On Suicide:—Age, Sex, and Method," *Social Science Review,* 1 (1861), p. 185. Although I am not aware of any journals other than those mentioned above, which took an interest in social science, there was much empirical research conducted in nineteenth-century England that will not be touched upon in this paper. Most important is that conducted by the government itself. The government sponsored and published voluminous reports on such subjects as the Sanitary Conditions of the Working Classes, and Factory Hours, and the like. These reports were issued in blue bindings and were called "bluebooks." A large portion of the research appearing in the *JRSS* was based on statistics published by the government. Another organization carrying on empirical research was the Charity Organization Society. Here, research was aimed at the "efficient" administration of charity and no pretense was made to being interested in "social science."

25 G. W. Hastings, *Transactions* of the SSA, 1 (1857), xxiv. Italics added.

26 Rev. Robert Everest, "On the influence of social degradation producing pauperism and crime, as exemplified in the free colored citizens and foreigners in the United States," *JRSS,* 18 (1855), 222-239, at p. 222.

27 Charles Booth, *Life and Labour of the People in London,* Vol. 2 (London and New York: Macmillan 1892), p. 16.

28 William Augustus Guy, "An attempt to determine the influence of the seasons and weather on sickness and mortality," *JRSS,* 6 (1843), 133-150.

29 Robert Giffen, *The Progress of the Working Classes in the Last Half-Century.* (London: Putnam, 1885), p. 4.

30 Richard Edmonds, "A Statistical Account of the Parish of Madron, contain-

ing the Borough of Penzance, in Cornwall. Digested from the Replies to the First Series of Questions Circulated by the Statistical Society of London," *JRSS,* 2 (1839), 198-233, at p. 231.

31   For one of the replies to this questionnaire see K. John Boyle, "An Account of strikes in the potteries, in the years 1834 and 1836," *JRSS,* 1 (1839).

32   T. S. Ashton, *Economic and Social Investigations in Manchester, 1833-1933* (London: P. S. King, 1934), p. 8. Here is another example of the use of sampling prior to Booth.

33   William Neild, "Comparative Statement of the Income and Expenditure of Certain Families of the Working Classes in Manchester and Dukinfield, in the year 1836 and 1841," *JRSS,* 4 (1841), 320-334, at p. 322.

34   Everest, *op. cit.,* p. 223.

35   See Jelinger Symons, "On Crime and Density of Population," *Transactions* of the SSA, 1 (1857), 265-270. Lack of space prevents me from going into the methods of data collection employed by Charles Booth, Frederick Engels, Francis Galton, and Leone Levi.

36   Jelinger Symons, *Tactics for the Times: As Regards the Conditions and Treatment of the Dangerous Classes* (London: John Olliver, 1849), p. 25.

37   Everest, *op. cit.,* p. 222.

38   Thomas Plint, *Crime in England, Its relation, character, and extent, as developed from 1801 to 1848* (London: Charles Gilpin, 1851), p. ii.

39   *Ibid.,* p. 132.

40   *Ibid.,* pp. 109-110.

41   Rev. John Clay, "On the Effect of Good or Bad Times on Committals to Prison," *JRSS,* 20 (1857), 378-388, at p. 381.

42   R. H. Walsh, "A Deduction from the Statistics of Crime for the Last Ten Years," *JRSS,* 20 (1857), 77-78, at p. 77.

43   *Ibid.,* p. 77. Later on in the century Leone Levi was to measure morality by the prevalence of broken homes and illegitimate children. "Levi presented a series of statistical snapshots, or better, of cinematographic pictures, illustrative of the moral condition of the nation. Statistics of divorces and separations, and those of illegitimacy, were taken as negative evidence of the sense of the 'duties of the affection'" (Ashton, *op. cit.,* p. 94).

44   Mary Carpenter, *Juvenile Delinquents* (London: Bennett, 1853). Miss Carpenter was also aware that treating juvenile delinquency as a "blanket concept" interfered with research.

45   Rev. Whitworth Russell, "Abstract of the 'Statistics of Crime in England and Wales, from 1839 to 1843,'" *JRSS,* 10 (1847), 36-61, at p. 39.

46   Plint, *op. cit.,* p. 12.

47   Joseph Fletcher, "Moral and Educational Statistics of England and Wales," *JRSS,* 10 (1847), 193-233, at p. 212.

48   An example of this type of criticism may be found in the article of Rawson W. Rawson, "Statistics of education among the criminal and general population of England and other countries," *JRSS,* 3 (1841), 331-352.

49   Plint, *op. cit.,* p. 31.

50   For such an analysis see Joseph Kay, *The social condition and education of the people in England* (New York: Harper & Row, 1864), p. 32. This book

was first published in England in 1850. The only reason why it could conceivably have been republished is because of its lengthy descriptions of the "bestial sexual sins" of the laboring classes. The book may have been read as a kind of Victorian Kinsey report.

51   Joseph Fletcher, "Progress of crime in the united kingdom," *JRSS*, 6 (1843), 218-240, at p. 232; italics added. Even though Fletcher correctly uses rates, he incorrectly suggests percentaging his table in the direction of the dependent variable.

52   William Augustus Guy, "On the relative value of averages derived from different numbers of observations," *JRSS*, 13 (1850), 30-45, at p. 43.

53   William Lucus Sargant, "On the Progress of Elementary Education," *JRSS*, 30 (1867), 80-137, at p. 86.

54   Leone Levi, "A Survey of Indictable and Summary Jurisdiction Offences in England and Wales from 1857 to 1876, in Quinquennial Periods, and in 1877 and 1878," *JRSS*, 43 (1880), 423-456, at p. 434.

55   He astutely tells us that although occupations may still have the same name, they may not really be the same occupation. "The people who have the same names at different times are not necessarily doing the same work. Some forms of work pass wholly away and wholly new forms come into existence. Making all allowances, however, and selecting the best comparative cases possible, some useful conclusion seems obtainable" (Giffen, *op. cit.*, p. 4).

56   David Chadwick, "On Free Public Libraries and Museums, and their usefulness, as Compared with Other Institutions for the Education of the Working Classes and the Improvement of their Social Position," *Transactions* of the SSA, 1 (1857), 574-588.

57   William Augustus Guy, "Contributions to a Knowledge of the Influence of Employments upon Health," *JRSS*, 6 (1843), 197-211, at p. 197.

58   William Augustus Guy, "Further Contributions to a Knowledge of the Influence of Employments upon Health," *JRSS*, 6 (1843), 283-304, at p. 291.

59   Edward Shepherd, "On the Reformation or Recommittal of Offenders," *Transactions* of the SSA, 3 (1860).

60   Plint, *op. cit.*, p. ii.

61   *Ibid.*, p. 6.

62   *Ibid.*, p. 7. Fletcher attempted to prove that ignorance was the main cause of crime.

63   Neither Fletcher nor Plint had at their side, as we do, a basket of statistical tools to measure the amount of the correlation between two variables. The application of the Spearman rank-correlation coefficient to the table analyzed by Plint shows that the relation between ignorance and crime in the counties Fletcher called "industrial" is −0.15. Plint is thus correct.

64   Plint, *op. cit.*, p. 24.

65   *Ibid.*, p. 19.

66   *Ibid.*, pp. 16-17.

67   *Ibid.*, p. 43.

68   *Ibid.*, p. 78.

69   *Ibid.*, p. 91.

70   *Ibid.*, p. 100.

71 *Ibid.*, p. 124.

72 *Ibid.*, p. 124.

73 *Ibid.*, p. 127.

74 *Ibid.*, p. 131.

75 For an interesting discussion of this topic see Anthony Oberschall, "Social Research in Great Britain Before Booth," unpublished paper, Yale University.

76 See C. C. Gillispie, *Genesis and Geology* (New York: Harper & Row, 1959) for a discussion of the growth of data collection in geology. It is impossible here to more than allude to the effect of the empiricist milieu on social research.

77 Frederick J. Mouat, "History of the Statistical Society of London," Jubilee volume of the Statistical Society, London, E. Stanford, 1885.

78 *JRSS*, 1 (1839), 8, italics mine. The comment that the age was "ripe" and that the "spirit" of the times favored statistical investigation can be seen throughout the sources I have used. Typical is the address of Sir Stafford Northcote to the statistical section of the British Association for the Advancement of Science. "To me it appears to be emphatically, and in the highest sense of the term, a statistical age; an age, that is to say, in which we are inquiring extensively and methodically into the facts by which we are surrounded, comparing ourselves with our neighbors, measuring our progress, and estimating our prospects with unprecedented care" [*JRSS*, 32 (1869), 265].

79 Nathan Glaser, "The Rise of Social Research in Europe," in Daniel Lerner, ed., *The Human Meaning of the Social Sciences* (New York: Meridian, 1959), p. 57.

80 *Ibid.*, p. 67.

81 Jelinger Symons, *Tactics for the Times: As Regards the Condition and Treatment of the Dangerous Classes* (London: John Olliver, 1849), p. 3. Italics added.

82 Sargant, *op. cit.*, p. 89.

83 See F. G. P. Neison, "Contributions to Vital Statistics Especially designed to elucidate the rate of mortality, the laws of sickness, and the influences of trade and locality on health, derived from an extensive collection of original data supplied by friendly societies and proving their too frequent instability," *JRSS*, 8 (1845), 290-343. Whether or not Neison's analysis of his data is accurate is not directly relevant here.

84 Joseph Fletcher, "Contributions to the Agricultural Statistics of the Eastern Counties," *JRSS*, 6 (1843), 130-133, at p. 132; italics added.

85 T. C. D. Lawson, "On the Connection Between Statistics and Political Economy," *JRSS*, 6 (1843), p. 322. Italics added.

86 See *JRSS*, 1 (1839), p. 8.

87 T. S. Simey and M. B. Simey, *Charles Booth: Social Scientist* (London, Oxford University Press, 1960), p. 64.

88 Charles Bowles Fripp, "Statistics of the City of New York," *JRSS*, 2 (1839), 1-25, at p. 2.

89 W. A. Graham, "Adaptation of Official Returns of Railway Traffic to the general purposes of Statistical Inquiry," *JRSS*, 8 (1845), 215-236, at p. 215.

90 Stephen Cole, "The Charitable Impulse in Victorian England," *King's Crown Essays,* 9 (1961), 3-28.

91 That separation of the classes was a grave concern of social researchers-reformers may be demonstrated by extensive documentation, which limitation of space prevents me from presenting here.

92 W. R. Deverell, "Statistics of the Population of the Kingdom of Saxony, to December 1837, including an account of the births, deaths, and marriages compared with those of the six preceding years," *JRSS,* 2 (1839), 103-114, at p. 104. This quotation illustrates the important influence that Benthamite utilitarianism had on the social researchers-reformers. "The Benthamites were active as the originators of reforms, and as the administrators who carried them out; to be effective as such they needed large quantities of precise evidence relating to the problems and the situations with which they were concerned. They thus created a demand for social information, and they produced much of the machinery for obtaining it. To a certain extent, therefore, the Benthamites laid the foundations on which the social sciences have been subsequently built; mainly as the result of their activities, the idea of painstaking inquiry into social problems was by no means new when Booth first went to work" (Simey, *op. cit.,* p. 244).

93 Sir Stafford Northcote, "Address," *JRSS,* 32 (1869), 260.

94 Crane Brinton points out that it was believed that it was "to ignorance rather than to other human weaknesses that present political evils must be traced. Ignorance of the science of economics on the part of too many Englishmen of all classes explains our present unrest" [*English Political Thought in the Nineteenth Century* (Cambridge, Mass.: Harvard University Press, 1949), p. 33].

95 E. D. P. Cheyney, *Modern English Reform* (Philadelphia: University of Pennsylvania Press, 1931), p. 52.

96 In a speech before the SSA Lord Shaftsbury told the audience: "We know the causes of many physical and moral evils, and we know the remedies for them; but we want a vast and constantly increasing accumulation of recent details to illustrate the power of present and approaching mischief, so as to force the public by copious particulars to come to the same view as ourselves, and so arrive at an effective conclusion." [From a speech by Lord Shaftsbury reported in the *Transactions* of the National Association for the Promotion of Social Science, 3 (1860), p. 12.]

97 Simey, *op. cit.,* pp. 47-48.

98 Thomas Beggs, *An Inquiry into the Extent and Causes of Juvenile Depravity* (London: Charles Gelpin, 1849), p. 4.

99 *Ibid.,* p. 3.

100 This is also the conclusion reached by Harold Westergaard in his history of statistics. "Many motives may have been leading to the foundation of these societies, but the most striking one seems to have been the interest in *social problems*" [*Contributions to the History of Statistics* (London: Staples, 1932), p. 141].

101 T. S. Ashton, *Economic and Social Investigations in Manchester, 1833-1933* (London: Staples, 1934), p. 2.

102   *Ibid.*, p. 4.

103   *Ibid.*, p. 11.

104   *JRSS,* 1 (1839), 45-46.

105   *JRSS,* 18 (1855), 97-103, at p. 101.

106   *Ibid.*

107   Sargant, *op. cit.*, p. 83.

108   *JRSS,* 33 (1870), 431-451, at p. 437. Many of Guy's papers on the conditions affecting the mortality rates of different professions emphasize the usefulness of such papers for sanitary and other reforms.

109   Symons, *op. cit.*, p. 6.

110   *Ibid.*, p. 18.

111   Simey, *op. cit.*, p. 90.

112   Space is unavailable for a discussion of the effect of the availability of data on empirical research. The two basic points to be made were (1) the fact that research problems were so closely governed by the existence of government statistics indicated that the "foci of attention" of empirical sociologists were not influenced very much by the "internal dynamics" of social science; and (2) the individuals most likely to engage in empirical research were those who came into contact with empirical data in the course of performing their jobs. Rawson, Fletcher, and Symons were all civil servants. Clay was a chaplain at the Preston gaol. Social research was at least partly a stylish hobby of Victorian civil servants.

113   This report is unavailable in the United States. From the references to it that I have seen, I believe that it was nothing more than a descriptive summary of the government tables.

114   Leone Levi, "A Survey of Indictable and Summary Jurisdiction Offences in England and Wales from 1857 to 1876," *JRSS,* 43 (1880), 423-456, at p. 432.

115   *Ibid.*, p. 433.

116   Occasional references are found to several other empirical researchers including Guerry, John Howard, and Sir F. M. Eden.

117   Karl Pearson, *The Life, Letters and Labours of Francis Galton,* Vol. II (London: Cambridge University Press, 1924), p. 148.

118   For another study of institutionalization in science see Harriet A. Zuckerman and Robert K. Merton, "Patterns of Evaluation in Science: Institutionalization, Structure, and Functions of the Referee System," Paper read at the annual meeting of the American Sociological Association, August 1968.

119   In Bernard Barber and Walter Hirsch, eds., *The Sociology of Science* (New York: Free Press, 1963), p. 9.

120   T. S. Simey and M. B. Simey, *op. cit.*, p. 98.

121   The most logical procedure would have been to take every third volume. However, during the course of the century the papers became increasingly longer and the contributors fewer, thus making it necessary to "oversample" the volumes in the latter half of the century. Also, as I originally began my sampling with a different procedure in mind, the volumes are not equally spaced. I believe that such a procedure has not in any way affected the results I have obtained. The volumes used for the sample were 2, 4, 6, 8, 10, 15, 18, 20, 22, 25, 28, 30, 32, 35, 38, 40, 43, 45, 47, 48, 50, 52, 55, 57, 60, 62.

122   It should be remembered that being a contributor did not necessarily mean that one did social research. Some contributions were not research reports. It might prove fruitful to have an occupational breakdown for the different types of contributions: research, nonresearch, descriptive, explanatory, programmatic, and so forth. Also other characteristics of the contributors such as religion and education might prove interesting.

123   Harriet A. Zuckerman, *Nobel Laureates in the United States,* unpublished Ph.D. dissertation, Columbia University, 1965.

124   Whether it is in fact true that "there are no schools in physics" is an interesting question. However, the mere fact that physicists should believe that schools do not exist is an indicator of great consensus on the substance of the discipline.

125   Plint, *op. cit.,* pp. 32-33.

126   The reasons for this are not of direct concern here. For an article that offers some interesting hypotheses see Joseph Ben-David and Abraham Zloczower, "Universities and Academic Systems in Modern Societies," *European Journal of Sociology,* 3 (1962), 45-84.

127   In *Transactions* of the SSA, 3 (1860), 437-438.

128   Mouat, *op. cit.,* p. 53.

129   Pearson, *op. cit.,* p. 416.

130   See J. R. Partington, *A Short History of Chemistry* (New York: Harper & Row, 1937), p. 56.

131   If we examine the 14 volumes of *L'Avant-Coureur,* published from 1759 to 1773, we can see the pattern of reporting scientific findings to journals becoming part of the scientific institution. In the early volumes of the journal scientific information was reported by reporters who had attended the meetings of scientific societies. In the last years of the journal's existence, the makers of discoveries themselves are more often the source of scientific information, and discoveries would be reported in the words of the discoverer rather than in those of the editor. Another early scientific journal, this one dealing exclusively with science, was *Observations sur la physique, sur l'histoire naturelle, et sur les arts,* which first appeared in 1771, edited by the Abbé François Rozier. Both these journals dealt with all the then current sciences. For comments on these two journals see W. E. Smeaton, *"L'Avant Coureur.* The Journal in Which Some of Lavoisier's Earliest Research Was Reported," *Annals of Science,* 13: 4 (1957), 219-234; and Douglas McKie, "The 'Observations' of the Abbé François Rozier (1734-1793)," *Annals of Science,* 13: 2 (1957), 73-89.

132   See N. R. Hanson, *The Concept of the Positron* (London: Cambridge University Press, 1963). For another interpretation of scientific continuity, see Thomas S. Kuhn, *The Structure of Scientific Revolution* (Chicago: University of Chicago Press, 1962).

133   A. Rupert Hall, "Merton Revisited," *History of Science,* 2 (1963), 1-15. The members of what Hall calls the "externalist school" explain the development of science by reference to such nonscientific factors as religion or economics.

134   Plint, *op. cit.,* p. 156.

135   *Ibid.,* p. 176.

reappraising
le play
•
walter l. goldfrank

No history of empirical social research in
France would be complete without a description and appraisal of the
contributions of one of its earliest practitioners, Frédéric Le Play.
Earlier secondary sources are inadequate, more recent accounts un-
balanced or special in focus, while most French studies of Le Play have
little use for the serious scholar.[1] So there is a modest gap to fill.

A brief biographical sketch will show how Le
Play came to fuse the growing empirical tradition in natural science
(which especially in its classificatory branches was already well developed by the end of the eighteenth century) with elements of
both the traditionalist Catholic reaction to the French and industrial
revolutions and the elitism of Saint-Simonian technocrats. This sketch
will lead to discussions of Le Play's conception of social science, his
theories of society, and his research methods.

Pierre Guillaume Frédéric Le Play was born in
1806 near Honfleur on the Normandy coast.[2] His father was a minor
customs official, his mother apparently a sturdy, simple, religious woman. The region itself was notable for its staunch loyalty to the old
order, even during the postrevolutionary period of Napoleonic rule.[3]
When Le Play's father died in 1811, the boy was sent to live with a rich
uncle in Paris, where he spent four years under the tutelage of an émi-
gré noble and a prerevolutionary magistrate. He returned to Honfleur
in 1815, studying at home in a period of economic prosperity for the
local fishermen. After receiving his baccalauréat in lettres in 1823, he
traveled with an old family friend, one of the first graduates of the
École Polytechnique, who impressed him with the duties of the new
engineers to the public interest, and whose prompting led Le Play to
study in Paris. After preparing at the Collège Saint Louis, he spent two

Walter L. Goldfrank is Assistant Professor of Sociology, Merrill College, University
of California at Santa Cruz. Born in New York City in 1940, he received his A.B.
from Harvard in 1962 and Ph. D. in Sociology from Columbia University in 1971.
Goldfrank is currently writing a book on the Mexican Revolution.

years at the École Polytechnique and then entered the École des Mines first in the incoming class. He completed the normally three-year course in two years, making the highest score up to that time on the comprehensive exam.

Le Play writes that he was unable either to share or to refute the Saint-Simonian doctrine current among his classmates. Thus, when he undertook the lengthy field trip required for completion of the program in metallurgy, he and a Saint-Simonian friend, Jean Reynaud, agreed to test their social ideas by observations en route. From May to November 1829 the two men trekked over 4000 miles through northwest Europe, visiting mines, factories, and families: While neither was convinced of the correctness of the other's opinions, they agreed that direct observation was a surer guide to thinking about society than deductive reasoning.[4] Although Le Play continued to oppose Saint-Simonianism, especially its notion of progress, his later writings reveal considerable borrowing from it. This is notably true for the doctrine of class harmony, the opposition to laissez faire economics, and the defense of private property as an economic arrangement carrying definite moral obligations.

In the spring of 1830 Le Play suffered severe potassium burns. His recollection of his eighteen-month convalescence reveals a process of reaffirmation of his conservative convictions. As friends brought him reports of the July rising, he vowed to study society scientifically in order to show the way to peace and prosperity. When he recovered he began dividing his time between research and teaching in metallurgy in Paris, and long trips on which he inspected mines and metal works and visited workers' families. Between 1831 and 1848 he traveled at least once through England, Spain, Italy, Germany, Austria, Hungary, Russia, and Scandinavia. During this period Le Play edited two mining journals, published numerous well-received works on metallurgy and geology, and from 1840 on held a chair at the École des Mines. He was proficient in statistics but later disavowed them as worse than useless for the social sciences because of their shallowness and their collection by untrained observers.[5]

Also during this period Le Play established relations with several influential aristocrats, including the then "Prince" Napoleon and the Czar Nicholas. He became one of the first "management consultants" on record, receiving from the Russian prince Anatol Demidov in 1837 a commission to survey and reorganize the prince's mineral and metal holdings in the Donetz region and the Urals, operations involving some 45,000 laborers. His intellectual circle in Paris was wide-ranging and of the highest order, including Thiers, Tocqueville, Arago, and Montalembert. After the 1848 revolution his old friend

Reynaud invited him to present the results of his social investigations to the Louis Blanc committee on unemployment. As a result of his testimony, Le Play was urged by men of divergent political opinions to publish the results of his family studies, from the radical left to the Catholic and liberal right. He decided to give up work on his metallurgical chef d'œuvre,[6] revisited many of the families he had seen in previous years, worked with friends to reorganize the data, and when Arago secured the backing of the Academie des Sciences, published under governmental auspices the first edition of *Les Ouvriers Européens*. An enormous folio volume, it contained an introduction, 36 family monographs and a short conclusion calling for social reforms; Le Play was forced to omit his conclusions, which were attacks on the revolutionary principles of 1789. He stayed at the École des Mines until 1854, then left to administer the Paris World's Fair in 1855. After his work received the Prix Montyon from the Academie des Sciences in 1856, his new career as social scientist and government servant began in earnest: Napoleon III named him *Conseiller d'Etat*, a post he held until 1867 when he was appointed to the Senate as a reward for his brilliant organization of the International Exposition. But the disaster of the Franco-Prussian War and the formation of the Third Republic brought his public career to an end.

Already Le Play had written at Napoleon's behest two books in which he presented his suggestions for reform,[7] discussing all the institutional realms of society from his peculiarly paternalistic, austere viewpoint. Now he worked in private life to achieve these reforms. Soon after the publication of *Les Ouvriers Européens* Le Play had founded the Société d'Economie Sociale and the Société Internationale des Etudes Pratiques d'Economie Sociale. His scientific prestige was then at its peak: The first three presidents of the societies —which seem to have been the same—were the great doctor Villermé, the noted mathematician Charles Dupin, and the famous chemist Jean-Baptiste Dumas. Originally formed to pursue the collection and publication of vast numbers of family monographs, the societies in 1864 began considering social reforms as well. But Le Play felt that this was not enough. In 1871 he thus organized the Unions for Social Peace, local groups throughout France and Belgium whose primary purpose was to disseminate the gospel according to Le Play, and incidentally to collect data on their regions. In 1875 Le Play published the quasiempirical *La Constitution d'Angleterre*[8] as a model "monograph" of a nation, for the Unions to follow in their own work. In 1877-1879 Le Play brought out a second, revised edition of *Les Ouvriers Européens*, in six volumes. The new edition contained expanded introductions and conclusions, 21 additional family monographs, and as a first volume, an autobiography and detailed methodological pronouncements that seem to have been virtually the only source from which later scholars drew. He died in 1882.

In his lifetime Le Play attracted scores of followers, many of whom learned his methods and contributed monographs to the series *Les Ouvriers des Deux Mondes*, which continued to appear every few years under the auspices of the society until after World War I. Le Play included several of the earlier monographs in this series in the second edition. In 1881 Le Play had founded a semi-monthly journal *La Réforme Sociale*; in 1886 a group of his younger disciples disassociated themselves from the society and started a separate monthly, *La Science Sociale*. Lazarsfeld has called attention to the growing ambivalence toward and rejection of Le Play on the part of this latter group.[9] With the exception of Émile Cheysson and Pierre du Maroussem, the group connected with the former journal drifted away from empirical research and from social science generally. Since 1945 survivors and descendants of both groups have published an undistinguished journal, *Les Études Sociales*. Although Le Play criticized as well as praised the Catholic church, his ideas had a certain resonance in Catholic circles. A sometime disciple of his, René de La Tour du Pin communicated his ideas to Pope Leo XIII, who is said to have been favorably impressed; there are clear echoes of Le Play in that Pope's social encyclicals.[10] Another follower of Le Play, Comte Albert de Mun, was instrumental in founding Catholic workers' associations.

The French corporatists claimed Le Play as a major fountainhead; during the Vichy regime a synthetic recapitulation of his ideas was published, showing—not without distortion—how Le Play prefigured the "sound" policies of Dolfuss, Mussolini, and Hitler.[11] Proudhon was probably the first to note the protofascist overtones of Le Play's thought when he characterized it as "the scientific organization of servitude."[12] The late President Salazar of Portugal was a member of the surviving Le Play society; at the conference commemorating the sesquicentennial of his birth, the Spanish Minister of Information gave a short paper tracing his influence in Spain.[13] It was also felt in prewar Rumania, and Lazarsfeld has given a brief account of the ramifications of Le Play's work in Britain, Canada, and the United States.[14] If little of it is remembered by contemporary social scientists, it is probably because in the end in the din of the turn-of-the-century marketplace of competing sociological approaches, his ideology and its derivatives overshadowed those aspects of his work that partake of modern scientific rationalism. And, of course, his followers were amateurs.

theoretical perspectives

At about the same time that Quételet and Comte were developing their respective notions of social physics and sociology, Le Play was conceiving of his social science. He meant two quite distinct things by "social science": practical wisdom applied to social organization, and a body of principles arrived at inductively after systematic comparisons of observed social facts. In an interesting way the two meanings were not refractory for him because he believed that his scientific work would demonstrate "how Societies are assured the Happiness that rests upon Peace and Stability,"[15] by providing "daily bread," and by adhering to the Decalogue. He himself pointed out that in the former sense social science was not new: "The eternal Decalogue is the supreme theory."[16]

Le Play's insistence that there is nothing to "invent" in social science was then one side of his objection to the speculative theories of Saint Simon and Comte. The other side of his objection to abstract theorizing, his method of observation, earned him a place in the history of social science. Most of the strengths—and a few of the weaknesses—of his work derive from this rigorous, if incomplete method, an application of his metallurgical training to the study of society.

Thus the analog for Le Play's social science is not the "lawful" natural science of physics, but rather the classificatory and eminently practical one of metallurgy. For Le Play each of the worker's families he observed was a mineral whose chemical composition could be stated quantitatively: The detailed breakdowns of the budgets of income and expenditure did just that, furnishing what for him was an objective exactitude.

Of course, his doctrine does not stop with the Ten Commandments, even if they constitute the supreme theory; nor do his observations and classifications stop with the budgets of workers' families. Yet this was the heart of social science as he conceived it. In 1877 he wrote that more than the 300 families thus far analyzed should be studied (think "where mineralogy would be if only 300 minerals had been analyzed"), but that the fundaments of the science would not be affected; "a host of secondary conclusions which also have their importance"[17] would however be found. As we proceed, it will be clear that from a contemporary viewpoint, his "secondary conclusions" were much more advanced than his "supreme theory."

In setting forth Le Play's conceptual perspective, it is useful to note what he rejected. He opposed Saint-Simonian rationalism and economic individualism. Like Comte, he stressed the desirability of consensus and harmony, and saw the family rather than the individual as the basic social unit. His envisioned consensus was not, however, to revolve around the priests of positive science; rather, it would mark a return to the eternal principles embodied in the Decalogue. For Le Play disputed the then voguish notion of unilinear progress, preferring to see history cyclically, as alternations of "good" and "evil," virtue and moral decay; he stressed the need for moral reform rather than economic reorganization, and in his time saw the strengthening of the French family as the single most important reform. Most objectionable for him were the revolutionary beliefs in the inherent goodness of man, and in systematic liberty, providential equality, and the right to revolt. Austere and puritanical, Le Play believed strongly in the doctrine of original sin, and asserted that hierarchy was the central principle of all social organization.

It is very difficult to separate ideology from sociology in Le Play's writing. His central concern was with happiness—a combination of morally correct action and prosperity—and he devoted his research to uncovering what he believed were the conditions under which it existed. He was convinced that peace and stability were assured when responsible, paternalistic elites ruled submissive, righteous, hardworking populations. In spite of these convictions—and in addition to their repeated expression—Le Play was a perceptive analyst. Thus while in one place he argued that the three "causes of suffering" are "vice, error, and the abuses of novelty," in another he said that suffering resulted from overpopulation, exaggerated traditionalism, and attempts at marriage regulation.[18] The former explanation is found in the hortatory conclusion to volume one of *Les Ouvriers Européens*, the latter in a family monograph about a specific region. His programmatic writings show a theory of social evolution quite as grandiose as those of Comte and Spencer (if somewhat more moralistic), yet he could be supple and undogmatic when discussing particular problems.

From his original focus on happiness and social peace, Le Play formulated a social theory that corresponded precisely to body-soul dualism: The good society exists where men enjoy their daily bread and practice the morality of the Decalogue. Economic geography and moral-religious culture are for Le Play the fundamental determinants of social life. His threefold classification of European societies followed from this conception. The "simple and happy" society features abundant food sources and a family organization in which the father is both priest and ruler; this type is superior to all others, Le Play wrote, because the father always looks after the interests of his kin. The "complicated and happy" society is more differentiated, the work necessary to secure sufficient food is such that the fathers are not equipped fully to teach moral precepts and to assure order; thus organized religion and organized government, in a paternalistic spirit, supplement rule by the father. So long as the public powers respect local customs, the society grows in wealth, knowledge, and power.

The third type is the "complicated and suffering" society (the fourth logical possibility is neglected; at least Durkheim named his "forced" division of labor); here Le Play cites Vico and introduces his cyclical view of (French) history. Whereas simple societies are likely to remain stable for centuries, complicated ones sooner or later suffer crises, when the elites violate local customs, forget their responsibilities, and thus encourage revolt. The dynamic force for him is elite egotism,[19] and the accession of Louis XIV is said to mark the entry of France into a period of decline, of which the Revolution and nineteenth-century crises were merely symptoms.

Thus in his own way Le Play recognized the epochal changes that most of the sociological founders characterized in their well-known distinctions, but he never put together the correlative features of the two types. In the design of the second edition of *Les Ouvriers Européens*, he moves from the rural East through the "mixed" North to the (relatively) urban West. The societies under consideration change from simple to complex social organization, from animal to mechanical technology, from tradition-bound to innovating in spirit, from religious to secular in ideology, from patriarchal and communal to unstable and isolated in family organization, from spontaneous to calculating in mentality, from prosperous to suffering in material and moral condition, and—it would not be Le Play without this judgment— from "good" to "evil" in the eyes of "social science."

But there are places where his observations and generalizations confute the dominant simplistic thrust. For example, he calls "an inveterate propensity to pastoral quietude" a major "vice" of the people of the steppes, and in discussing a wine-growing region near La Rochelle remarks that some rural areas are "even worse than the cities," which have the good example of the "sober bourgeois" and are the home of more and more elite clergy.[20] Among Russian peasants living under a manorial system Le Play greatly admired, religion is said to be very strong; yet intemperance, fraud, and unchaste women are common (Vol. 2, No. 2). Closer to Moscow, a patriarchal family studied had split because of "internal dissension." A the supposedly exemplary mining enterprise at Hartz, the illegitmacy rate is alarming (Vol. 2, No. 3); here Le Play shows that this was a consequence of the directors' attempt to limit the population by prohibiting marriage before 25. And although his hortatory passages urged "respect for paternal authority" as a keystone of rectitude, his data on authority relations within families in all parts of Europe indicate that women tended to dominate, and with happy effect.[21]

Although he seems to have been sympathetic to a system of fixed social classes,[22] Le Play was acutely sensitive to the nuances of social mobility (as an individual, rather than structural phenomenon). His own career was an instance of great upward movement, but in his writing he concentrated on intra- and intergenerational climbing from manual to petit-bourgeois occupations. In 18 of the 45 family monographs mobility is mentioned as either having occurred, in the process of occurring, or likely to occur; and it is implicitly referred to in most of the others. Le Play worked with a rudimentary notion of what contemporaries call "delay of gratification," and although he held the self-serving idea that personal qualities outweighed external circumstances in producing mobility, he did show considerable shrewdness in assessing the effects of property relations, inheritance laws, and the availability of models to emulate.[23]

A famous but overemphasized element of Le Play's conceptual apparatus is his classification of family types (it is ironic that he chose to study families as shortcuts, as indicators of societal conditions, and was little interested in them for their own sake). Again we find three types, each with its characteristic geographical environment, each with its characteristic form of inheritance, each corresponding to a social type. Following the above order, first was the patriarchal family, with property held in common and passed from generation to generation. Married offspring lived close to the ancestral home, and in times of duress, the family might migrate as a unit. Le Play called this type of inheritance "forced preservation"; the property remained intact.

The second type he distinguished was the stem family ("famille-souche"), in which one heir inherited all the land while siblings were helped to migrate. This was possible with primogeniture, although Le Play thought freedom for the father in designating his heir preferable. The outstanding feature of this type of family was that it maintained continuity, providing a place where the other children could return in times of stress, and balancing tradition and innovation. This arrangement was likely to increase mobility. Le Play put his greatest hopes for reforming France on ridding the Civil Code of the equal inheritance provision and instituting the stem family, but the matter failed to pass the Senate. Thus French families continued to be of the third type, the "unstable" family. This type he held to develop from overintense forest clearance, from compulsory division of property, and from rapid urbanization. The family in this form tended to cease being transgenerational when there was no property to transmit, and it was especially likely to be without resources in times of stress. Because the children lived apart from their parents, there was little support for the aged.

The distinction between family types led Le Play to distinguish types of migration. This was a topic that interested him greatly, because he believed that actively organized migration from overcrowded areas would have a salutary effect on the society. Like social mobility, it was a matter he considered extensively but for which he is little known. Again, this is because his discussions occur in the family monographs themselves, rather than in his programmatic statements.

Basically, Le Play distinguished two types of emigrants, rich and poor, corresponding to the stem and unstable family types. The former is organized and supported by the home branch of the family, and was found in Scandinavia, Saxony, and the Basque country. The latter is random, inevitable, and disastrous, for its central feature is rootlessness. It resulted from overparceling land into plots that could not support a family.

These two types of out-migration are in turn related to two sorts of in-migration. Poor emigration produces unskilled laborers often fleeing debts or bad reputations; he conscientiously avoids describing the most degraded forms of life.[24] Rich emigration produces two types: the temporary and the permanent. The former comes in order to earn and save enough for the eventual purchase of land in his home region; he usually lives in the city with young men from his area, thus preserving local customs and reinforcing resistance to the temptations of the city. The latter type comes to stay: Le Play notes that he is likely to make his way successfully by hard work, his rural sobriety keeping him from mischief.[25] Of course, there are no frequencies to buttress such asserted correlations.

To summarize: Beyond—although not uninfluenced by—his nostalgic Catholic elitism, Le Play developed a series of classifications that were easily par for his century, even if they lacked the dynamic sweep and historical range of the greatest theorists. His empirical reports were dotted with distinctions and hypotheses that have been rediscovered by more recent sociologists because no one ever bothered to read past the more prominent, and less deserving, pomposities, programs, and special pleadings for a return to a past that probably never was.

methods and methodology

Le Play is best remembered today for his contributions to methodology and for his early insistence on field work. The specific trigger for his decision to undertake empirical social research was his distaste for the Saint Simonian notions voguish in the Paris of his youth and hence for deductive theory. His radical departure from previous travelers' accounts—surely a well-used genre—came with his eventual crystallization of systematic observational procedures; after ten years he arrived at the final outline of the family monograph.

On his travels he carried out three types of study. First he observed mining and processing, including a rare interest in the commercial and labor structure of the operations. Second were his talks with the elites who commissioned his metallurgical studies: He claimed to derive great intellectual benefit from an impressive roster of aristocratic notables. Third, of course, were his studies of workers' families. He said he made 300 such detailed studies, although no more than 30 ever appeared in print. On occasion he lodged with the families under scrutiny, and reported that he spent from a week to a month with each. His methods, then, developed under the influence of these three sorts of inquiry: The "natural" leaders he called "social authorities" seem to have guided him to certain observations to the exclusion of others, and it was with these men that Le Play identified. His quest for facts was motivated by desires for reforms which he thought the authorities would carry out.

observation and interviewing

Le Play related that his first observations and discussions with various local elites discouraged him, because he did not readily find differentiating characteristics between "prospering" and "suffering" societies.[26] But he persisted in his empirical work, and in the late 1840s concluded, on balance, that politics was less important than simple material satisfaction and moral respect. (One suspects that his reading of de Maistre was more important than his observation.) Let us look more closely at what he did, as well as what he said about it.

The family case studies were conceived as indicators of the material and moral well-being of large geographical regions and/or national societies. Le Play rejected the use of statistics such as those then available on crime for several reasons. They were collected by unscientific administrators; they failed to reveal the complexities of "man's intimate nature"; they were not cross-nationally comparable because institutions differ from country to country; finally, they were often misleading because "the art of grouping the figures allows one to demonstrate with a semblance of truthfulness any conclusion established a priori."[27] Although he praised the English parliamentary surveys, he preferred direct observation, which not only gets to the bottom of things; "sometimes, an unexpected idea, indicated by the spontaneous declaration of a respondent, suddenly forces the research in a new direction."[28]

Given his ambitious comparative purpose, Le Play's reliance on case studies of single families represents the limiting case of a sample survey. Viewed this way it is highly unsatisfactory. In only 2 of the 45 full-length family monographs is any evidence given of representativeness; for the remainder, we must take on faith the assertion that the families, selected with the help of local social authorities, were typical of the region under discussion.[29] One class of exceptions to the rule of alleged typicality includes families consciously chosen to illustrate an untypical feature—a clear foreshadowing of "deviant case" analysis. As one might expect, they all depart from the norm in a "positive" direction, showing ways in which environmental obstacles to well-being may be overcome. Several are well-off families in rundown areas; others are more interesting, like that of a carpenter (Vol. 5, No. 9), through whose example Le Play explored the functions of the religious brotherhoods of carpenters: They were the only workers who did not strike in the aftermath of the 1830 revolt, and when they did strike in 1845, the dispute was quickly and amicably settled. Obviously, it is impossible to assess the degree to which model families were included. However, comments on the community context are included in most of the monographs, and the ones selected for publication were done with the help of local elites.[30]

Once selected, the families were then observed and interrogated. A first difficulty was the sheer volume of detail necessary to establish an accurate annual budget: Persistence overcame it. Then came the need to ask delicate personal questions, which might take on the character of "an intolerable inquisition." Further, the observer, in an unfamiliar milieu—and especially if he had difficulty with the local language—had to ask many questions and thus used valuable time, or "impose(d) great mental fatigue on people little practiced in serious thinking and inept at coordinating their ideas."[31] But, Le Play claimed, long experience showed that these problems were by no means insurmountable; although he alleged that the virtues of the method itself accounted for its success, his letters—and others, descriptions of him—point to his great empathic capacity. Here is his description of how to win a family's good will:

Not to risk an investigation that might be unwanted without securing . . . an introduction from a wisely chosen authority. To assure himself first the confidence, then the sympathy of the family in making it aware of the aim—public utility—and the devotion that inspire the observer. To keep up the respondent's attention by telling interesting stories. To pay them for the loss of time occasioned by the investigation. To praise with discretion the wisdom of the men, the grace of the women, the gentleness of the children, and to distribute judiciously small gifts to all.[32]

It would create an unduly favorable impression if one failed to add that he closes the section with the moralistic warning that respect for science is imperative: Like logic in the hands of a sophist, the method of direct observation used by a "false *savant*" can lead to corruption.

In the account of Le Play's procedure thus far, one notes several sources of probable error in both the selection of families and in what we now call interviewer effect. Le Play made most of his studies on visits to mining installations where he was in close contact with the owners and directors of the enterprises, or on visits to large landowners. It is thus likely that some of the families were chosen on the basis of proximity to an installation and more important, that they were likely to be families that the local elites, anxious to impress favorably, wanted him to see. Furthermore, he made the visits under the sponsorship of the families' overseers (in some cases, their virtual owners), causing some skepticism about the truthfulness of their responses.

Further doubt is cast on the reliability of the monographs by the fact that Le Play himself was responsible for gathering the data for only 22 of the 45 full-length monographs published. Some of his collaborators did very few investigations, and thus can be assumed to have been less skilled.

Finally, the likelihood of considerable error is suggested by three checks on his research made after his death. One intended to study changes in Norway's family structure over a century.[33] The authors suggest from accounts of labor troubles in 1847, two years after Le Play's visit (Vol. 3, No. 2), that he exaggerated the well-being of the workers. They further state that they could not find a family of the same name and age-sex pattern as that in Le Play's monograph; they hypothesize that Le Play either disguised his family or invented a composite.

In 1897 a contributor to the Le Playist journal, *La Réforme Sociale*, attempted to analyze fifty years of change by studying the Hartz region (Vol. 3, No. 3). He wrote: "It hurts me to admit that [Le Play's conclusion that the workers preferred their rude existence to that of city people] was never completely just."[34]

One piece of research however aimed to attack the veracity of Le Play's account.[35] Alfons Reuss revisited a German town and interviewed two children of a previously observed family. He also consulted local newspapers, and arrived at a severe indictment of Le Play for having neglected facts that did not

fit his ideas, such as his subject's activities in local politics, which accounted for the large sum spent in pubs, a sum that appeared in the
budget under "drinking." Le Play had failed to mention the unfortunate
consequences integral inheritance had upon the younger children. Most
out of line was his picture of working conditions in a town that experienced repeated riots.

    We are thus left with the sense that Le Play's
claim to scrupulous observation is dubious. Or did he simply not see
what he was steered away from?

family monographs

    As noted above, Le Play brought out an ex-
panded second edition of his work in 1879, in six thick volumes. The
first, also published separately under the title *La Méthode Sociale*, contains an autobiography, an overview of the conclusions, and a detailed
account of research procedures. The remaining five follow a geographical version of Le Play's basic societal typology: eastern Europe and
the periphery (2), the North—Saxony, Scandinavia, Britain (3), the
stable West (4), the "disturbed" West (5), and the disorganized West,
including of course Paris (6).

    Each volume consists of an introductory dis-
cussion of the societal type involved, nine full-length and one or two
précis monographs (the latter for explicit comparative purposes), a
glossary of Le Play's scientific vocabulary and a conclusion relating
changes that occurred in the region in the twenty years since he stopped
his travels. Seven of the 36 monographs from the first edition have been
reduced to précis size; 16 full-length and 5 condensed ones have been
added, all from the *Ouvriers des Deux Mondes* series.

    The first part of a monograph was the title:
the location, the "Situs," the worker's rank in the occupational structure, and the nature of his tie to an employer or to the market. Le Play
worked with six types of occupational positions because he dealt only
with manual workers (the bulk of the population). The classifications
fail to allow for independent variation of the several dimensions they
imply, but they are nonetheless apt and useful: (1) domestic workers,
living in master's household; (2) day laborers, who may own or rent
homes, be paid in cash or in kind; (3) contract workers, higher ranking
than the former because surer of employment; (4) tenants, who range
from the poorest to the best off of workers, depending on the quality
of land, the arrangements, and so forth; (5) small holders, who likewise
vary greatly in status; and (6) master craftsmen, farmers in agriculture,
artisans in manufacture.

However, for Le Play, the wage or rent is not so important as the nature and duration of the agreement binding the worker to his employer; he distinguishes three types of relationship, noting that they are attributes of societies rather than of individuals. First are compulsory agreements, characteristic of the Middle Ages and persisting in eastern Europe. Second are permanent voluntary agreements, which followed the former historically in northern and western Europe but which since 1830 tended to be replaced by the third type, short-term agreements. Le Play saw this last type as correlative with class antagonism and instability, and largely a result of the Revolution. (He overlooked the fourth logical possibility: short-term compulsion, as in the corvée, or military draft.)

Part two was the budget of income and expenditures; Le Play called it "the monograph proper," and it has generally been held to be his most important methodological innovation. Borrowing by analogy from mineralogy the scientific principles of direct observation and comparison, he sought "guarantees of exactitude" in describing the material and moral conditions of workers by a quantitative technique, the budget:

A mineral is known when the analysis has isolated each of the elements of its composition, and when it has been verified that the weight of all these elements is exactly equal to that of the mineral. A numerical verification of the same sort is always available to the *savant* who systematically analyzes the existence of the social unit constituted by the family.[36]

The mineral kingdom, with only a few hundred species, and the human race with millions of individually distinct exemplars, merely represent extremes of the simplicity and the complex. This dissimilarity "does not exclude the analogy in methods of verification . . . [because] every act making up the existence of a worker's family ends up, more or less directly, in a receipt or an expenditure." Thus, he continued, "an observer possesses complete knowledge of a family when having analyzed every element comprised in the two parts of the household budget, he arrives at an exact correspondence between the two totals."[37] This then was the badge of science Le Play wore. He argued that while it might seem at first that the budgets reduce social science to the material aspect of life, in reality this is not so: Here he cites as one of *only five instances* in six entire volumes the fact that a Parisian longshoreman spends 12 percent of his income on alcohol and not a sou for the education of his five children.

Lazarsfeld has distinguished three primary ways to use budget data—analytical, synthetic, and diagnostic;[38] Le Play clearly falls in the third category. When he uses specific figures they are superfluous, coming in lengthy, descriptive passages, generally about religious or educational expenditures. Given the infrequent use of budget items in the discussions, it appears that Le Play expected his readers to wade through the tedious compilations. The German economist Ernst Engel used them in his consumption calculus, first published in 1857, in which he stated the law that as income rises, the proportion spent for food declines. Michel Chevalier's report, on the first edition of *Les Ouvriers Européens*, to the Academie des Sciences Morales et Politiques shows that he too read the budgets. His interest was in reporting to the Academy that the diets of workers were not correlated with the degree of culture and civilization attained.[39] And one of Le Play's followers used the budgets to generalize the hypothesis that the closer a worker lived to an industrial center, the higher the proportion of his income derived from wages.[40] None of Le Play's contemporaries or followers used the budgets in the diagnostic way Le Play had; the group of disciples who collaborated on *La Science Sociale* criticized the budget method sharply and eventually abandoned it altogether.[41] The budgets never attracted the following that Le Play hoped for, and given the quality of his description, his use of budget data is unnecessary. Only in the sense of "breaking down into components" can it be said that Le Play "analyzed" the family budget "as a quantitative expression of all aspects of family life."[42]

On balance, the budgets appear peripheral to Le Play's larger concern with drawing implications for reform in France from comparative research. Yet one can strongly suggest that the budgets served a crucial heuristic purpose in the field work itself, insuring that observers would gather ample data. First, the structures imposed by itemizing virtually everything led to extensive questioning. Second, it may well have eased the discussion of personal matters to introduce them in the abstract context of income or expense. In this sense, the budget outline that would eventually be completed was certainly the most comprehensive interview guide of the first half of the nineteenth century.

Part three of the monographs included 13 categories of "Preliminary Observations" (these preceded the budgets proper) and a various number of remarks under the heading "Diverse Elements of the Social Structure." About 20 pages of text were devoted to each of these sections, with about 12 pages of budgets. The preliminary observations did little more than spell out the budget items: (1) state of the soil, industries, population; (2) names, ages, sexes of family members; (3) religion and moral habits; (4) hygiene and medical care; (5) rank; (6) property; (7) subventions; (8) work and domestic industry; (9) diet and meals; (10) lodging, furnishings, clothing; (11) recreation; (12) principal phases of family's history; (13) customs and institutions assuring physical and moral well-being.

The latter sections, under "Diverse Elements of the Social Structure," varied considerably from monograph to monograph in length and number. They range from cross-national comparisons of laws designed to punish violators of marriage contracts, to recipes for local dishes and instructions in regional orthography. Most of them make no reference to the family being considered. Some are drawn from books, others from observations, others from discussions with "social authorities." Many are utterly irrelevant to the subject of the work, and show clearly the heritage of the traveler's account of curiosities: for example, a charming description of the life cycle of the Norwegian salmon.

For the most part, however, they describe institutional arrangements—of guilds, mutual societies, labor association, organized emigration, inheritance laws—and discuss their consequences. They form the most interesting, vivid, and revealing sections in all of Le Play's writings. Various trends and social processes are examined, though without benefit of a consistent theoretical apparatus. Though he considered them mere appendages to the glory of the family budgets, these sections of his monographs are much more interesting to the contemporary sociologist.

qualitative indicators

Le Play never drew up for his collaborators a list of suggestions for field observation. Nor did he report having confirmed his inferences by asking his respondents directly, for example, whether their small family meant they were anxious to save money and to rise socially. He made common-sense diagnoses, as we all do, but was particularly good at it—sensitive to conversational detail, to home furnishings, to anomalous occurrences.

The qualitative indicators cited by Lazarsfeld[43] all involve inferences about the workers of their families: Religious indifference is inferred from incapacity to find a minister in an emergency (Vol. 3, No. 6); respect for women from a husband's tolerance of interruption (Vol. 2, No. 1); social alienation from envious gossip about town dignitaries (Vol. 4, No. 4). Most common are inferences from style of life observations to mobility aspirations.

But other examples show Le Play inferring characteristics of the wider social system from field observations. Thus the adoption of orphans by many Lyonnais families (Vol. 6, No. 3) led him to report that in spite of widespread apostasy, good moral qualities persisted there. He contrasts Castile and San Sebastian (Vol. 4, Nos. 5 and 6) in terms of cross-class solidarity, by noting that in the former area, benches in church are not assigned according to social rank, whereas in the latter place they are so assigned.

To summarize: Although Le Play was among the earliest to do systematic field research, his data were not always reliable. In organizing and presenting them, the most interesting discussions are the least systematic. His overevaluation of the budget as a precise means of portraying essentials is betrayed by the fact that his interest was not in the families per se but rather in what they would reveal about the larger society. Beyond a repeatable outline, he had no method of comparison, however, so that the budgets served a heuristic function in data collection. His use of qualitative indicators was never pursued as a conscious strategy, but it attests to great perceptiveness and ingenuity.[44]

the social structure of england

After the publication of *Les Ouvriers Européens*, Le Play wrote only one empirical work in addition to the succession of tracts he turned out on social problems, labor reform, and family reform. That work, *La Constitution d'Angleterre*, he intended as an example of what the national and regional chapters of the Unions for Social Peace could do as "monographs of societies," just as the earlier work had shown the correct way to prepare "monographs of families." So far as one can tell, only one other was ever done, Claudio Jannet's *États-Unis Contemporains*.

The scientific nature of the monograph, however, was less a product of a striking method or of an advanced theoretical view than the result of a clear classificatory outline, providing rubrics under which a little bit of everything can be described. Le Play of course recognized the need to limit inclusion to the essentials; England was the society he knew best, having traveled often and long there, and having used the *relatively* stable pattern of English development as a foil for his diatribes on France.[45] The classification or "nomenclature" scheme entailed 12 "books," further subdivided into 127 chapters; they are preceded by a glossary of terms and followed by 9 appendices (including some demographic data and selected local and national budgets!).

The twelve books are (1) geography and population—land use, labor force, mineral and power production, climate, and the like; (2) history—here Le Play distinguishes five alternating periods of good and bad times; (3) political subdivisions; (4) "Principles of good and practice of evil"—Henry VIII breaking with Rome, the structure of the Anglican church, customs, laws, and after praise for the English trait of keeping up worthwhile traditions, an attack on Adam Smith for treating labor as a commodity; (5) family—here he draws on relevant family monographs; (6) "association and hierarchy in private life"; (7) "foreign relations in private life"; (8) local government; (9) provincial government; (10) the national state—"interior peace"; (11) national governmental structure; and (12) "prosperity and suffering"—a summary.

Books eight through eleven represent the greatest departure for Le Play: his increased interest in government can probably be attributed to the public role he had come to play. However, these sections are hopelessly dull, being thorough and complete accounts of each major office in the government—executive, judiciary, police, prisons, asylums, civil engineering and public works, financial arrangements, and budgets. But here Le Play claims no special virtue for the budgets, and there is no evidence of any intent to use them for diagnostic or comparative purposes.

The only virtue of *La Constitution d'Angleterre* is its clarity in classification. No attempt is made to show connections among the institutions described. No use is made of the statistical data. Lazarsfeld's characterization of the "nomenclature" developed 11 years later by Le Play's disciple Henri de Tourville applies to the work on England as well: It represents "a major wave of categorization, similar to that of Hermann Conring and the school of German university statistics."[46] The comparison with Conring is more apt for Le Play than for Tourville, because the former was actively attempting to influence political leaders and in fact served the state in various capacities.

To summarize, in developing his methods over twenty years, Le Play fused the long tradition of the curious traveler with those of the paternalistic landowner and the benevolent overseer. To those older orientations he added a concern for scientifically grounded social reorganization prevalent among many of his generation, and a conception of science drawn from metallurgy, emphasizing observation, classification, and quantitative measurement. His social theorizing was permeated by ideological conservatism, pastoral Catholicism (he never cared about theology), and paternalistic elitism. Yet he was not antimodern in a pervasive way; he found merit in the use of mechanical technologies for agriculture and manufacture, was very much a man of science, and admired the socially mobile. Interestingly, his less ideological conceptions prefigure some of Durkheim's most notable ideas, and his analyses of families, migration, and mobility were usually acute. When the received mythology is cleared away, Le Play emerges as a curiously contemporary figure: the upwardly mobile conservative (liberal) technocrat hoping to solve "scientifically" problems perpetuated by the very ruling groups he begs to serve.

notes

1 Standard histories of sociological thought are misleading. Howard Becker and Harry Elmer Barnes, *Social Thought from Lore to Science*, Vol. 3 (2d ed.; New York: Dover, 1961), pp. 817-819, draw their summary from the lengthier discussion in P. A. Sorokin, *Contemporary Sociological Theories* (New York: Harper & Row, 1928), pp. 63-98. This discussion seems largely taken from a critical follower of Le Play, Paul de Rousiers, whose article "La Science Sociale" [*Annals* of the American Academy of Political and Social Science, 4, 1894, 620-646] contains serious distortions. The article on Le Play in the first *Encyclopedia of the Social Sciences* Vol. 11 (New York: Macmillan Co., 1936), I, pp. 411-412, pays almost no attention to Le Play's research. The account of his ideas in Carle C. Zimmerman and Merle Frampton, *Family and Society* (New York: Van Nostrand Reinhold, 1935), pp. 73-120, is unexceptional for the most part, but defensively attempts to refute apt criticism of Le Play's moralizing and ideology; the truncated translation of Volume 1 of *Les Ouvriers Européens* is biased, expurgating all references that might be thought offensive. Details on this translation may be found in Paul F. Lazarsfeld, "Notes on the History of Quantification in Sociology," ISIS 52: 2 277-333, 323-324.

   Lazarsfeld's article concentrates fruitfully on Le Play's methods. Nathan Glazer, however, makes the mistake of taking Le Play's methodological preachments for his actual practice in "The Rise of Social Research in Europe," in Daniel Lerner, ed., *The Human Meaning of the Social Sciences* (New York: Meridian, 1959), pp. 43-72, at p. 55. Although neither seems to have consulted the original family monographs, both Jesse Pitts in the new *International Encyclopedia of the Social Sciences* (New York: MacMillan, 1968) and Matilda White Riley in her *Sociological Research* (New York: Harcourt Brace Jovanovich, 1963) give better rounded treatments.

   Of the French sources, the less said the better. On the one hand are encomia by latter-day Le Playists, collected as *Recueil d'études sociales publié à la mémoire de Frédéric Le Play* (Paris: Mercure de France, 1943). On the other hand is Andrée Michel's "Les Cadres sociaux de la doctrine morale de Frédéric Le Play [*Cahiers internationaux de Sociologie*, 34, (1963), 47-68], which neglects any mention of his methodological advances. In addition is the sophisticated discussion of the family budgets by Maurice Halbwachs in *La Classe Ouvrière et les nivaux de vie* (Paris: Alcan, 1912), pp. 157-175, 484-487, and some early, commonplace summaries: P. Collingnon, *Frédéric Le Play: sa conception de la Paix Sociale* (Paris: Domat-Montchrestien, 1932); Paul Escard, *Frédéric Le Play* (Arras et Paris: Sueur-Charruey, 1903); Pierre Maline, *P. G. F. Le Play* (Paris: Bloud, 1912).

2   The best sources on Le Play's life are *Recueil, op. cit.*; Louis Baudin, preface, in his *Le Play, Textes Choisis* (Paris: Dalloz, 1947); Dorothy Hebertson, *The Life of Frédéric Le Play* (Ledbury: The Le Play House Press, 1946); various articles in *Réforme Sociale*, 52 (1906, commemorating the centenary of his birth; and Le Play, *Les Ouvriers Européens*, (2d ed.; Tours: Alfred Mame, 1877-1879), 6 vols. This last will hence be referred to as *OE*, with parentheses in the text indicating the volume number and the number of the family monograph being discussed.

3   See Paul Farmer, "The Social Theory of Frédéric Le Play," in H. S. Hughes *et al.*, eds., *Teachers of History* (Ithaca, N.Y.: Cornell University Press, 1954), pp. 58-78.

4   Le Play's typological habit of mind is well illustrated by his description of the journey as containing five types of day: 80 days of "stationary study" (10 km/day); 40 days of "excursions" in the surrounding area (30 km/day); 40 days of geological exploration (50 km/day); 20 days of "general" explorations (60 km/day), and 20 days of comparatively rapid travel (80 km/day). See pp. 37-38, *OE*, 1.

5   *Les Ouvriers Européens* (1st ed., Paris: Imprimerie Impériale, 1855), p. 11.

6   Notes for this work, *L'art métallique au XIXe siècle*, reveal that Le Play planned to include detailed breakdowns of the costs of processing one ton of each mineral—a device analogous to his family budget technique.

7   *La Réforme Sociale en France*, (Paris: Dentu, 1864-1867), 3 vols.; *L'organisation du travail* (Tours: Alfred Mame, 1870).

8   Tours: Alfred Mame, 1875. Mame was himself a member of the Society for Social Economy and distributed Le Play's works at cost.

9   Lazarsfeld, *op. cit.*, pp. 317-321; for more detail see Catherine Bodard, *A Contribution to the History of Empirical Social Research in France: The Study of the Group "La Science Sociale,"* unpublished M.A. thesis, Columbia University, 1967.

10 Baudin, *op. cit.*, p. 56.

11 Thomas, *op. cit.* This is also manifest in the work of Baussan, *op. cit.*, especially, pp. 212-246. Alexander Farquharson's Foreword to the Herbertson biography mentions that other followers of Le Play were active supporters of Marshal Pétain.

12 Maxime Leroy, *Histoire des Idées sociales en France*, Vol. 3 (Paris: Gallimard-nrf, 1954), p. 278.

13 At the end of his article the Minister notes that when he taught sociology at the University of Madrid (1947-1953), he had his students prepare "several hundred Le Play-type family investigations, which [he] considers the most formative work a sociology student can do." *Recueil, op. cit.*, p. 34.

14 Lazarsfeld, *op. cit.*, pp. 321-326. One addition to his list of misinformed followers of Le Play is the group of *soi-disant* family monographs written by the Barnard College (N.Y.) students of the anthropologist Elsie Clews Parsons around the turn of the century. See Elsa G. Herzfeld, *Family Monographs* (New York: James Kempster Printing Company, 1905).

15 *OE*, 1, p. 475.

16 *Ibid.*, p. 627.

17 Charles de Ribbe, "Frédéric Le Play d'après sa correspondance," *Réforme Sociale,* 7 (1884), 173.

18 *OE*, 1, p. 574; 6, p. 26.

19 Curiously, Pareto, in *The Mind and Society,* §2234, fn. 1., suggests that "monographs along the line of Le Play's would be of great use in determining the character of the persons belonging in our S group [speculators], and those belonging in our R group [rentiers]." Le Play, of course, never studied the bourgeoisie or nobility.

20 *OE*, 2, p. 5; 6, pp. 176-178.

21 See, for example, *OE*, 4, p. 297; 6, pp. 110-112.

22 *OE*, 6, p. 43.

23 See, for example, Vol. 2, No. 4; Vol. 3, No. 8; Vol. 4, Nos. 4, 5, and 6; Vol. 6, Nos. 6 and 8; Vol. 6, No. 2. It is peculiar that Sorokin, who devoted much space to Le Play in his survey of sociological schools, made no mention of this aspect of his work, his pioneering *Social Mobility* (New York: Harper & Row, 1927) noted merely that Le Play had great understanding of the family.

24 Le Play's prudishness deprives the reader of any descriptions of life among the lowest classes. See *OE*, 6, p. 109, for justification of this.

25 See *OE*, 6, No. 7.

26 *OE*, 1, pp. 215-216.

27 *Les Ouvriers Européens*, 1st ed., p. 11.

28 *Ibid.*, p. 12. No examples of "serendipitous" findings are given, however.

29 The two are a Parisian tailor who lives with a mistress (Vol. 6, No. 8), like 10 of every 11 tailors; and a Nivernais laborer who is nearly bankrupt, like 9 of every 10 such laborers. In neither case is the source of the figures given, and they, of course, indicate representativeness on but one of many potentially relevant dimensions.

30 *Les Ouvriers Européens*, 1st ed., p. 5.

31 *OE*, 1, pp. 220-224.

32 *Ibid.*, p. 223.

33 Thomas D. Eliot, Arthur Hillman et al., *Norway's Families* (Philadelphia: University of Pennsylvania Press, 1960), pp. 3-35.

34 Edouard Julhiet, "Le Mineur du Harz 50 années après Le Play," *Réforme Sociale*, 33 (1897), 73-84, at p. 83.

35 My discussion of Alfons Reuss, *Frédéric Le Play in Seiner Bedeutung fur die Entwicklung der Sozialwissenschaftlichen Methode* (Jena: Gustav Fischer, 1913), is drawn from Lazarsfeld, *op. cit.*, p. 325. Lazarsfeld erroneously cites the Le Play monograph examined by Reuss as Vol. 6, No. 6; it appears to be Vol. 3, No. 4, the arms-maker in Solingen.

36 *OE*, 1, p. 224.

37 *Ibid.*, p. 225.

38 Lazarsfeld, *op. cit.*, p. 327.

39 Michel Chevalier, "Rapport Verbale sur un Ouvrage de M. F. Le Play," *Séances et Travaux de l'Acad. Sci. Morales et Polit.*, 34 (1855), 139-147.

40 Émile Cheysson, "Le Salaire," *Réforme Sociale*, 8 (1884), 159-172.

41 Lazarsfeld, *op. cit.*, pp. 328-329.

42 Becker and Barnes, *op. cit.*, p. 817.

43   Lazarsfeld, *op. cit.*, pp. 329-330.
44   It is worth noting that Le Play's family monographs earned him a place in the recent textbook on research methods by Matilda Riley (*op. cit.*, pp. 112-119; the quote is at p. 114). From her discussion it appears that she did not look far into the monographs, if at all. More important, her consistent attempt to coopt Le Play for didactic purposes leads to an unwarranted use of contemporary methodological language which gives the impression that his research was more careful and better rationalized than we have seen it to be. Her juxtaposition of Le Play and two long-term field studies (Whyte on Cornerville, Malinowski on the Trobriand Islands) with quite different purposes leads her to such statements as "he does not limit himself to one case or just a few, but deals with 300 cases, widely diversified by nationality and type of worker. These decisions have the effect of enhancing both the reliability and generality of his findings." Methodology is more properly examined by studying what a person did than by looking at his dicta; the bulk of Riley's text attests to that.
45   Especially in *La Réforme Sociale en France, op. cit.*
46   Lazarsfeld, *op. cit.*, p. 331.

émile durkheim
and the
french university:
the
institutionalization
of sociology
•
terry n. clark

Between 1870 and 1914, a great deal of crea-
tive sociological research was completed in France. But this activity did
not follow any sort of regular, coherent process of development; there
were several quite separate lines of investigation, which generally corresponded to distinct social groupings.

The first of these was composed of Frédéric
Le Play's various followers, who after the death of the master had split
into two subgroupings, one of which rallied around Henri de Tourville
and published in *La Science Sociale*, introducing a number of new ideas
including their famous Nomenclature; and another, less revisionist in
outlook, which published in *La Réforme Sociale*. In their family monographs, community and regional studies, and historical and general
theoretical contributions, the Le Playists evidenced continuing creativity
and intellectual vitality.

Terry N. Clark is Associate Professor of Sociology at the University of Chicago.
Born in 1940, he received his B.A. degree from Bowdoin College in 1962 and his
Ph.D. in Sociology from Columbia University in 1967. Clark has published articles
on community power and decision making, French social scientists, and innovation
in higher education, in particular French higher education. He is the editor and coauthor of *Community Structure and Decision Making: Comparative Analyses*
(1968) and *Community Politics: A Behavioral Approach* (1971).

This paper is part of a larger project concerned with the emergence of the social
sciences in France. Support for preparation of the manuscript was provided by the
Social Science Research Committee of the University of Chicago.

A second grouping, even less unified than the Le Playists, was that of the social statisticians. These were largely governmental administrative officials with an interest in developing the quantitative, empirical studies which they conducted for various governmental bureaus into more systematic and coherent research. Some of their best studies—such as those by Jacques Bertillon or Émile Levasseur on population growth—remained classics for many decades.

René Worms was a highly active figure who did his utmost to create a third grouping by organizing journals (especially the *Revue Internationale de Sociologie*), scholarly societies (the International Sociological Institute, the Paris Sociological Society), congresses, and publishing enterprises. He was, however, only partially successful. While a core of persons participated in many of these activities—of which the most eminent were Tarde, Novicow, de Roberty, and Kovalevsky—their collaboration was never so close as that of the other groupings. Still, marginal and eclectic, they were also in many ways quite innovative.

The fourth and last grouping, and the one with which we are most concerned in this paper, consisted of Émile Durkheim and his followers.

If these four groupings of researchers had grown up in the United States, we might speculate that, after a few years of struggle, altercation, and self-definition, all four of them would have ended in reasonably comfortable positions in universities of one sort or another. In Great Britain, on the other hand, certainly Oxbridge, and perhaps the rest of the universities, would have remained lofty and inhospitable to virtually all of these gentlemen. But in France, the Durkheimians alone succeeded in entering the university; the Le Playists have been scorned to this day; certain offshoots of the statisticians were eventually accepted at a later date; and the international sociologists around Worms gradually dispersed or found refuge in foreign universities. How then are we to explain (1) the institutionalization within the French university system of any sociology at all, but then (2) only the Durkheimian version? Answering these questions is the primary task of the present paper. We consider first certain general characteristics of French society.

general societal conditions

Durkheim himself emphasized two basic features of French society as functional imperatives for the development of sociology: first, the decline of traditional belief-patterns and institutional arrangements—what one might designate the legacy of the Revolution—and second, the strength of belief in reason—or what might be termed the legacy of Cartesianism:

Sociology could have been born and developed only where the two conditions which follow existed in combination: First, traditionalism had to have lost its domain. . . . Second, a veritable faith in the power to reason to dare to undertake the translation of the most complex and unstable of realities into definite terms was necessary. . . . We are and shall remain the country of Descartes; we have a passion for clear ideas.[1]

Though the traditionalism of the *ancien régime* declined following the 1789 Revolution, the more or less authoritarian political regimes that ruled until the inauguration of the Third Republic in 1870 restricted free inquiry, hindering intellectual development in general, and the social sciences in particular.[2]

The 1870 war with Bismarck's Prussia, the consequent fall of the Second Empire, the butchering during and following the Paris Commune, and the loss of Alsace and Lorraine to the "colossus across the Rhine" were events that, coming in rapid-fire succession, caused Frenchmen to reconsider many of their national institutions: In politics, the Third Republic replaced the Empire; in education—for the educational institutions were felt to be singularly outdated and a major factor in the French defeat—a program was put into effect reorganizing the system from primary school through graduate and research institutions. To the widespread sentiment that training in the political and social sciences was deplorably weak, one response, in 1871, took the form of the École Libre des Sciences Politiques—designed to train governmental officials, diplomats, and journalists who should direct the affairs of state more rationally than had their predecessors.

The major structural modifications in French society related to the educational system concerned restricting the activities of the Roman Catholic Church, especially the replacement of many Catholic schools by state institutions with lay teachers.[3] The principal legislation was the Primary Education Law passed in 1882, providing free, obligatory, nonreligious education for all children from ages 6 to 13.[4] It led to opening new schools as well as expanding the student body; these in turn created strong demands for additional teachers. The debasing of Catholic orthodoxy—the prior foundation for moral and civic training in the schools—created a void that educational administrators actively sought to fill during the 1880s and 1890s.[5] Several accounts report that Louis Liard, Director of Higher Education, had a conversation with Durkheim in 1886 in which he learned of Durkheim's ardent Republicanism and desire to formulate a secular morality based on science.[6]

The next year a Ministry of Education fellowship permitted Durkheim to study with Wilhelm Wundt at Leipzig and at the University of Berlin. Durkheim published several incisive articles on scientific morality in Germany, and in 1887, Liard arranged for him to become *chargé de cours*, or university instructor, in Social Science and Pedagogy at the Bordeaux Faculty of Letters.[7] He was reappointed each year for seven years, offering courses on social solidarity, the sociology of the family, suicide, physiology of law and ethics, and other subjects. In 1893, he defended, vigorously,[8] *De la division du travail social* and *Quid Secundatus politicae scientiae instituendae contulerit* as his doctoral theses at the Paris Faculty of Letters, and the next year was given a permanent appointment, as *professeur adjoint*, or assistant professor, at Bordeaux.[9] At that point, in addition to the two theses, Durkheim had published a dozen articles and reviews in Ribot's *Revue philosophique*, criticizing sociological works and outlining the need for a scientific foundation of ethics. The same year that he was given a permanent appointment he published the programmatic *Rules of Sociological Method,* thus defining the ideology for a new cluster.[10] In 1896, he became *Professeur de Science Sociale,* assuming the first such chair in France,[11] and launched the *Année sociologique.*

In articles, lectures, and conferences, Durkheim distinguished himself as an outstanding university figure and a particularly clear spokesman on ethics and public morality. In the mounting Dreyfus affair, he was a prominent *intellectuel.*

In 1902, when Ferdinand Buisson left his Sorbonne chair of *Science de l'Education* for the Chamber of Deputies, Durkheim was invited to substitute as *chargé de cours.*[12] This continued each year until 1906 when he was named to the chair. In 1905, *"morale et sociologie"* became one of four possible subjects for the written section of the philosophy *license.* In 1906, his course on pedagogy became mandatory for all *agrégation* candidates in the Faculty of Letters, the only such course in the Faculty. The title of Durkheim's chair was changed to *Science de l'Education et Sociologie* in 1913; he died four years later.

Sociology, in Durkheimian guise, thus penetrated the university. In the rest of this chapter, we examine some of the more important factors contributing to its success. We focus first on how the status of sociologist came to be defined, then on the rise of Durkheim inside the university system, the creation of a cluster around the *Année sociologique*, and Durkheim's relations with the intellectual community and the broader society.

professionalism and the
durkheimian conception of sociology

Although existing social science organizations and journals would have welcomed Durkheim, he started his own journal, the *Année sociologique*, drawing to it an intelligent, committed group of young scholars. Another short-lived publication in sympathy with the Durkheimians was edited by François Simiand while he served as librarian at the Ministry of Commerce, *Notes critiques: sciences sociales.* For about four years after 1900, *Notes critiques* published monthly "critical notes" on new books similar to those in the *Année.* Contributors were largely the same as for the *Année*, including Durkheim, who published an important review there of Simmel's *Philosophie des Geldes.* Lucien Herr also published several reviews of Durkheim's works in *Notes critiques.*

In their writings and other activities, Durkheim and his colleagues showed great disdain for most persons not collaborating with the *Année*; they thereby contributed to crystallizing French social scientists into outwardly aggressive and inwardly self-satisfied schools.

We shall say more of relationships among the Durkheimians in discussing the *Année sociologique*; here we simply note that, in contrast to the groupings considered thus far, the Durkheimians were not united through a professional organization; Durkheim never created a formal organization as the basis for a cluster. Some Durkheimians occasionally participated in organizations overlapping with their concerns. Thus, Durkheim, Mauss, and a few others met with Léon Brunschvicg, Elie Halévy, and Xavier Léon in the Société Française de Philosophie. Lucien Lévy-Bruhl, Robert Hertz, Henri Hubert, Marcel Mauss, and Durkheim met (infrequently) at the Institut Français d'Anthropologie, founded in 1911.[13] After Durkheim's death, the remaining cluster members continued participating in these organizations, and founded their own Institut Français de Sociologie. But by that time the cluster had changed considerably.

Durkheim and most *Année sociologique* collaborators had impeccable pedigrees for a university career. The ideal type included an outstanding secondary school record and study at the École Normale Supérieure; *agrégation* (state examination for teaching posts) in philosophy; several years of teaching philosophy in provincial *lycées* (secondary schools); fellowship term in Germany; *Doctorat-ès-Lettres* (Ph.D.). Nonacademic but significant personal characteristics were petty bourgeois family origins (ideally with a father as a primary-school teacher), passionate devotion to the Republic, militant anticlericalism, and Radical Socialist or Socialist political preferences.[14] The Jewish background of Durkheim and certain associates does not appear to have been directly important inside the university; the over shadowing religious issue was clericalism versus anti-clericalism.[15]

Last, but of obviously great significance, was Durkheim's intellect. Even at the École Normale he was considered a remarkable student. Although he ranked next to last on the *agrégation,* this reflected the well-known conservatism of the examining committee —comprised not of his innovative teachers at the École Normale, but of older men from outside.[16] After the turn of the century, he was exceptionally active in national university affairs, wrote indefatigably in general publications, and ranked in the popular eye with such intellectuals as Bergson, Jaurês, or Lanson.[17] As the epitome of the brilliant *universitaire*, his magnetic intellect attracted some of the best young normaliens, or graduates of the *École Normale.* Their combined talents did a good deal to raise the general status of sociology and to facilitate its diffusion.

In sharp contrast to many who merely dabbled in social science, the Durkheimians were thorough professionals. Because they were committed to largely traditional university careers— or, to be more precise, because Durkheim invited only such persons to collaborate—their major activity was creative research. But although full-time self-supporting *universitaires*, generally they were not destined for chairs labeled sociology. Certain faculties were prepared to modify titles for some chairs, but just how far the system would expand remained unclear at least until the 1920s. The possibility that sociology might become a lycée subject, implying considerable expansion of university posts, seemed quite real for many years. But a realistic young man could not plan his career on that eventuality. In 1900, the only sociological position in France was Durkheim's chair in Bordeaux. In 1914, there was the Bordeaux chair, and at the Sorbonne Durkheim's chair of *Science de l'Éducation* and Bouglé's position as *maître de conférences*, or seminar leader, in *Economie Sociale*. But there was still not a single chair entitled sociology. It was therefore necessary, if only temporary, to develop a specialized competence to be named to existing positions in the system.

This career structure seems to have been significant in leading Durkheim to define sociology as broadly as he did, for in this way professors of law, education, linguistics, religion, and other subjects could legitimately consider their work sociological. Durkheim was thus able to draw on a pool of talent of up to forty persons; if he had collaborated uniquely with potential professors of sociology, the cluster would have been drastically reduced.

Three comprehensive sociological utopias ante-dated Durkheim: Saint-Simon and his disciples, particularly Auguste Comte, were among the most flamboyant; organismic theorists such as Schaeffle and Fouillée also shared a taste for the grandiose; if Marxists are included, although they seldom claimed the title of sociologist, the choice of themes broadens still further. Indeed, social theorists of the nineteenth century characteristically painted vast frescos of humanity, postulating fundamental laws for past, present, and frequently the future.

In contrast to these immodest predecessors, Durkheim was a systematic student of very circumscribed phenomena; and, in fact, he saw himself largely in this light. But the ideological stamp of his work was conspicuous next to certain contemporaries as well as later sociologists. He was by no means immune to quasi-utopian pronouncements. The original preface of his first book contains perhaps his best known passages in this respect:

This book is preeminently an attempt to treat the facts of the moral life according to the method of the positive sciences. . . . We do not wish to extract ethics from science, but to establish the science of ethics, which is quite different. . . . Although we set out primarily to study reality, it does not follow that we do not wish to improve it; we should judge our researches to have no worth at all if they were to have only a speculative interest . . . for we shall see that science can help us adjust ourselves, determining the ideal toward which we are heading confusedly. . . . Finally, comparing the normal type with itself—a strictly scientific operation—we shall be able to find if it is not entirely in agreement with itself, if it contains contradictions, which is to say, imperfections, and seek to eliminate them or to correct them. . . . The passage from science to art is made without a break. Even on the ultimate question, whether we ought to wish to live, we believe science is not silent.[18]

Positions more ideological than utopian were taken by disciples in later works aimed at popularizing the faith, such as Georges Davy's *Sociologues d'hier et d'aujourd'hui*[19] and Bouglé's *Bilan de la sociologie française contemporaine.*[20]

Their precise designation was of great concern for the Durkheimians. Followers of Le Play, for example, spoke of *"la science sociale"* to refer only to contributions from their own grouping. "Sociology," for the Le Playists, included only the doctrines of Auguste Comte and writers building on them.[21] The Durkheimians sought to redefine sociology to cover their own work and significant social science contributions by others, including many who did not label themselves sociologists. This "imperalism" led to more than one misunderstanding.

Nomenclature for subfields also generated no

little debate. The section in the *Année* entitled "social morphology" contained works identical with the "human geography" of Vidal de La Blache and his followers.[22] Much work termed "economic sociology" by Simiand and Halbwachs was claimed by the economist and historian.[23] "Juridical sociology" overlapped with law and political science. Much of "moral sociology" was essentially philosophy. Finally, on a conceptual level, ethnology and sociology remained close to synonymous until the 1930s.[24]

Such terms as "collective conscience," "collective representations," "collective memory," "social solidarity," and "suicideogenic current," among others, became identified with the Durkheimians. These matters of nomenclature were important in defining relationships with adjoining fields.

Less pretentious than Comte's "queen of the sciences," Durkheim's conception of sociology was still more audacious than that of most sociologists today. His dogmatic proclamations on these matters also did not help relations with neighboring fields. Probably the most acrimonious disputes were those between sociologists and psychologists. They originated in Comte's failure to include psychology in his list of sciences, and were sharpened when Durkheim virtually reasserted Comte's position that ultimate principles of human behavior lay in the social, not the individual, realm. These intellectual issues were aggravated by the direct competition between sociology and psychology for the few university positions in pedagogy and "scientific" philosophy. The controversy did not subside until close to World War II.[25] Perhaps less detrimental to ongoing research than the struggle with psychology, territorial disputes with such young disciplines as human geography, social history, and political economy were still far from negligible.[26] More than one philosopher also felt that sociology was only a branch of that august discipline.[27]

For Durkheim, sociology neither claimed a subject matter separate from the individual social sciences, nor did it approach the same subject matter with a distinctive methodology; sociology comprised the "system" or the "corpus" of the individual social sciences.[28] But the total content of every social science was not included, only those elements that were "sociological." Specialists working with economic or political materials unsociologically were not sociologists. But his emphasis on social factors led Durkheim to deny that such nonsociological research was fruitful; he dismissed such specialists as largely misguided or incompetent.[29]

The manifesto and handbook for proselytes was *The Rules of Sociological Method*; it defined the Durkheimian approach to sociological analysis, founded on "social facts." The two basic criteria for social facts were exteriority and constraint. Defined as "every way of acting, fixed or not, capable or exercising on the individual an external constraint,"[30] social facts are those elements in a society that are more than merely present in individual psyches; they are, as contemporary sociologists would say, institutionalized. Social facts are to be analyzed as external data, *comme des choses* (as physical objects) and not introspectively in the consciousness of the observer; complete objectivity is imperative for true science. The efficient cause producing each social fact should be isolated, and the functions specified that it fulfills. In every case, however, the analytical level is social: Adopting Boutroux' theory of emergent levels, Durkheim would admit no cause for a social fact except another social fact; similarly, functions performed by social facts are preeminently social. Sociology was thus the study of economic, legal, religious, and other social facts gleaned by specialists, and the summation of principles from these areas into a systematic and integrated theory.

This conception of sociology contrasted with two others of the period. The first, supported by Worms and Tarde, among others, held that sociology was not the aggregate but only the "philosophy" of the social sciences, the body of general principles subsuming the individual disciplines.[31] This conception, they pointed out, did not arouse charges of imperialism by other social scientists. The Durkheimians retorted that such an approach, adequate for grandiose systems of earlier years, was too superficial for an adequate general theory, and too general to be useful to specialists.[32]

The second conception contrasting with Durkheim's held that sociology was parallel to other social sciences, and distinguished by its formal approach to patterns of social relationships. Although this conception was supported by few French sociologists, an outstanding German proponent, Georg Simmel, published a major programmatic paper in the first *Année sociologique*. Durkheim did not conceal his disagreement with Simmel, however, and Simmel never published again in the *Année*.

While engendering conflict with some, the Durkheimian conception was consistent with the goals of career-conscious *universitaires*. A distinction must still be made between employing sociological analysis and becoming a sociologist. Durkheim inspired many persons to apply sociological analysis to traditional fields, but trained only a handful of sociologists without some qualifying adjective. How he brought sociological analysis to these fields had a good deal to do with his role in both national and university politics.

the rise of the durkheim cluster:
the dreyfus affair and the new university

Many potential political issues may have been
slighted during the Third Republic,[33] but those that were raised involved public education to a remarkable degree.[34] It was through
scholarships created for secondary and higher education in the first
decades of the Third Republic that many persons of petty bourgeois,
and occasionally working-class and peasant, background completed
higher degrees. Many of these became teachers in state institutions, and
constituted for many observers the core of active support for the Third
Republic.[35] The national educational system thus selected a meritoc-
racy which in many respects became a new "establishment," based not
on titles, land, or industry, but on examinations. Represented in the
Radical and Radical Socialist parties, its political dominance grew after
1880, and became consolidated during the Dreyfus affair. The trial of
a Jewish officer by the aristocratically oriented military was a perfect
symbol around which to mobilize opponents of the traditional order.
The rising *professeurs* used the issue to topple their adversaries and
continued to dominate the political scene until the 1930s.

It was no coincidence that the success of the
Durkheimians paralleled that of the *république des professeurs*; and
the Dreyfus affair was a benchmark for both. Students in the Latin
Quarter have a long tradition of street and classroom violence, and
under the impact of the Dreyfus affair disturbances between Dreyfusard and anti-Dreyfusard occurred almost daily.[36] The leadership of
the Dreyfusards was at the École Normale Supérieure where the socialist
librarian Lucien Herr directed his lieutenant, Charles Péguy, in daily
battles, using *normaliens* as shock troops.[37] The Sorbonne as a whole
was pro-Dreyfus, but Latin Quarter students were split almost evenly so
that conservative, anti-Sorbonne, anti-Dreyfusard critics would spread
violence around the Sorbonne and disrupt lectures of Dreyfusard professors. Elaborate quasi-military systems of spies, runners, messengers on
bicycles, rowdies, shock troops, and defense guards were organized by
both sides and prepared to mobilize on less than half an hour's notice.[38]

Durkheim and his associates were among the
most active of Dreyfusards. Simiand and several younger Durkheimians
participated in the activities organized by Herr.[39] Durkheim became
secretary general of the Bordeaux section of the *Ligue pour la Défense
des Droits de l'Homme*, the leading Dreyfusard organization, soon after
its founding in 1898.[40] He was a favorite speaker at rallies in the Bordeaux area.[41] In conjunction with his colleague Hamelin, Durkheim
founded an association of university teachers and students called *"la*

Jeunesse Laïque," which met weekly. Meetings were ideological discussions with socialist, antimilitarist overtones which stressed the importance of science as an alternative to Christianity.[42] Along with Radical and Radical-Socialist deputies, senators, and educational administrators, Durkheim was a leading speaker at the *Congrès International de l'Education Sociale,* held at the Paris World's Fair of 1900.[43] At the Congress, at the institutions created by Dick May, and elsewhere, republicanism, Dreyfusard ideology, and the emergence of the new social sciences became combined as a single effort.

We do not have precise information about public opinion concerning the New University,[44] the Dreyfus affair, and the emergence of romantic nationalism. But from about 1880 to 1900, there appears to have been considerable support among the intellectual public for the ideas, men, and institutional arrangements associated with the New University. These years also saw the greatest activity of the Société de l'Enseignement Supérieur. Numerous articles in the Society's *Revue internationale de l'enseignement (RIE)* favored the New University and the new social sciences. Contributions were included from Durkheim and Tarde on general intellectual issues and from René Worms and Dick May on organizational questions. These RIE discussions provided important links between strictly intellectual debates and organizational changes and appointments.

One issue continually discussed in the *RIE* was pedagogy, *"la science de l'éducation."* Many felt that developments in sociology and psychology bearing on education made university instruction in the area worthwhile. Thus, in 1883, Henri Marion became *chargé de cours* at the Paris Faculty of Letters, lecturing on *science de l'éducation*. He was given a chair with the same title in 1887; he occupied it until his death in 1896, when he was replaced by Ferdinand Buisson.[45] In Buisson's lectures and most public debates, *la science de l'éducation* consisted less of educational theories than the social, political, and philosophical beliefs which should inform the general educational process.[46] To teach this mixture of secular morality, republican ideology, and the "art of forming good citizens," the incumbent of such a chair had to remain in close touch with more general political and ideological developments. Buisson clearly did. As Director of Primary Education for 15 years before assuming the chair, he had been the major individual to enforce the laws of Jules Ferry establishing general secular public education. He later served as president of the *Ligue pour la Défense des Droits de l'Homme.* After six years in the Sorbonne, in 1902, he was elected deputy and took a temporary leave from the chair; in 1906, he abandoned it definitively. When he left the important chair vacant, it was imperative to find a substitute possessing the appropriate ideological, philosophical, and social scientific elements.

      The year 1902 witnessed several developments that made Durkheim a logical choice. After a widely publicized campaign for donations, a statue of Auguste Comte was erected which dominated the Place de la Sorbonne. The 1902 reforms were enacted, merging the École Normale with the Paris Faculties of Letters and Sciences and increasing attention to the nonclassical subjects in the licence sequence. During the same year at Dick May's École des Hautes Études Sociales, Dean Alfred Croiset and Ferdinand Buisson were conducting their seminar on pedagogy and their *enquêtes* on the teaching of ethics in primary, secondary, and higher education. Durkheim had impressed the Dean of the Faculty of Letters and the incumbent of the chair; he seems to have been respected by the professors of philosophy, especially Boutroux, whose student he had been at the École Normale.[47]

      When Buisson's chair was declared vacant, six persons presented their candidacies. Durkheim was the unquestioned choice of Buisson, whose opinion was seconded by Boutroux, professor of history of modern philosophy, Brochard, professor of history of ancient philosophy, and Espinas, professor of social economy. Durkheim was elected "first line" candidate.[48]

      Durkheim's success was a combination of many intellectual and ideological factors. To emphasize the ideological elements is in no way to denigrate the intellectual qualities, but it is essential to explain how many administrators and faculty evaluated him, and how many of his followers advanced their careers. Critics like Hubert Bourgin, Pierre Lasserre, Charles Péguy, and Henri Massis no doubt exaggerated the ideological elements; the Durkheimians themselves stressed the intellectual qualities; both factors contributed, reinforcing each other so as to make their segregation most difficult.

      Clearly, Durkheimians had to be both ideologically and intellectually outstanding to make headway in a system so structurally unresponsive. Nevertheless, several types of positions were amenable to definition, or redefinition, as at least partially social scientific. *La science de l'éducation* was one such field. Another was "*l'économie sociale.*" Considered by some as the study of the distribution of wealth in contrast to political economy's focus on the production of wealth,[49] in the 1890s the concept attracted the Comte de Chambrun. Not only did Chambrun found the Musée Sociale, he also created courses and chairs in social economy. A course at the *École Libre des Sciences Politiques* in 1893 (by Cheysson) was followed by others at the Paris Faculty of Law in 1898 (by Charles Gide) and the École des Ponts et Chaussées in 1900 (also by Gide).[50] Most important for present purposes, however, was the chair he endowed in the history of social economy at the Paris Faculty of Letters in 1894.[51] Alfred Espinas, then professor of philosophy and dean at the Bordeaux Faculty of Letters, was called to Paris in 1894 as *chargé de cours* in the area of the chair. He became *professeur adjoint* in 1899 and *titulaire* in 1904. But in 1907, he took a leave of absence for reasons of health. The ambiguous nature of the chair then became evident in discussions of the *Conseil*. Following an interesting debate, Bouglé was elected to the chair.

The case of Bouglé illustrates well the role of ideology in advancing a career. Older than most other Durkheimians, he had attended the École Normale in the early 1890s, placed first in the *agrégation* for philosophy in 1893, and consequently spent the next year with a fellowship in Germany.[52] He became *maître de conférences* at the Montpellier Faculty of Letters in 1898. The next year he defended his most important work, *Les idées égalitaires*, as his thesis and became *chargé de cours* (1900) and then professor (1901) of social philosophy at the Faculty of Letters of Toulouse. He completed several insightful articles in the *Année*, in particular on the Indian caste system. But with the Dreyfus affair, he began publishing more ideological works (*La crise du libéralisme*, 1902; *Solidarisme et libéralisme*, 1902; *Le solidarisme*, 1907; etc.). His publicist reputation derived from these works, frequent lectures and debates, and his activities as journalist and editor of the important leftist newspaper, *La dépêche de Toulouse*. By 1907, when he entered the Sorbonne, his ideological activities had almost supplanted the scientific; these continued while he substituted in the chairs of Espinas and later Durkheim until 1919, when he became professor of history of social economy.

Durkheim and Bouglé were the two central members of the cluster before 1914, although they were increasingly supported by Lucien Lévy-Bruhl. Durkheim's other collaborators remained outside the Sorbonne before 1914, but nevertheless increased in numbers and advanced quite impressively in their careers (see tables 1 and 2).

When the first volume of the *Année* appeared in 1898, it included as collaborators (there was never an editorial board) Georg Simmel, Emanuel Lévy, and Célestin Bouglé in junior university positions; Gaston Richard who had completed his *Doctorat* but still was awaiting an appointment; and eight *agrégés* (those having passed the *agrégation*), most in lycée posts. The last prewar issue included contributions from 9 of the original 13 collaborators. Durkheim and Bouglé were then at the Sorbonne; Paul Lapie and Emmanuel Lévy had become faculty professors; Henri Hubert and Marcel Mauss were *directeurs adjoints* at the *École Pratique des Hautes Études*; Paul Fauconnet was *chargé de cours* at Toulouse; François Simiand and

table 1 · number and rank of *année sociologique* collaborators, 1898-1913

status	I 1898	II 1899	III 1900	IV 1901	V 1902	VI 1903	VII 1904	VIII 1905	IX 1906	X 1907	XI 1910	XII 1913
Chairholders in faculties or *Collège de France*; EPHE directors	1	1	1	2	4	5	5	5	6	7	5	5
Nonchairholders in faculties; EPHE staff below directors	2	3	2	3	3	4	4	4	4	2	4	4
Administration (inspectors, librarians)	–	–	–	–	–	1	1	2	2	2	2	2
Agrégé or *docteur*	9	8	8	8	8	5	7	8	7	8	12	12
No *agrégation*	–	–	–	–	–	–	–	–	–	–	2	2
Foreigners	1	–	4	–	–	–	–	–	–	–	–	–
Total	13	12	15	13	15	15	17	19	19	19	25	25

table 2 · new collaborators of *année sociologique*, 1898-1913

I 1898	II 1899	III 1900	IV 1901	V 1902
Durkheim, professor of social science, Bordeaux Faculty of Letters Lévy, *chargé de cours*, Toulouse Faculty of Law Bouglé, *maître de conférences*, University of Montpellier Fauconnet, Hubert, Lapie, Mauss, Milhaud, Muffang, Parodi, Simiand, Richard, *agrégés* Simmel, a.o. professor, University of Berlin	Foucault, *agrégé*	Ratzel, professor, University of Leipzig Sigel, professor, University of Warsaw Steinmetz, professor, University of Utrecht J. T. Stickney (Harvard)	Charmont, professor, Montpellier Faculty of Law Aubin, H. Bourgin, *agrégés*	Meillet, director, EPHE Hourticq, E.-Cl. *Maître agrégés*

VI 1903	VII 1904	VIII 1905	IX 1907	X 1910
Huvelin, professor, Lyon Faculty of Law	Lalo, *agrégé*	Halbwachs, Hertz, Vacher, *agrégés* G. Bourgin, *archiviste-paleographe*	Bianconi, *agrégé*	David, Davy, Gernet, Ray, Reynier, *agrégés* de Felice, Lafitte

Dominique Parodi were still listed as *agrégés*; Gaston Richard, Georg Simmel, H. Muffang, and Albert Milhaud no longer collaborated. Additional contributors included Antoine Meillet, professor at the Collège de France; Paul Huvelin, professor of law at Lyon; A. Aubin, *Inspecteur*; Georges Bourgin, *archiviste-paléographe*; Bianconi, Hubert Bourgin, Maxime David, Georges Davy, Louis Gernet, Maurice Halbwachs, Robert Hertz, R. Hourtig, Jean Ray, and Jean Reynier, *agrégés*; and Ch. de Felice and J. P. Lafitte who had not completed an *agrégation*. What did collaboration with the *Année* mean to these persons?

the structure of the durkheim cluster:
the année sociologique and socialism

The *Année sociologique*, to use Durkheim's term, was a phenomenon *sui generis*. Félix Alcan, the enterprising publisher of the *Revue philosophique* and Durkheim's books, apparently decided that the material on "scientific philosophy" in the *Revue philosophique* was sufficient to warrant separate publication. Alfred Binet and H. Beaunis were thus asked to edit an *Année psychologique*, and Émile Durkheim an *Année sociologique*, each of which followed the same format. But the organizations of the two journals were strikingly different. The *Année psychologique* included considerable material by Alfred Binet, who remained isolated in his École Pratique des Hautes Etudes laboratory, and contributions by a wide range of persons whom he had difficulty attracting.[53] The *Année sociologique* became instead the center of a powerful cluster. How did the *Année sociologique* develop in this distinctive manner?

The research institute, as found in many German universities, was one organizational model which inspired it. While a student at the University of Leipzig, Durkheim had been impressed by Wilhelm Wundt's famous institute.[54] The general association of research in Germany with the research institute[55] lent this structure considerable prestige. Durkheim did not, however, adopt that institution closely allied with the research institute in Germany—the seminar. While the ideal of collective research was greeted with enthusiasm,[56] the form it assumed in the *Année* was more rigidly hierarchical than in Germany. The more authoritarian professor-student relations in the French university,[57] and Durkheim's authoritarian personality,[58] reshaped the research institute from the German model.

The model for a seminar had existed even closer to home: In 1891, Léon Duguit, professor at the Bordeaux Faculty of Law, had organized a seminar on sociology. But Durkheim apparently had nothing to do with Duguit's seminar.[59] Nor did he ever organize a seminar of his own.[60]

The *Année* was thus far more than a journal. It shared many goals and performed many functions of a modern social research institute. As a collectivity it could—and did—realize two of Durkheim's basic ideals: scientific objectivity and intellectual excellence. As a firmly established social fact, the *Année* provided both exteriority to minimize subjective bias, and constraint from association with hyper-critical minds, to maintain standards at a consistently high level. These two goals overshadowed the others.

The principal manifest goal of the *Année* was still compilation of sociologically useful contributions of the previous year. Between 1895 and 1912, out of what might easily have become a mechanical abstracting service, Durkheim and his collaborators pro-duced 12 of the most significant volumes in the history of sociology. Like contemporary research institutes specialized in secondary analysis, they synthesized studies of such varied subjects as French industrial plants, Bavarian peasant villages, Australian tribes, New York slum dwellers, and Sicilian criminals, as well as theoretical contributions from practically every country in the world. From this heterogeneous clay, the Durkheimians molded a vigorous and proud sociology, unsur-passed in many respects for years to follow.

In this collective enterprise, Durkheim also achieved another ideal essential to transcend earlier superficiality: specialization of task through division of labor. Individual specialization was complemented by a common master scheme. Durkheim's methodol-ogical works, especially *The Rules of Sociological Method*, were basic guides; the *Année* itself promoted further unity. Its *mémoires originaux* amalgamated major advances of specialists.

Beyond these manifest goals—reviewing the literature, enforcing scientific objectivity, maintaining high intellectual standards, promoting specialization, and providing integration into an overall pattern—the *Année* performed four more latent functions: re-cruitment, training, social integration, and the exercise and legitimation of authority.

Reviewing a single book or article was a simple enough task to delegate to a student in one of Durkheim's courses or to others that *Année* collaborators might contact. A young man thus could try his hand at a limited task and learn about the cluster. In this way, Durkheim created a channel for recruiting new talent.

Providing external checks for advanced collabo-rators, collective activity also facilitated evaluation of younger men. Weak points could be remedied through suggested reading, direct in-struction and criticism, and informal example. Apprentice-like training thus complemented more didactic lessons of formal lectures. Such activities reinforced informal relationships; these in turn furthered social and intellectual integration.

Finally, Durkheim's authority was extended and legitimated through the *Année*. Group pressures against deviance are generally stronger than those of even an eminent individual. Division of labor led to elaboration of Durkheim's ideas by others who in turn enforced the master's authority. He was thus freed for other tasks.

Durkheim still played a considerable role in compilation of the *Année*. He had no office for the *Année* except his personal study, and no administrative assistance except his wife, who assumed numerous menial tasks; Alcan provided only minimal support in these matters. It appears, although we have no conclusive evidence,[61] that the *Année* was financially self-supporting.[62]

The standard procedure for compiling the *Année* was as follows:[63] Bibliographies from publishers, newspapers, and various professional journals were scanned for appropriate titles; more came from associates in France and abroad. After this stage, Mauss took most responsibility for the religious section and Simiand for the economic, but Durkheim still had the greatest burden. All three would write to publishers for review copies of the works. Upon arrival, they were examined briefly and sent to specialized collaborators, or the director of the section would review it himself. Individual reviewers sent manuscripts to the section directors, who would edit them and perhaps return them for revisions.[64] Eventually manuscripts were assembled and sent to Alcan for printing. Proofs were sent to the director of each section who sometimes returned them to individual authors for final editing. Durkheim, aided by Mme. Durkheim, would go over almost every page, critically.[65] When proofs had been corrected by various authors and section directors, they were returned to the publisher for final printing. Because Durkheim was in Bordeaux from 1896 until 1902, these activities took place through the mails. Even after that time, however, with collaborators scattered throughout France,[66] most communication remained confined to the mails.

Only Durkheim assured coordination among the many collaborators. In keeping with his authoritarian preferences, no staff meetings were held; he would see people one at a time. Certainly, informal contacts emerged between collaborators of similar age and speciality, but for many—particularly younger men in provincial lycées—most work was done in isolation. Mauss and Simiand each led subclusters, but despite the cluster's remarkable *intellectual* integration, *social* integration was much less developed. Many contemporary descriptions of the *Année* reflect the background from which it developed: Inasmuch as advanced collective work remained infrequent, the relative integration of the *Année* understandably impressed outside (and inside) observers.[67] When there was finally one meeting of the entire staff in 1912[68] —a unique occasion in the prewar period—it was a collective ritual charged with all the emotion that Durkheim had described in the totemic ceremonies of Australian aboriginals. Cognizant of the importance of religious symbols and rituals, the tribe would have found the ceremony incomplete without the erection of a totem. There was no disappointment that day, for a bust of Durkheim had been executed for the occasion!

It is interesting to inquire how Durkheim coordinated the many persons around the *Année*, with no professional organization or editorial board meetings, no funds to dispense, no seminars, and no research institute in the traditional sense. Most groupings discussed in earlier chapters consciously strove toward integration— employing these and other mechanisms for institutionalization that Durkheim eschewed—but they largely dispersed within a decade or two, and almost none achieved the intellectual integration of the Durkheimians.

One major factor integrating the Durkheimians was of course the centralized structure of the national educational system: For the reasons outlined previously, the system tended to generate clusters. Even lacking direct support for the *Année*, Durkheim's missionary zeal for sociology led him to devote time to lectures, public debates, committee meetings, and other activities that made him into a leading *patron universitaire*, an academic patron. He thus assisted his collaborators in obtaining positions throughout the educational system. There was also, of course, Durkheim's unquestionable intellect. In addition, he had a remarkable ability to formulate problems strategic both for sociological theory and pressing moral and political concerns. His prestige with both his collaborators and the general public was enhanced by the timeliness of his theoretical works for definition of a secular morality, development of a theory of solidarity, and isolation of causes of social deviance. The Durkheimians also shared a common training and career pattern. They were brought together again by a series of important political experiences.

Their militant pose and internal cohesion were strengthened by serving in the Dreyfusard army. When attacks on the master took the form of loud jeers, thrown objects, and manhandling of students at the lecture hall entrance, his defenders understandably closed ranks and assumed a belligerent pose. Political continuity after the Dreyfus affair came through socialism. National transformations were doubtless important in this metamorphosis, but a major influence must be attributed to Lucien Herr.

A graduate of the École Normale in philosophy (four years after Durkheim), Herr began research for a possible thesis (never completed), and in 1888, was named librarian at the École Normale. Long fascinated by politics, Herr eventually joined the relatively undogmatic *possibiliste* socialists led by Jean Allemane. He attended weekly cell meetings and wrote a weekly article for the party organ *Le parti ouvrier*. His role in the Dreyfus affair achieved legendary proportions.[69] As a bachelor Herr lived for many years near the École, usually dining with students in residence; he was also in frequent contact with them through the library. These close relationships with students led to a considerable number of converts to socialism (including Jaurès himself).[70] By the late 1890s, the École had become a citadel of socialism. And many leading converts came to collaborate with Durkheim.[71]

For many at the time, socialism, social science, and sociology were related closely enough to make confusion a frequent occurrence.[72] This tendency was facilitated by the active socialism of the majority of *Année* collaborators. Marcel Mauss, François Simiand, and Lucien Lévy-Bruhl were all involved with Herr and Jaurès in founding *l'Humanité*, and they, Halbwachs, and Fauconnet contributed to the paper for many years.[73] In the École Socialiste, founded to instruct workers in socialist doctrines, Emmanuel Lévy, Simiand, Mauss, and Fauconnet all served as teachers.[74] Simiand and Hubert Bourgin sat with Herr, Mario Rocques and Léon Blum on the board of a socialist publishing house founded by Herr and managed by Péguy,[75] thirteen contributors to the *Année* became stockholders in subsequent years.[76] Henri Hubert and Robert Hertz were also socialists.[77]

The closeness of the Durkheimians' scholarly work to socialism was underlined when sections of their academic writings were republished with fiery introductions in a series of socialist tracts.[78] Bouglé spent a good deal of his time with socialist activities, and edited an annotated version of the works of Proudhon.[79]

Durkheim's own relations with socialism were extremely complex and have been the subject of considerable scholarly controversy.[80] His original thesis topic had been the relation of individualism to socialism, and although changed to the individual and society, socialism was never far below the surface of *The Division of Labor in Society*; nor was it in *Suicide* or several other works.[81] He planned a history of socialist thought, although he completed only the section on Saint-Simon.[82] Jaurès came to Durkheim's home for Sunday dinner several times[83] and he was in close contact with Lucien Herr, who first directed him to Frazer's work on religion. He was known to arrive at lectures and to walk out of the Sorbonne conspicuously carrying *l'Humanité*, a political act in itself.[84] He never joined a socialist party, how-

ever, nor did he participate in partisan activities with his younger collaborators. Repelled by the emotion and lack of rigor of most socialist
writers, he remained deeply concerned with many phenomena they
treated. But to many less concerned with these subtleties, there was no
doubt that Durkheim was a socialist.[85]

relations with the intellectual community

The combination of petit bourgeois family ori-
gins, the École Normale, philosophical training, collaboration on the
Année, common career lines, the Dreyfus affair, and socialism bound
the Durkheimians to one another and to the national university system.
But such cohesion also helped unite their opponents. The many reforms leading to the New University were not made without considerable resistance. The very criticisms, however, illuminate the Durkheimians' success.

Four types of critics of the New University
may be discerned. Traditional Catholics, incensed by abolition of the
Faculty of Theology, regarded the new secularism as undermining religious values. Second, upper-class groups abhorred the left-of-center
orientation of most Sorbonne professors and students;[86] upper-class
children consequently preferred the Faculties of Medicine or Law, a
Grande École, or the École Libre des Sciences Politiques. Third, humanistic litterateurs resented the intrusion of scientific attitudes into
fields that traditionally favored intellectual flair and intuitive brilliance.[87] This was one element of the aristocratic heritage that opposed
the bourgeois style—calculating, rational, and unpolished.[88] Petty
bourgeois students at the École Normale and the Sorbonne were assailed
as *Berufsmenschen* (vocationally oriented). Finally, superpatriots attacked the reforms as imports from an alien and barbaric foreign
culture, woefully lacking the effervescent *esprit latin*.[89] The old tensions
between Cartesianism and spontaneity were quite clear.

The *Geist* of the Sorbonne also opposed that
of the Collège de France, at least as then expressed from certain chairs
in philosophy. Facing each other across the Rue Saint Jacques, the two
buildings housed sharply contrasting philosophies, personalities, and
styles. This temperamental conflict was reflected in many facets of the
notorious debates between Durkheim and Gabriel Tarde. Tarde had
been elected to the chair of modern philosophy at the Collège in 1900,
defeating Henri Bergson by only a few votes.[90] Upon Tarde's death four
years later, Bergson acceded to the chair, and in the decade before 1914
came to symbolize for many all that the Sorbonne lacked.[91] Georges
Sorel, the *polytechnicien* (graduate of the *École Polytechnique*) turned

revolutionary, drew heavily on Bergson in his mystique of violence. He would come into Paris from his suburban residence on Friday afternoons, stop by the *Cahiers de la Quinzaine* to meet Charles Péguy, Daniel Halévy, Julien Benda, Berth, and Peslouän, whence they would proceed past the Sorbonne to the Collège de France to attend Bergson's weekly lecture.[92]

Among others frequenting the crowded lecture hall were Gabriel Tarde's son (who, unlike his father, insisted on the aristocratic particle), Guillaume *de* Tarde, and a close friend, Henri Massis. Using the *nom de guerre* of Agathon, the two collaborated on several pamphlets and books in which the four above criticisms were combined in lashing diatribes against the Sorbonne, and especially that diabolical figure and family enemy, Émile Durkheim.[93] It was also at the Collège de France that Jean Izoulet was professor of social philosophy, the Izoulet who wrote the damning phrase so widely quoted by Durkheim's adversaries: "the obligation of teaching the sociology of M. Durkheim in 200 Normal Schools in France is the gravest national peril that our country has known for some time."[94]

Over a period of twenty years, Durkheim and his thought thus rose from near obscurity to dominate the university system to the extent that for critics he symbolized its very essence, with all the advantages and problems that this implied. If at the outset Durkheim had been in harmony with the music of the university, by the end of his career he became one of its major composers.

Although Durkheim published most scientific work in the *Année sociologique* and in separate books, he also wrote about 75 articles for magazines and journals of more general circulation, such as the *Revue bleue*, and the *Revue des deux mondes*.[95] His ideas on scientific ethics were widely debated by philosophers, educators, and the general public.[96] At meetings of the French Philosophical Society, he debated the epistemological and ethical aspects of sociology.[97] Several polemics, including those with Tarde, took place in more popular publications. This was especially true of social problems involving legislative action, such as the causes of crime, the effects of the press on public morality,[98] suicide, divorce, and depopulation.[99] Durkheim's role in the Dreyfus affair has already been discussed.

The impact of the Durkheimians on the Latin Quarter climate, their influence on the ideological tenor of the educational system,[100] and their success in promotions and appointments must still be sharply distinguished from structural change of the system. The success of the Durkheimians, for the most part, took place within established structures. Before 1914, only one chair was created in the entire system for them, that of Durkheim in Bordeaux; those assumed by Durkheim and Bouglé in the Sorbonne, and most assumed by Durkheimians in later years, had existed for some time. Attacked as ideologues by political critics outside the university, inside it they were more often condemned as academic imperialists. The internal criticisms were enhanced not because the Durkheimians tried to create new posts and then failed, but because they were named over non-Durkheimian philosophers, historians, and others who sought the same existing chairs.[101] Such imperialism made possible a large and powerful cluster; but without a *license-agrégation* foundation it remained structurally insecure. The constraints of the national system prevented creation of full-fledged examinations and chairs in sociology, even with administrators as sympathetic as Paul Lapie in the Ministry of Education. Lacking the foundation on which other fields built, the Durkheimians were forced to maintain leadership through moralizing and political debate. This they did with considerable success, for a time.

notes

1   Émile Durkheim, "La sociologie," *La science française* ["Exposition universelle et internationale de San Francisco" (Paris: Librairie Larousse, 1915)], Vol. 1, trans. by Jerome D. Folkman as "Sociology," in Kurt H. Wolff, ed., *Émile Durkheim, 1858-1917* (Columbus: Ohio State University Press, 1960), pp. 383-384. Nisbet stresses the importance of the French Revolution of 1789 and the Industrial Revolution as background factors for the development of sociology. See Robert A. Nisbet, *Émile Durkheim* (Englewood Cliffs, N. J.: Prentice-Hall, 1965), pp. 19 ff.; and *The Sociological Tradition* (New York: Basic Books, 1966).

2   For example, when a group of scholars around Paul Broca, a dynamic young doctor at the Paris Faculty of Medicine, requested governmental permission to form an Anthropological Society in 1858, it was only after a great deal of difficulty that they were authorized to hold meetings on condition that (1) no more than 20 persons attend at one time, (2) there be no discussion of politics or religion, and (3) an Imperial Police officer attend all meetings.

3   Jean-Marie Mayeur, "La France bourgeoise devient républicaine et laïque (1875-1914)," in L. H. Parias, *Histoire du peuple français* (Paris: Nouvelle Librairie de France, 1964), pp. 178-199.

4   See the three-volume series on anticlericalism by Louis Caperan, *Histoire contemporaine de la laïcite française, la crise du seize mai et la revanche républicaine* (Paris: Marcel Rivière, 1957); *La revolution scolaire* (Paris: Marcel Rivière, 1959); *La laicite en marche* (Paris: Nouvelles Editions Latines, 1961), as well as the brief study by Georges Duveau, *Les instituteurs* (Paris: Sueil, 1961), pp. 102 ff.

5   On the general importance of positivism in this task, see Louis Legrand, *L'influence du positivisme dans l'œuvre scolaire de Jules Ferry* (Paris: Marcel Rivière, 1961).

6   Raymond Lenoi, "L'œuvre sociologique d'Émile Durkheim," *Europe,* 22 (1930), 294.

7   See René Lacroze, "Allocuation: Émile Durkheim à Bordeaux (1887-1902)," *Annales de l'Université de Paris,* 30 (January–March 1960), p. 26, and Harry Albert, "France's First University Course in Sociology," *American Sociological Review,* 2 (June 1937), 311-317.

8   On the thesis defense, see L. Muhlfeld, *Revue universitaire,* 1 (1893), 440-443.

9   The Rector wrote to the Ministry on November 19, 1894 that "I have the honor of sending you, with a very favorable recommendation, a copy of the minutes . . . in which the Council of the Bordeaux Faculty of Letters unanimously nominates M. Durkheim, now in charge of a *cours complémentaire* in social science and pedagogy, for the position of *professeur adjoint*." A footnote added that of 11 titulary professors, one, M. Radel, either abstained or was absent from the meeting. Whether informal influence had been exercised from Paris is thus unclear; all official documents show the initiative coming from the Bordeaux *Conseil.*

These, other letters and information about Durkheim's salary advances, teaching schedule, and other administrative matters are included in the Dossier Durkheim, compiled by the Ministry of Education. It was transferred to the Archives Nationales and first became available for consultation 50 years after his death, in 1967.

10 We use the term "cluster" to refer to the basic unit of French academic life, as analyzed in our *Revue française de sociologie,* 12 (1971) paper. A cluster was generally composed of a patron, normally a Sorbonne professor, and a dozen or so followers—professors in provincial universities, research institute members, École Pratique des Hautes Études staff, advanced lycée professors.

11 The official papers are included in the A.N. Dossier Durkheim. The appointment was made as smoothly as that to *professeur adjoint* of two years before.

12 Durkheim had earned 4000 francs annually as *chargé de cours* after 1888; 5000 as *professeur adjoint* in 1894; and 6000 as *professeur* in 1896. When he left his chair in Bordeaux, he still received one-half the salary from it. In Paris he earned 9000 francs as *chargé de cours* from 1902 to 1904. Salary information after 1904 is not available in the A.N. Dossier Durkheim.

13 Institut Français d'Anthropologie, *Comptes rendus des séances,* (1911-1913), 129-131.

14 Paul Gerbod, *La condition universitaire en France au XIXe siècle* (Paris: Presses Universitaires de France, 1965), pp. 535-582.

15 École Normale director Fustel de Coulanges wrote that Durkheim was an "excellent student, a vigorous mind, at the same time just and original, and remarkably mature, high aptitude for philosophical studies, especially for psychology . . . his instructors have a high opinion of him."

Later in the lycée St. Quentin he was evaluated by S. M. Lachelier as possessing "a very serious and somewhat cold" personality. A.N. Dossier Durkheim.

16 Cf. Charles Andler, *Vie de Lucien Herr* (Paris: Rieder, 1932), pp. 13-30.

17   When Durkheim was first called to Paris, the normally laconic minutes of the
      Conseil de l'Université de Paris noted that Buisson was being replaced by
      Durkheim, "whose name and studies are universally recognized." Ministère
      de l'Instruction Publique et des Beaux-Arts, *Enquêtes et documents relatifs
      a l'enseignement superieur,* 80 (Paris: Imprimerie Nationale, 1902), 11.

18   Émile Durkheim, *The Division of Labor in Society* (New York: Macmillan,
      1933), pp. 32-35. Cf. also *ibid.*, p. 23, and Durkheim's response to an *enquête*
      on "L'elite intellectuelle et la democratie," *Revue bleue,* 5th series, 1 (June
      4, 1904), 705-706.

19   Paris: Alcan, 1931. Cf. p. 2.

20   Paris: Alcan, 1935.

21   See the priority claims set forth in Philippe Robert, "Le progrès contempo-
      rain, en géographie humaine, en sociologie, en histoire, et l'anteriorité des
      découvertes de la science sociale," *La science sociale,* 2d series, 100-101
      (January and February 1913).

22   M. C. Elmer, "Century-Old Ecological Studies in France," *American Journal
      of Sociology,* 39 (July 1933), 63-70; Jean Stoetzel, "Sociologie et demogra-
      phie," *Population,* 1 (1946), 79-89; Louis Chevalier, "L'école géographique
      française et la demographie, *Population,* 2 (1947), 149-153.

23   Some of the polemical discussion is contained in François Simiand, "Methode
      historique et science sociale," *Revue de synthèse historique,* 2 (1903), 1-157;
      and Simiand, *Statistique et experience, Remarques de méthode* (Paris: Mar-
      cel Rivière, 1922).

24   "Anthropology" in France has been used more frequently than in the United
      States to refer strictly to physical anthropology. Claude Lévi-Strauss, "La
      sociologie française," in Georges Gurvitch and Wilbert E. Moore, *La sociol-
      ogie au XXe siècle,* Vol. II (Paris: Presses Universitaires de France, 1947),
      pp. 513-545. See also his "Ce que l'ethnologie doit à Durkheim," *Annales de
      l'université de Paris,* 30 (January-March 1960), 47-52.

25   Thorough documentation on the controversy was compiled by Daniel Essertier
      in *Psychologie et sociologie* (Paris: Alcan, 1927); *La Psychologie* (Paris:
      Alcan, 1929); and *La sociologie* (Paris: Alcan, 1930).

26   Philippe Robert, "Le progrès contemporain . . . ," Henri Berr, *La synthèse en
      histoire* (Paris: Alcan, 1911), Part II; Jacques Faublée, "Henri Berr et *l'Année
      sociologique,*" *Revue de synthèse,* 3d series, XXXV (July-September 1964),
      68-74; Robert N. Bellah, "Durkheim and History," in Robert A. Nisbet, ed.,
      Émile Durkheim, (Englewood Cliffs, N. J.: Prentice Hall, 1965), pp. 153-
      176.

27   Cf. Émile Durkheim, *Sociology and Philosophy* (New York: Free Press,
      1953), and the introduction by J. G. Peristiany.

28   See Harry Alpert, *Émile Durkheim and His Sociology* (New York: Columbia
      University Press, 1939; Russell and Russell, 1961), pp. 163-173, and Durk-
      heim's works cited there; also Guy Aimard, *Durkheim et la science économi-
      que* (Paris: Presses Universitaires de France, 1962), pp. 3-114.

29   Émile Durkheim, "prefaces to *L'Année socologique,*" republished and trans-
      lated by Kurt H. Wolff in Wolff, ed., *Émile Durkheim, 1858-1917* (Colum-
      bus: Ohio State University Press, 1960), pp. 344-348; "Notre Siècle: La

sociologie en France au XIXe siècle," *Revue bleue,* 4th series, 13 (May 19, 1900), 648.

30 Émile Durkheim, *The Rules of Sociological Method* (New York: Free Press, 1938), p. 13.

31 René Worms, *Philosophie des sciences sociales* (Paris: Giard and Brière, 1903, 1904, 1907), 3 vols.; Gabriel Tarde, "La sociologie," and "Les deux elements de la sociologie," in *Etudes de psychologie sociale* (Paris: Giard and Brière, 1921), chaps. 3-5.

32 René Worms, *La sociologie; sa nature, son contenu, ses attaches* (Paris: Giard Brière, 1921), chaps. 3-5.

33 Cf. Stanley Hoffman, "Paradoxes of the French Political Community," in Stanley Hoffman et al., *In Search of France* (Cambridge, Mass.: Harvard University Press, 1963), pp. 1-117.

34 See the sections by Jean-Marie Mayeur, François Bedarida, and Antoine Prost in *Histoire du peuple français, cent ans d'esprit républicain* (Paris: Nouvelle Librarie de France, 1964); John Edwin Talbott, *Politics and Educational Reform in Interwar France, 1919-1939,* unpublished Ph.D. dissertation, Stanford University, 1966.

35 The standard argument is presented in Albert Thibaudet, *La république des professeurs* (Paris: Bernard Grasset, 1927), especially pp. 21 ff.

36 Cf. Eugen Weber, *Action Française* (Stanford, Calif.: Stanford University Press, 1962).

37 Charles Andler, *Vie de Lucien Herr,* pp. 112-150; Romain Rolland, *Péguy* (Paris: Albin Michel, 1944). On Péguy's criticisms of the Durkheimians, see Charles Péguy, *Œuvres en prose, 1898-1908* (Paris: Gallimard, Bibliothèque de la Pléiade, 1959), pp. 991 ff.

38 Péguy would mobilize shock troops by banging on students' doors at the École Normale with a heavy cane that he used in street fights during the affair. See Rolland, *Péguy,* 1, 306 ff.; Daniel Halévy, *Péguy et les Cahiers de la Quinzaine* (Paris: Bernard Grasset, 1941), pp. 68-80.

39 Herr had been highly critical of *The Division of Labor in Society* when it first appeared, writing in the quasi-official *Revue universitaire* 3 (1893), 447-478, that Durkheim had eliminated the sources of acting and feeling from individuals by investing them in the abstraction of society, concluding that "not only do I not adhere . . . but I do not comprehend and I refuse to recognize as scientific anything that could be constructed on such a foundation, with these materials." Herr's strong support for Durkheim and his associates during and after the Dreyfus affair was presented by critics like Hubert Bourgin as a clear demonstration that Durkheim was called to Paris because of his Dreyfusard activities. Cf. also Pierre Laserre, "La sociologie de Sorbonne ou l'école du 'Totem,'" *Revue de l'Action Française,* 33: 1, 412-414.

40 Although she was either a very distant relative of Captain Dreyfus or entirely unrelated, the fact that Dreyfus was the maiden name of Durkheim's wife was still of symbolic importance. Lucien Lévy-Bruhl was a cousin of Captain Dreyfus.

41 A Bordeaux newspaper account of a June 6, 1900 meeting of the Ligue remarked that M. Stapfer, Honorary Dean of the Bordeaux Faculty of Letters,

was "no less applauded when he spoke of M. Durkheim, professor at the Faculty of Letters of Bordeaux, whose fiery speeches bring supporters to the Ligue from far and wide." Clipping in Durkheim's dossier, University of Bordeaux, cited in Steven Lukes, "Émile Durkheim: Socialism, The Dreyfus Affair and Secular Education," unpublished manuscript.

42   "The speaker [Durkheim] at a meeting of 'La Jeunesse Laique' proposed to treat the problem scientifically. He declared that while he predicted the triumph of science, he realized that one could not eliminate religion with the stroke of a pen. The only possible reconciliation between Science and Religion consisted in discovering within Science itself moral ends." *La Petite Gironde*, May 24, 1901, in Durkheim's dossier, University of Bordeaux, cited in Lukes, *op. cit.*

43   Durkheim also presented a motion, adopted by the Congress, that more courses in "social economy" should be created in the universities. Henri Hauser, *L'enseignement des sciences sociales* (Paris: Chevalier Maresq, 1903), p. 165.

44   The "New University" refers to the merging of the École Normale with the Paris Faculty of Letters and Sciences. Cf. below.

45   See F. Buisson, "Leçon d'ouverture du cours de science de l'education," RIE, 32 (July-December 1896), 481-503; also E. Boutroux, "Henri Marion," *ibid.*, pp. 289-311.

46   See Ferdinand Buisson, *Un moraliste laïque* (Paris: Alcan, 1933). The work contains enthusiastic prefatory statements by Édouard Herriot and Bouglé in which Bouglé remarks that "he always remained the 'militant,' the propagandizer *par excellence*," p. 2.

47   *The Division of Labor in Society* was published with the dedication *"A Mon Cher Maître, M. Émile Boutroux, Hommage respectueux et reconnaissant."*

48   Here is the exact summary of the meeting from the minutes kept by the Secretary of the Faculty: *Conseil de la Faculté: mardi 24 juin 1902.*

The Conseil de la Faculté met on Thursday, June 24, 1902, under the chairmanship of M. A. Croiset, Doyen; present were MM. Gebhart, Lavisse, Bouché-Leclercq, Cartault, Boutroux, Lichtenberger, Decharme, Luchaire, Aulard, Collignon, Dubois, V. Henry, Brochard, J. Martha, Buisson, Vidal de la Blache, Séailles, Lemonnier, Thomas, Brunot, Beljame, *professeurs*— Guiraud, Gazier, Espinas, Lafaye, Denis, Dejole Egger, *professeurs adjoints.* . . .

As a result of the election of Professor Buisson as deputy [to the National Assembly], the faculty had to decide in what manner to fill the vacancy of the chair in the science of education tion. Six candidates presented themselves: MM. Durkheim, Lefèvre, Malapert, Mauxion, Payot, and Pinloche. The dean invited Professor Buisson to be the first to express an opinion. Buisson reviewed the candidates in succession; his conclusion is that M. Durkheim ranks far above the others by the sum total of his publications, by the power and objectivity of his instruction, and by the originality of his method. M. Durkheim is a first-class sociologist, and is not pedagogy a province of sociology. Therefore, even though MM. Payot, Pinloche, Lefèvre, Malapart possess also impressive credentials, M. Buisson does not hesitate to state that in his opinion M. Durkheim is the outstanding candidate. This is also the opinion of MM. Boutroux, Brochard, and Espinas; the latter recalled that as a colleague of M. Durkheim, he saw him in action at Bordeaux University where the young professor exercised a great influence on his audience and on his disciples.

The Council was sufficently informed on the matter and proceeded to a vote with the following results:

Number of voters:

For first choice:	M. Durkheim:	21 votes
	M. Malapert:	8 votes
For second choice:	M. Malapert:	16 votes
	M. Payot:	10 votes
	M. Lefèvre:	2 votes
	M. Pinloche:	1 vote

Source: Archives of the Paris Faculty of Letters.

49 See the discussion of the concept in Hauser, *L'enseignement des sciences sociales*, pp. 155, 170, 198.

50 See Dick May, *L'enseignement social á Paris* (Paris: Arthur Rousseau, 1896), pp. 53 ff.; *RIE*, 31 (1896), 89; Hauser, *loc. cit.*; and scattered announcements in the *RIS*.

51 Ministère de l'Instruction Publique et des Beaux-Arts, *Enquêtes et documents relatifs à l'enseignement supérieur,* 106 (Paris: Imprimerie Nationale, 1913), 11.

52 A summary of his observations was published as *Les sciences sociales en Allemagne* (Paris: Alcan, 1895).

53 See Theta Wolf, forthcoming study on Alfred Binet.

54 Alpert, *Émile Durkheim and His Sociology*, p. 35.

55 Friedrich Paulsen, *The German University* (New York: Macmillan, 1894), pp. 126-173.

56 The visit to Germany by some of Durkheim's collaborators helped to socialize them to collective research, not a negligible task given the traditional individualism of French intellectual life. Bouglé writes apropos of his trip to Germany: "What I was able to see of German intellectual organization made me clearly understand the degree to which a collective effort could be useful to French sociology, an effort in groups (note Bouglé's use of the plural) that Durkheim would guide. I was thus fully prepared to offer him my collaboration, to recruit collaborators for him, in order to swell the ranks of this 'École de Bordeaux' that he had formed" [C. Bouglé, "L'œuvre sociologique d'Émile Durkheim," *Europe*, 22 (1930), 283].

57 Paulsen contrasted the German situation with the French: "Only a few years before, in 1808, Napoleon had reorganized the French universities, consistently following the opposite principle. . . . The professors were teachers and examiners rather than scholars, and all individual initiative was restricted to the smallest minimum. . . . The fact that, two generations afterwards, the French people began to reorganize their universities on German lines would seem to afford a strong proof of the superiority of the idea of liberty as compared with the principle of rules and regulations." Friedrich Paulsen, *German Education, Past and Present* (London: T. Fisher Unwin, 1908), pp. 185-187.

58 His nephew Marcel Mauss experienced such authority most directly. He began with a unique education: not at the École Normale, but the Bordeaux Faculty of Letters, where he prepared the *agrégation* directly under the surveillance of his uncle. But Mauss never quite internalized the Durkheimian moral education. Durkheim frequently had to lock him in his room to keep

him at his books. Even when Mauss was a grown man, Durkheim remained a very external and highly constraining social fact. For example, one hot summer day not before 1909 (Mauss was thus at least 37), he and Georges Davy stopped work for a beer in a café on the Place de la Sorbonne. Durkheim then walked out of the Sorbonne courtyard, to the horror of his nephew, who immediately whispered to Davy, "Quick, hide me! Here comes my uncle!" He escaped behind an orange tree decorating the café, and at least that time evaded the eye of the stern taskmaster. (Personal communication, M. Georges Davy.)

59　"I use . . . [the term 'seminar'] instead of some other because my goal has been to follow as closely as possible the method and procedures of German seminars." It brought together a small number of advanced students, one of whom would present a paper at each meeting, which would be discussed by the other participants. They dealt with such general questions as "Does there exist a sociological science?" "Is there a sociological art, and what are its relations with a sociological science?" "Is there a social conscience?" and "What are the subsections of a sociological science?" Léon Duguit, "Un seminaire de sociologie," *RIS,* 1 (1893), 201-208, at p. 201.

60　Every faculty member submitted an annual report to the ministry indicating the subjects and scheduling of courses and the number of students attending. To these reports, the rector would occasionally add a few comments. Durkheim's reports from Bordeaux between 1888 and 1902 indicated that from 19 to 40 students attended his one-hour course on pedagogy. He also offered a one hour *"conférence d'agrégation,"* generally attended by less than ten students. These first two courses were scheduled in mornings or afternoons during the week. The third course, on some aspect of sociology, was on Saturday at 5:30 P.M. in 1902, and attended by 30 students. There were almost no comments by the rector in earlier years, but in 1901, he noted that "He is moved by an ardent and *militant* proselytism." (A blue pencil, presumably in the ministry, underlined the comment and added a line in the margin next to it.) He wrote in 1902 that "He interprets his role of teacher as a sort of apostolate that must continue to influence his students outside of the university and must follow them in later life. Superior intelligence. . . ." A.N. Dossier Durkheim. The reports after 1902 are not included in the dossier.

　　For (incomplete) listings of Durkheim's courses, see *RIS,* 23 (1915), 468-469, and Alpert, *Émile Durkheim and His Sociology,* pp. 65-66.

61　Personal communication, M. André Davidovitch, *Secrétaire de la rédaction* of the *Année sociologique.* Official support to the *Année* in postwar years was carefully acknowledged.

62　As a leading academic publisher, Alcan could justify a loss on certain ventures. By supporting outstanding journals such as the *Revue philosophique, Année psychologique,* and *Année sociologique,* Alcan both enhanced its prestige and provided announcements of its own publication. Alcan was suppressed by the Nazis, and the list and format were taken over by Presses Universitaires de France, which revived the *Année sociologique* after World War II. The *Année psychologique* changed publishers several times.

63　In addition to the published accounts of the *Année,* this section draws on conversations with Georges Davy and André Davidovitch.

64   This continual reworking of manuscripts led to more jointly written articles than was typical of other journals. Of every other article sampled from four volumes between 1886 and 1914 of each of three other journals—the *Revue internationale de sociologie*, the *Science sociale,* and the *Journal de la Société de Statistique de Paris*—there was not one jointly written paper. In just the 1912 issues of the *Année sociologique*, however, a total of 334 articles included 6 by 2 authors and 1 by 3.

65   Georges Davy recalled one instance when he had written a critique of just one short article. Durkheim returned it with a note to reread the article and rewrite his own contribution, as an argument had been misinterpreted.

66   In later years, Hertz, Fauconnet, Bouglé, Davy, and Halbwachs also took on some of the responsibility for subsections of the *Année.* (Personal communication, Georges Davy.) See also Georges Davy, "Émile Durkheim," *Année sociologique*, 3d series (1957-1958), vii-x, and H. Lévy-Bruhl, "Marcel Mauss," *Année sociologique*, 3d series (1948-1949), 1-4.

67   Perceptions of cohesiveness still varied with the observer's vantage point. Alfred Espinas, for example, saw the group around Durkheim as "a militia organized for the propagation of political theories or an engine of politics, and also as a secret society. . . . having its mysteries to cover its ambitions, and its police, its reports, its admissions, its white and black lists." Quoted in Hubert Bourgin, *De Jaurès à Léon Blum, l'École normale et la politique* (Paris: Arthème Fayard, 1938), p. 91.

Davy, in contrast, asserted that

There were, in effect, certain persons around him who formed a sort of spiritual family, united by the tie of common method and of a common admiration for their master. [Note that Davy does not mention ties among individuals.] They constituted . . . the clan of the *Année sociologique.* Durkheim created and maintained the spirit of unity of this little society, without the least tyranny, leaving to each his entire liberty. He only acted through the enormous supremacy of his mind and of his method. Everyone liked to go see him to receive his advice and experience the affectionate interest he had for all. But there were no court sessions, no meetings, no slogans. How many have been wrong in having thought to see in him the apostle of tyranny and the despiser of the individual. . . .

If Durkheim was thus the chief of a school, it is because he instituted a new doctrine. It is he who in fact was, despite illustrious predecessors such as Montesquieu and Auguste Comte, the true founder of French sociology. [Georges Davy, "Emile Durkheim," *Revue de metaphysique et de morale*, 26(1919), 194-195.]

68   *Ibid.,* p. 195.

69   In one climactic incident, a letter from Herr describing police brutality in 1899 was quoted by Édouard Vaillant in an address to the Chamber of Deputies; it led to collapse of the Dupuy ministry. Waldeck-Rousseau's government which followed ordered the retrial of Dreyfus. See *Vie de Lucien Herr*, pp. 143-147.

70   "Jaurès began to set his thought in order, to organize his social theories systematically. His petty bourgeois republicanism had succumbed to disappointment, and he was ready for socialism. In a crucial interlude in 1889, he struck

up a friendship with the erudite librarian of the École Normale Supérieure, Lucien Herr, who guided him toward a new affirmation. . . . Equipped with a staggering mastery of sources and endowed with a great personal warmth, Herr, who had become socialist by 1889, directed successive generations of *normaliens* to the important treatises on socialist theory. 'Here was the man, whom the public did not know,' Léon Blum once exclaimed, 'yet under whom the socialist *universitaires* were formed, from Jaurès to Déat, including my generation and that of Albert Thomas.'" Harvey Goldberg, *The Life of Jean Jaurès* (Madison: University of Wisconsin Press, 1962), p. 62.

71 Mauss noted in an obituary of Herr in the *Année* that "Until his last days and including this particular volume, he has been for us a constant advisor who we listened to. . . . His personal authority, his enthusiasm, his encouragement decided for many of us our vocation." "Notices biographiques," *Année sociologique*, new series, 2 (1927), 9.

72 Until as late as 1925, there was a combined heading of "Socialisme; Science Sociale" in Otto Lorenz, *Catalogue générale de la librairie française*, the major bibliography of books published in France.

73 Andler, *Vie de Lucien Herr*, pp. 169-182. A particularly compelling but little known case of the influence of socialist ties was that of Maurice Halbwachs during his fellowship term in Germany. After about three months in Berlin, Halbwachs, acting as correspondent for *l'Humanité* while collecting material for his thesis, published an article in *l'Humanité* criticizing the brutality of the Berlin police at a mass demonstration. The Prussian authorities saw the article, and, following a perfunctory interrogation, gave Halbwachs one week to leave Prussia. He was forced to complete his fellowship term in Vienna. The affair aroused attention in France, and was criticized by Jaurès in *l'Humanité*, December 23, 1910, and in *Le Temps*, January 2, 1911. The *Humanité* of February 15, 1911, carried an article by Liebknecht denouncing the affair, although Halbwachs affirmed that he had not been in personal contact with Liebknecht, being closer to the socialism propounded by Bernstein. The entire affair is discussed in a four-page closely written document by Halbwachs, entitled "Une expulsion." It was written just a few months before he was deported in 1944, not, however, because of his family background, but because he, and even more his son, had been deeply involved in underground activities during the war. The two were sent to Buchenwald, and although neither was put to death, the father did not survive the miserable living conditions. (Personal communication from Madame Maurice Halbwachs and André Davidovitch.) I am extremely grateful to Madame Halbwachs—herself a sociological researcher at the Centre d'Études Sociologiques in former years —for her hospitality and patience in going through her husband's papers and files, filling in many unpublished details.

74 Andler, *Vie de Lucien Herr*, p. 163.

75 *Ibid.*, pp. 151-168.

76 The complete listing of stockholders can be found in the Archives Nationales, 40 AQ 1, 2, reproduced in Robert John Smith, *The École Normale Supérieure in the Third Republic*, unpublished Ph.D. dissertation, University of Pennsylvania, 1967.

77   Hubert Bourgin, *Le socialisme universitaire* (Paris: Delamain and Boutelleau, 1942), p. 107.

78   The series Les Cahiers du Socialiste was founded by François Simiand, Robert Hertz, and Hubert Bourgin a few years before World War I (Bourgin, *Cinquante ans d'experience democratique*, p. 85). Halbwachs published an abridged version of his law doctorate on population movements in the series [*La politique foncière des municipalités* (Paris: Les Cahiers du Socialiste, No. 3, 1911)].

79   Bouglé tells us: "In fact, the majority, the near totality of the collaborators of the *Année sociologique*—the most moderate among them can affirm it— were great friends of the celebrated librarian of the École Normale named Lucien Herr, were enrolled in the socialist party, and more than one was also a collaborator of *l'Humanité*" [*Humanisme, sociologie, philosophie: remarques sur la conception française de la culture generale* (Paris: Hermann, 1938), p. 34]. Apparently Bouglé himself never joined a socialist party.

80   See Filloux, "Durkheimism and Socialism," *The Review*, 10 (1963), 66-85.

81   See *Suicide* (New York: Free Press, 1951), pp. 361-392.

82   Émile Durkheim, *Socialism* (New York: Collier, 1962).

83   Personal communication, Georges Davy. Jaurès also attended the tenth anniversary celebration of the *Année* (Goldberg, *The Life of Jean Jaurès*, p. 85).

84   Personal communication, Georges Davy and Armand Cuvillier. On the evolution of *l'Humanité* from socialism to communism, see Annie Kriegel, *Aux origines du communisme français 1914-1920* (Paris: Mouton, 1964).

85   See Filloux, "Durkheimism and Socialism," and Raymond Aron, "Sociologie et socialisme," *Annales de l'Université de Paris*, 30 (January-March 1960), 30-37. Aron's thesis—". . . in a simplified formula that we will seek to rectify, one could say that he conceived sociology as the scientific counterpart of socialism" (p. 33)—is similar to that of Bourgin in *Le socialisme universitaire*, pp. 72-79.

86   "The real grief against the Sorbonne, that which united against her so many different passions, is not in fact, whatever may be said, either literary or pedagogical. It is political. It is religious. She has against her conservatives and clericals of every shade. . . . She is an alarming specter for those who want to subject youth to the old political and religious dogmas. . . ." *Le Temps*, June 16, 1911, quoted in Eugen Weber, *The Nationalist Revival in France* (Berkeley: University of California Press, 1959), p. 81.

87   This scientific preoccupation . . . has swept away our Faculties of Letters. Professors of Literature no longer base their judgments on precisely observed facts. They are doing the work of historians, thus of scholars. . . .
       Philosophy in turn has followed this same evolution. Metaphysics occupies a modest place in our Faculties. . . . Disciplines are also developing here that were formerly confused with general philosophy. Psychology, pedagogy, sociology, have their chairs and their laboratories. The teaching of the Faculty of Letters is becoming penetrated by the same mentality as the Faculty of Science. [Theodore Steeg, "Ancienne et Nouvelle Sorbonne," *Revue bleue*, 48 (1910), 64 ff.

       Steeg cites three major *promoteurs* of this movement: Lavisse, Lanson, and Durkheim.

88 See Priscilla P. Clark, *The Bourgeois in the French Novel 1789-1848* (unpublished Ph.D. dissertation, Department of French, Columbia University, 1966), for a discussion of these and related themes.

89 The Sorbonne had sided with the British during the Hundred Years War, thus opposing Joan of Arc. Péguy, in whose works Joan was a recurrent subject, at one point presented an image of her trial where such "Sorbonnards" as Durkheim and Lanson mingled with their fifteenth-century predecessors, dressed in the same robes, and condemned the undisciplined girl. Halévy, *Péguy et les Cahiers de la Quinzaine*, p. 287.

90 Bergson also submitted his candidacy for Sorbonne positions in 1894 and 1898; he was defeated both times. See the file of unpublished documents on Tarde in the library of the Centre d'Etudes Sociologiques. The competition with Bergson is treated in the "Dossier Bergson," consisting largely of documents from the Collége de France.

    The mutual sympathy of Bergson and Tarde is well known. See, for example, Gabriel Tarde, *The Laws of Imitation* (New York: Holt, Rinehart & Winston, 1903), p. 145, and Bergson's preface to the memorial volume on Tarde, *Introduction et pages choisies par ses fils* (Paris: Louis-Michaud, 1909).

91 "Certainly Sorbonne professors no longer take account of the intimate life of *chefs-d'œuvre*. They wish to reduce history, literature, philosophy to some sort of dead and dry knowledge. . . .

    "One well understands the animosity they feel for M. Bergson. It is a pleasure to note, during lectures, during thesis defenses, unfavorable allusions to 'outside influences,' in general, and to that great thinker in particular." "Les tendences de la nouvelle sorbonne, lettre d'un étudiant," *l'Action*, n.d., signed Jacques Jary, student in philosophy at the Sorbonne. Cf. also Rolland, *Péguy*, 1, 35, and Henri Chevalier, *Henri Bergson* (New York: Macmillan, 1928).

92 Georges Goriely, *Le pluralisme dramatique de Georges Sorel* (Paris: Marcel Rivière, 1962), pp. 172-182. Sorel was a major influence in turning Péguy toward Bergson and away from Lucien Herr and the Durkheimians. Sorel detested the university and its "pretentions of furnishing, through sociology, a new and definitive foundation for the Republic. . . . It is Durkheimian sociology which appeared to constitute the major arm of this *'parti intellectuel,'* which, thanks to Dreyfusism, had conquered certain high university posts. . . ." *Ibid.*, pp. 175-177.

    Bergson, in contrast, fascinated them: "Seated on the higher benches of the room [an amphitheater], we would listen to the fascinating words, subtle, precise, always simple and always creative. All ears, all eyes too, for the teaching of Bergson had to be watched as well as listened to. The philosopher worked alone in front of his audience like an artisan alone at his bench. The whole man applied himself in front of us. Concentrating intensely, he would bend forward, straighten up again, sometimes as if overwhelmed with the difficulties in rising. To a meticulous analysis he would add, as if he had received an inspiration, an image. What marvelous lessons!" Halévy, *Péguy*, p. 111. See also Georges Sorel, "Les théories de M. Durkheim," *Le devenir social*, 1 (1895), 1-26, 148-180.

93   Several articles published elsewhere were reprinted as *L'esprit de la Nouvelle Sorbonne: la crise de la culture classique, la crise du français* (Paris: Mercure de France, 1911). One passage on Durkheim is the following:

Would it be M. Durkheim that M. Liard has charged with elaborating the new doctrine? The powers that he has conferred to him in the organization of the New Sorbonne leave us with some basis to fear that this is the case. He has made of him sort of a *préfet d'études*. He has given him his entire confidence and had him called, first to the *Conseil* of the University of Paris, then to the *Comité Consultatif,* which permits M. Durkheim to survey all appointments within the field of higher education. The case of Durkheim is a victory of the new spirit. Charged with university pomp, he is the regent of the Sorbonne, the all-powerful master, and it is known that professors in the section of philosophy, reduced to the role of humble civil servants, follow his every order, oppressed by his command. One is forced to recall Cousin, who spoke to the professors of philosophy as 'my regiment' and of his doctrine as 'my banner.' But Cousin, although fanatical in his way, had suppleness, capriciousness, and a persuasive eloquence.

    Dogmatic, authoritarian, M. Durkheim . . . has created his own domain, *pedagogy*. This is the grand creation (should we say the great thought?) of the New Sorbonne. . . . The importance attributed to this subject is proven by a simple fact: It is the *only obligatory course* for all students preparing the *agrégation,* and those who miss two or three lectures are not permitted to pass exams. Does he in this way have as his goal the rational formation of a future professor? . . .

    M. Durkheim has firmly established his intellectual despotism. He has made of his teaching an instrument of domination. [*Ibid*., pp. 98-100.]

       Similar diatribes continue for pages. Cf. also Agathon, *Les jeunes gens d'-aujourd'hui*, pp. 77 ff.

94   Cited in M. Goyau, *Comment juger la "sociologie" contemporaine* (Marseille: Editions Publioror, 1934), p. 184.

95   The most complete published bibliography is in Alpert, *Émile Durkheim and His Sociology*, pp. 217-224. Steven Lukes had prepared a more complete listing which is to be published shortly.

96   A volume attacking Durkheim's secular morality was written by a professor at the Catholic university in Louvain, Simon Deploige, *Le conflit de la morale et de la sociologie*, (2d ed.; Louvain and Paris: Alcan, 1912). The second edition contains two letters by Durkheim attacking Deploige's work. See also Ferdinand Brunetière, *La science et la réligion* (Paris: Firmin-Didot, 1895); and Georges Weill, *Histoire de l'idée laïque en France au XIXe siècle* (Paris: Alcan, 1925), especially chaps. 7-14.

97   See D. Parodi, *La philosophie contemporaine en France* (Paris: Alcan, 1920), pp. 113-160; and Durkheim, *Sociology and Philosophy*.

98   Émile Durkheim, "Crime et santé sociale," *Revue philosophique*, 39 (1895), 518-523, is an incensed reply to an article by Tarde of the same title.

99   See Émile Durkheim, "Suicide et natalité," *Revue philosophique*, 26 (1888), 446-463, and Durkheim "Le divorce par consentement mutuel," *Revue bleue*, 5th series, 10 (1906), 549-554. These were attacks on such statisticians as Bertillon.

100   A 1907 questionnaire survey of philosophy professors in secondary schools led Alfred Binet to conclude that "The majority of our correspondents assure us, in different ways, that 'sociology inspires in their students a passionate

interest.' This is one of the facts most clearly revealed in our questionnaire. Disenchantment with metaphysics, interest for abnormal psychology, and especially for sociology, are characteristics of the present generation." "L'évolution de l'enseignement philosophique," *Année psychologique*, 14 (1908), 210.

101   One Gilbert Maire (pseudonym?) suggested that Bouglé's biography might be entitled *La carrière d'un arriviste*, or *De Montpellier à Paris par Dreyfus*, which would include a central chapter on *De l'usage du faux en philosophie*, or *Les moyens de parvenir*. Indeed, he suggested, opportunism was too mild a characterization for Bouglé: "He is supposed to be a professor; yet he is more of an electoral agent. . . . I believe that he will serve each regime with the same zeal, but we will be on our guard, since with the coming of Philippe VIII, he will no doubt propose to us a monarchist Rousseau." "Un politicien en Sorbonne: M. Bouglé," *Revue critique des idées et des livres*, 19 (1912), 161-180.

the institutionalization of american sociology

•

anthony oberschall

guiding ideas

In contrast to the difficulties of establishing sociology as an autonomous academic discipline in Europe, its institutionalization in the United States can only be described as a smashing success. This fact is all the more noteworthy because the founding fathers of U. S. sociology did not develop any original ideas and intellectual systems that have withstood the test of time. Much of their theoretic work as well as their methodology were taken over from European thinkers and modified to suit an American audience. Nor were the processes of rapid industrialization and urbanization, the growth of slums, the labor question, and other associated social problems unique to this side of the Atlantic, with the single exception of massive immigration into the United States. The crucial difference for sociology was rather the rapid expansion of higher education in the United States with unprecedented resources at its command, and its growth as an extremely competitive system, favorable to innovation. Moreover the novel and amorphous discipline of sociology received the backing at this opportune time of groups in favor of social reconstruction: the Protestant clergy (especially its social gospel wing); the municipal reformers; the various groups and organizations active in the areas of philanthropy, charities and correction, social settlement, and social

Anthony Oberschall is Associate Professor of Sociology at Yale University. Born in Budapest in 1936, he received his B.A. from Harvard University in 1958 and his Ph.D. in Sociology from Columbia University in 1962. Oberschall is the author of *Empirical Social Research in Germany, 1848-1914* and a book on social conflict to be published in 1972 by Prentice-Hall. He has also been studying social change in East and Central Africa.

work; and the backers of other Progressive causes, all of whom were
seeking an academic foothold and scientific justification. It is true that
in Europe as well, many sociologists were intellectually affiliated and
identified with a political orientation of the left sympathetic to the
problems of working people, and with liberal reform and change more
generally. The crucial difference was that the reform movement in the
United States during the Progressive era was pursued by respectable, old
American, Protestant, middle- and upper-middle-class groups having
influence with the universities' boards of trustees and the heads of
foundations, whereas the European sociologists were seen as potentially
subversive and did not have the backing of the organized labor movements either. Thus in Europe, with the exception of France where Durkheim and his group received the French government's support for
political and ideological reasons, no powerful groups sought the academic
establishment of sociology. Even so the new discipline of sociology had
no easy sailing in the United States. It was met by widespread hostility
in the university faculties, and it is only because of the massive
scale on which it was introduced that it eventually managed to
break through into the kind of discipline that we now recognize as
sociology.

   The theoretic ideas that inform this essay are
simple and few in number, and have been developed in the sociology of
science, though not yet applied to the case of sociology itself, so far as
I know. The institutionalization of sociology as an ongoing academic
enterprise, with permanent positions, a sense of professional identity,
intellectual distinctness and continuity, cannot be explained with reference primarily to the history of ideas, their origin, diffusion, modifi-
cation, inherent worth or excellence. To be sure, there existed toward
the end of the nineteenth century widespread intellectual dissatisfaction
with the approaches of the several existing disciplines—economics,
psychology, law, the philosophy of history—in the sense that their concepts, methods, and concerns did not adequately deal with an entire
order of social phenomena. But this intellectual malaise and the widespread concern with the social problems of an urban-industrial society
were also present in Europe and by themselves did not provide the
opportunity for the establishment of sociology in universities, although
it allowed for sociology to be pursued as a semirespectable intellectual
enterprise. Following Ben-David[1] it is hypothesized that the wide
resource base and competitive nature of the rapidly expanding higher
education system in the United States, together with the sponsorship
and active backing of the new discipline by influential and organized
groups who perceived sociology in their interest, were the crucial factors

enabling the institutionalization of sociology in the United States. Moreover, the opportunity provided by sociology was exploited not just by intellectually dissatisfied and socially concerned scholars, but by a group of upwardly mobile men who otherwise could not have moved into university positions through the already established disciplines. Such an opening was therefore seized, and a group of professors with a vested interest in the continuity and the differentiation of the new discipline was formed. The multiple starts of sociology at several universities and the sheer quantity of sociologists then made for a high probability that at least some would be successful in this process of intellectual differentiation and innovation, thus benefiting the others as well.

While these processes do explain the academic entrenchment of sociology in the United States, they do not shed much light on the content of the early U.S. sociology. Following Wirth,[2] Merton,[3] and Shils[4] and others on this matter, it will be demonstrated that the pressing question of academic legitimacy in the face of skepticism and hostility, the previous intellectual background of sociologists in political economy, philosophy, and charities and corrections, and finally the supportive audience of social reformers and social workers, shaped the sociologists' choice of subject, techniques of inquiry, presentation of results, in short the substance of their sociology and their concerns. The dual constituency that sociologists had to satisfy led to an obsessive concern with academic legitimation as a science and to the demonstration of practical usefulness in social problem solving, that is on the one hand to abstract system building, the stress on "science" and occasional "sociological imperialism," and on the other, to popularized, atheoretical investigations without any methodological sophistication.

Many other points of a more specific nature also need clarification, and can for the most part be filled into the existing theoretic framework, though the length of this essay allows but for sketchy treatment. A striking feature of U.S. sociology was that it was institutionalized before it had a distinctive intellectual content, a distinctive method, or even a point of view, to echo the words of Small.[5] What then was and is the significance of the fact that early sociology was more a "movement" than an intellectual discipline? Why was it at Chicago, and not some other university, that sociology was transformed into the discipline we recognize today? And why, despite the vast changes in content and method, not to speak of the size and prosperity of the sociological enterprise, are some of the early feelings of insecurity and excessive self-awareness of the early sociologists still with us?

the age of reform[6]

Rapid urbanization and industrialization to-
gether with immigration, and their associated urban and labor problems,
marked the period from the end of the Civil War to World War I and
served as the context in which sociology was established in the United
States. The growth of trusts and monopolies, corruption on an unprecedented scale, widespread labor and agrarian unrest culminating in long
and violent strikes and labor-management wars and the Populist movement were all characteristics of the latter nineteenth century. Laissez-
faire individualism was the economic orthodoxy of the day. Its social
policy implications were reinforced by the spread of Social Darwinism.
The two together constituted a powerful ideology favorable to big business at the expense of labor, the consumer and the small businessman.
Somewhat independently of these trends, higher education was completely revolutionized after the first genuine graduate schools were
established, new colleges founded, existing colleges upgraded, the curricula secularized and modernized, and university instructors with higher
degrees, many of them from German universities, displaced the teaching
clergy.

These broad trends reshaped the stratification
and prestige structure of the United States. The clergy, previously near
the top of the status ladder and the moral leaders of the community,
were successfully challenged in their intellectual and moral leadership
and were separated from and unable to communicate meaningfully with
the new immigrant working-class city population. The solid, native,
Protestant middle class of professionals and businessmen fell in economic
position and political influence to the gain of the new business tycoons
and industrial magnates, and somewhat later their grip on local politics
was wrested from them by the machine politics of the immigrants. The
young, foreign-trained university graduates had to wage an uphill battle
against their entrenched and intellectually inferior elders while at the
same time fighting the battle for academic freedom against the university trustees. It is the reaction of these adversely affected social strata
that gave rise to the powerful reform movement which found its most
organized and political expression in the Progressive party. These groups
saw America as they once knew it being transformed beyond recognition, and their position in it insecure. They organized to stop and re-
verse these trends unfavorable to them and to reestablish their grip upon
society. They sought actively to bring about social betterment and reconstruction. In these reform endeavors, a portion of the Protestant
clergy, the middle-class reformers (many of them college graduates and
products of the new education), and the academics were strongly influenced by both British and German precedents, not to speak of their own

consciences and Christian social teachings. It was these groups loosely allied with the reform movement that were directly instrumental in the institutionalization of the new discipline of sociology.

The reform impulse needed, however, intellectual legitimacy and respectability because it was in contradiction to the dominant ideology of the time and in fact constituted the most powerful challenge to it. Samuelson describes the economics of the period as optimistic, theological in character, protectionist, nationalist, and pro-business: ". . . the typical textbook writer seems to have been an ordained clergyman teaching as an amateur economist in a college," who took progress for granted and as in the nature of things, and who assumed that the "harmonies of the economic system were the harmonies of . . . ruthless competition."[7] Max Lerner calls this period "the triumph of laissez-faire" diffused through economics departments, during which "the main theses of economic theory had been so long reiterated and accepted that they had the character of a tradition."[8] According to the orthodox view, private charity and government intervention to correct social evils would in fact lead to collective harm for the entire society, not to its improvement or cure. Reform in all its aspects stood condemned as a socially harmful activity inspired by sentimentalism and irrationality.

Reformers found even less solace in the Social Darwinist current that at this time captured American intellectual life and popular thought. In its ethical teachings and social policy implications, Social Darwinism reinforced orthodox economic thought. Spencer and his ideas were more popular in the United States than they ever became in Britain and on the continent.[9] Even its opponents were influenced by it, including of course many of the founding fathers of sociology. In Hofstadter's words, "Darwinism was used to buttress the conservative outlook in two ways. The most popular catchwords of Darwin, 'struggle for existence' and 'survival of the fittest,' when applied to the life of man in society, suggested that nature would provide that the best competitors in a competitive situation would win, and that this process would lead to continuing improvement."[10] Progress was a natural law of the competitive struggle, whose slow development should not be interfered with by government action or reform to protect the weak, the incompetent, the inefficient, and the poor.[11] Spencer, the major spokesman of Social Darwinism in the United States, "ridiculed schemes for quick social transformation . . . and punctured the illusions of legislative reformers."[12] His views were put forward in a succession of books with large American printings, preceded by the serialization of some of his works by his publisher in the *Popular Science Monthly* (where Giddings first read Spencer) in 1872-1873, and in other periodicals.

Upon his visit to America in 1882, Spencer got an enthusiastic reception that culminated in a magnificent banquet in New York's fashionable Delmonico Hotel attended by the cream of New York society. In speeches and pronouncements, Carnegie, Rockefeller, Hill, and other business giants echoed his philosophy.[13] No wonder that the reformers during this time were on the intellectual defensive. By a curious and illogical twist, however, sociology, the new science championed by Spencer, became the intellectual ally of the reformers.

the revolution in higher education

A decade and a half after the end of the Civil War, the United States underwent a revolution in higher education on an unprecedented scale. Before that time the typical institution was a small, sectarian college of a few buildings and six to eight faculty members, usually clergymen teaching multiple subjects.[14] To be sure, as Flexner wrote, "In the Eastern States, fairly well-organized state systems of education existed. Colleges—Harvard, Yale, Columbia, Williams, and others—meagerly endowed and meant mainly to give a modest 'higher education' to prospective preachers, teachers, lawyers, and doctors, had been in operation for centuries, more or less,"[15] but "a university in the sense in which I use the term, an institution consciously devoted to the pursuit of knowledge, the solution of problems, the critical appreciation of achievement and the training of men at a really high level—we did not possess until the Johns Hopkins University modestly opened its portals in 1876."[16] Students went to Germany for a graduate education and the valuable Ph.D. degree, many of them in the social sciences.[17] And no wonder. In his autobiography, Richard Ely recalls that in 1872 the Dartmouth Library was unheated and open only for one hour twice a week. The Columbia Library was but little better. When Ely sailed for Germany with a Columbia fellowship in 1876, the corresponding chapter title reads "I sail to Germany in quest of the truth."[18] Many economists and future sociologists, including Small, Ross, Park, and Thomas, did and felt likewise.

The transformation in higher education was most immediately brought about through the willingness of businessmen to endow several universities just at a time when the state universities were also being founded and expanded. As Flexner later wrote, "Sums (of money) of which no one could then have dreamed of have been assembled, buildings, apparatus, books have been provided."[19] The new universities were headed by formidable president-entrepreneurs. The highly competitive system among the various universities provided for rapid horizontal and vertical mobility, salary increases for professors, and opportunities for introducing new subject matter and to innovate in a general fashion.

The first competitive spurt was initiated with the founding of the first graduate school at Johns Hopkins in 1876 under Gilman's presidency and with $3.5 million in endowments. Gilman attracted top men at high salaries of up to $5000 a year for full professors, double the salary of the average Yale and Harvard professor.[20] Gilman's successful formula in the social sciences was to make use of the German seminar method, a lighter teaching load to allow time for research, publication of doctoral dissertations in the *Johns Hopkins Studies in Historical and Political Sciences*, and the creation of other scholarly journals to report faculty research, steps later repeated by other universities, notably Columbia under Burgess and Chicago under Harper.[21] Gilman succeeded in attracting top students and young instructors, many of them already with a German degree, notably Woodrow Wilson, Richard Ely, Albion Small, and E. A. Ross.

While Johns Hopkins was strongest in the new history and political science and subsequently experienced a decline, it provided the impetus for innovation elsewhere. As President Eliot of Harvard later testified:

President Gilman, your first achievement has been . . . the creation of a school of graduate studies . . . which has lifted every other university in the country in its departments of arts and sciences. I want to testify that the graduate school of Harvard University, started feebly in 1870 and 1871 did not thrive until the example of Johns Hopkins forced our faculty to put their strength into the development of instruction for graduates.[22]

More decisive yet was the response of Columbia University in letting John W. Burgess go ahead with his plans for a School of Political Science in 1880. When Johns Hopkins opened in 1876, Columbia College was a day school with no afternoon classes, no dormitories, and a library open only two to three hours a week. Burgess succeeded in building it up to a national university and the leading graduate school of the day. Burgess' method was to send his most promising pupils from Amherst and Columbia abroad for further instruction, each in a different specialty, and upon their return to appoint them to a Columbia post. He also had the library enlarged, permitted course choices for students, founded an academy of political science with the Ph.D. degree needed for entry, introduced fellowships and scholarships to attract top students, created a publications series for dissertations and the highly successful *Political Science Quarterly* for faculty research. In 1899-1900 Columbia graduate enrollments topped those of other universities. Columbia and Johns Hopkins graduates spread out to found or staff social science departments at universities and colleges all over the United States.[23]

The Columbia challenge was immediately met by the University of Michigan where a School of Political Science was started in 1881 because of President Angell's interest in the political sciences "and the conspicuous example of Columbia."[24] This was shortly followed at the University of Pennsylvania by the Wharton School of Finance under Edmund James, who repeated the earlier Johns Hopkins and Columbia patterns of founding an academy. Its journal established itself as the highly successful *Annals of the American Academy of Social and Political Science.*[25]

Just when the competition generated by the Hopkins and Columbia undertakings, as well as the founding of Vanderbilt in 1875, Tulane in 1884 and other institutions, was beginning to dampen, the second and even more extensive round of competition and innovation was started with the founding of the University of Chicago, as well as the more modest undertakings at Stanford in 1891 with a $20 million endowment, and of Clark University.[26] If there ever was an academic innovator and entrepreneur, it surely must have been William R. Harper, first president of the University of Chicago and former professor of Greek and Hebrew at Yale. When fellow Baptist John D. Rockefeller offered him $1 million to start a college, Harper replied he needed $15 million to create a truly great university.[27] He eventually got $30 million, and delivered on his promise in a remarkably short time. The immense resources of the new university and Harper's aggressive tactics immediately threw other universities on the defensive. As Small recalled it, "The mystical belief spread at once that this upstart institution had the intention and the resources . . . to do for the older institutions what the Standard Oil Company had done for many of its rivals."[28] Harper offered $7000 to department heads, an unprecedented sum at the time. Otherwise his salary scale was twice that prevailing elsewhere. He recruited to the faculty eight former college presidents, including Small, had double the proportion of faculty members with a Ph.D. degree of Harvard, reduced the teaching load to 8 to 10 hours per week, and publicly proclaimed that promotion would depend more on research than teaching.[29] As to his faculty-raiding techniques, they are best illustrated in the words of one of his victims, G. Stanley Hall of Clark University:

Very soon after this, President Harper of the University of Chicago appeared on the scene. He had made many proposals to eminent men to join his staff but they had been turned down because of a critical attitude towards a "Standard Oil" institution. . . . Dr. Harper, learning of the dissatisfaction here, had at Professor Whitman's house met and engaged one morning the majority of our staff. . . . Those to whom we paid $4000 he gave $7000; to those we paid $2000 he offered $4000, etc., taking even instructors, docents, and fellows.[30]

The competition created a heavy demand for young social scientists with a Ph.D., whether a German degree or one acquired in the new graduate schools. Those who saw their progress blocked at the prestige universities would be received with open arms in the newer state universities or out West. Alvin Johnson, later the editor of the *Encyclopedia of the Social Sciences*, felt cramped at Columbia because his seniors were still in their prime. As a result, he resigned in 1906 and went to teach in rapid succession at Nebraska, Texas, Chicago, and Stanford where President Jordan offered him the chairmanship in economics. Yet in 1912 Johnson preferred to come back East to Cornell, whence after three years he resigned to join the staff of the *New Republic*.[31] Edward A. Ross, after two years in Germany and a further stay at Johns Hopkins, had offers from Cornell, Northwestern, Indiana, and Stanford, and later recalled that "salaries (in the 1890s) were equivalent to salaries 70 percent to 90 percent higher today (in 1936)."[32]

Besides rapid advancement, another consequence of demand exceeding supply was the relative ease with which professors could stand up to the trustees and university presidents in academic freedom cases. Indeed the very diversity of the American system was such that at any given time there were bound to be several liberal universities of high caliber that were glad to recruit and protect professors with antiestablishment views. At Stanford, Ross stood up to the Southern Pacific Railroad, Mrs. Stanford, and the trustees by publicly opposing Oriental immigration—cheap labor for the railroad designed to keep wages low and make unionization difficult for native labor—by endorsing municipal ownership of public utilities, and by being prosilver and pro-Democrat. When he was eventually fired, many of his colleagues resigned in sympathy. Ross found no difficulty getting a position at the University of Nebraska, whence in 1906 he was called to the University of Wisconsin in the model Progressive state.[33] At Wisconsin, Richard T. Ely, a notorious academic radical, recruited other social scientists with unorthodox views like John R. Commons and Ross into economics because he did not want "armchair economics" at Wisconsin.[34] The University of Wisconsin during several Progressive administrations worked hand in hand with the LaFollette forces for reform. Even in this favorable atmosphere Ely's departmental building efforts were not easy because Wisconsin and other leading universities were already part of a nationwide competitive market for scarce intellectual resources: ". . . the necessity to stay competitive with Harvard, Yale, Michigan, meant that standardization (of salaries) had to be abandoned.

When Frederick Jackson Turner was called to Stanford, his salary was promptly matched at Wisconsin."[35]

Social science, not just sociology, profited from the competitive and expanding system of higher education. Political science was able to differentiate relatively painlessly from history, political economy, and general social science, a process successfully completed by 1900. Burgess and H. B. Adams, from Columbia and Johns Hopkins, substituted for the earlier deductive approach that derived "laws" from a priori principles the historical and comparative approach of the German *Staatswissenschaften*. There were the usual debates on what was the most appropriate subject matter of political science, what were its boundaries with sister disciplines, and the like, so typical of the process of differentiation, yet they occurred with less frequency and during a shorter period than subsequently in sociology. Political science included the ancient and respectable core subjects of political theory, constitutional law and public law, and was traditionally an upper-class subject matter, so that the problem of legitimacy never arose in an acute form.[36]

Economics had been relatively more differentiated from general social science and moral philosophy already before the revolution in higher education. In the 1880s there occurred a confrontation between the older, established, British-trained or -oriented deductive economists who were advocates of laissez faire, and the younger, ethically committed, German-trained "institutional" economists using the historical and inductive method, who were critical of the status quo and had frequently sympathies for labor, the farmer, and the consumer. The reception of the younger economists with a German Ph.D. was often hostile, especially when they associated themselves openly with socialist and prolabor positions and organizations. The American Economic Association (AEA) was created for the organized defense of the younger economists under attack. Richard T. Ely, one of its founders, later wrote, "in 1885, Adams, Clark, Patten, James, Seligman, and I, fresh from our studies in Germany were regarded as a group of young rebels . . . we felt the urgent necessity for uniting into a solid group in an effort to break the 'crust' which had formed over economics. . . ."[37] And Small was equally explicit in recognizing behind the AEA movement the conflict of generations resulting from blocked mobility quite apart from the intellectual and value differences between the two groups:

The men who promoted the movement for organization of progressive economists had the very definite belief that they must fight for their scientific and academic existence. . . . They felt that these men (the older, established economists) were virtually if not avowedly a trust to control the opportunities for economic recognition in this country, and that the alternatives were to be either stifled by the current orthodoxy or to combine for the preservation of independence.[38]

At the 1885 meeting of the American Historical Association, to which nearly all economists belonged, the American Economic Association was founded. For a while the older Yale-Harvard group boycotted the new association, but not for long. Shortly its constitution was toned down and by 1890 the leading academic members of the old school had joined.[39] The reconciliation was accomplished speedily and painlessly because of the rapid increase in economics departments, positions, and enrollments resulting in an abundance of opportunities for the young rebels. The AEA acted as a clearinghouse for research projects, information, and publications. Standards of inquiry were raised. Economics became fully institutionalized and professionalized. Samuelson observes that "By the turn of the century, economists were ceasing to be amateurs and were making their livelihood as college professors. This professionalization may have had as one of its by-products a toning down of radical feelings, for the university environment and the full-time study of economics may make for a reduction of utopian ardor."[40]

For the emergence of sociology, the decisive significance of the professionalization and institutionalization of economics by 1900 was that it had narrowed its subject matter to the exclusion of the philosophy of history, abstract methodological discussions about the nature of the social sciences, and evolutionary speculation. Economists also did not wish to become directly involved and bogged down in the rising demand for courses on philanthropy, charities, and corrections, and on the 3 Ds: the defective, dependent, and delinquent classes. At the same time economics was firmly enough entrenched in the universities and enjoyed sufficient prestige to allow a breakaway group of economists who were sociologically oriented a certain amount of departmental and intellectual autonomy. At Columbia, for instance, "As early as 1891 Burgess and Mayo-Smith suggested the need for a chair of sociology because many special questions of penology, charity, and poor relief could not be treated from the standpoint of pure political economy and many problems of social ethics could not be studied from the point of view of individual ethics."[41] Giddings, who had been a journalist and had no higher degree, but who was active in the AEA and already teaching sociology at Bryn Mawr, was recruited for the position, and in 1894 his lectureship was changed to a professorship of sociology. The Columbia case is by no means atypical of the process of differentiation of sociology from other disciplines.

the protestant ministry and sociology

The fact that the emergence of sociology was intimately linked with Christian social reform and the social gospel movement has been noted by Hofstadter.[42] Of the early presidents of the American Sociological Society (ASS), Giddings', Thomas', and Vincent's fathers had been ministers while Sumner, Small, Vincent, Hayes, Weatherly, Lichtenberger, Gillin, and Gillette had presociological careers in the Protestant ministry.[43] Twenty-one ministers were among the founding members of the AEA in 1885,[44] and five influential clergymen-educator-reformers were members of the American Sociological Society (ASS) when it was founded in 1905: Francis G. Peabody, dean of the Harvard Divinity School; Graham Taylor, professor, author, and president of the Chicago School of Civics and Philanthropy; Josiah Strong, author of the best-selling *Our Country* (called the *Uncle Tom's Cabin* of the urban reform movement)[45] and general secretary of the Evangelical Alliance for the U.S.A., one of the principle associations for social Christian discussion; Samuel Dike, occasional contributor to the *American Journal of Sociology* and secretary of the Divorce Reform League; and S. Z. Batten, leader of the Baptist Christian Social Movement.[46] The linkage of careers and personnel between the Protestant ministry and early U.S. sociology is thus well documented. It remains to describe the institutional structures and the intellectual and reform activities that brought the two groups together, the reasons behind their alliance, and its consequences for the establishment of sociology.

Henry May, the historian of the Protestant churches in the post-Civil War period, writes that "organized Protestantism supported the dominant economic beliefs and institutions even more than it accepted the existing form of government. . . . in 1876 Protestantism presented a massive, almost unbroken front in defense of the social status quo. Two decades later social criticism had penetrated deeply into each major church."[47] The transformation in Protestantism was broad in scope and deep in substance. Writing about the progressive movement, Hofstadter states that "no other major movement in American political history had ever received so much clerical sanction."[48] The increased violence of labor conflict, the rapid growth of cities, and their associated social problems acted as a jolt to the clergy's conscience even while the new masses of urban wage workers stayed away from the church and some means had to be found to bring them into the fold. The clergy were the major losers in the status revolution.[49] Secularization of thought and of higher education meant for them a loss of intellectual and moral leadership. The boards of trustees and college presidencies, at one time the prerogative of ministers, were taken over by businessmen, bankers, and lawyers. The income of the clergy did not keep up with the rising cost of living. Thus, the social gospel movement and Christian social reform can be understood as an "attempt to restore through secular leadership some of the spiritual influence and authority and social prestige that clergymen had lost."[50]

The Christian reform movement proceeded on a wide front and with numerous links to progressive and socially concerned social scientists. There was a popular literature on urban problems and projected reforms written by clergymen that complemented the work of muckraking journalists and novelists; there was a movement for introducing college settlement work into the training of ministers; clergymen participated in the recently formed civic improvement associations; denominational and interdenominational organizations were created to advance the cause of Christian reform, such as the Christian Social Union, the Evangelical Alliance for the U.S.A., and the Church Association for the Advancement of the Interests of Labor, including more radical groups such as W. D. P. Bliss's Society of Christian Socialists. Each of these had its own periodicals, and several had social scientists on their editorial staffs. There were also more scholarly and intellectual formulations of the new Protestantism, such as John R. Commons' *Social Reform and the Church* (1894), Washington Gladden's *Applied Christianity* (1886), Richard T. Ely's *Social Aspects of Christianity* (1889), and T. H. W. Stuckenberg's *Christian Sociology* (1880).[51]

One of the basic texts resulting from the joint collaboration of ministers and social scientists was the comprehensive *Encyclopedia of Social Reform*, edited by W. D. P. Bliss.[52] This work of over 1000 pages enlisted the participation of noted clergymen like the Reverend E. E. Hale; reformers like Robert Woods of the Andover House Settlement in Boston, Charles Kellogg, general secretary of the Charity Organization Society of New York, and Frances Willard, President of the Women's Christian Temperance Union; radical social scientists like Frank Parsons of Boston University, John R. Commons and E. W. Bemis of the University of Chicago; as well as respectable academic figures of the stature of President Andrews of Brown, Arthur Hadley, professor of political economy and later president of Yale, William Dunning and Giddings of Columbia, and Carroll Wright, U.S. Commissioner of Labor. The topics covered included anarchism, charities, civil service reform, currency reform, land and legislation reform, penology, socialism, social purity, trade unions, and women's suffrage, as well as entries for political economy, political science, sociology, and statistics. The general tenor of many articles was to assemble facts and figures in the cause of reform by pointing up the quantitative magnitude of social problems. Other entries were written in the manner of popular exposés. A list of

4047 American millionaires is classified by occupational and industrial group and the manner of acquiring their wealth. About one fortune it is specifically written that it was "made in the Tweed Ring in New York City." More generally, 1125 fortunes are alleged to have been made in "protected" industries. A bar chart in the appendix contrasts the distribution of wealth in the United States with the population distribution. The origins of social problems are assigned primarily to socioeconomic causes and are treated as subject to correction by organized intervention rather than as resulting from biological and mental defects or from personal shortcomings. For instance, in the analysis of the causes of poverty (page 1073) 74 percent of the cases are put down to "misfortune" and only 21 percent to "misconduct." The volume of quantitative data, mostly from census publications and the reports of municipal and private agencies, is impressive. Numerous unfavorable comparisons are made between the United States and European countries. The techniques of analysis are almost entirely based on simple descriptive statistics in tabular form. The data are marshaled to present an unfavorable view of the state of U.S. society and their presentation is followed by persuasive arguments and specific programs for change and reform.

Aside from intellectual collaboration, there were institutional networks linking reform-minded clergy and social scientists together and specifically sociology and the sociologists as they were coming into being. These were the Chautauqua movement, Christian sociology, and the introduction of sociology courses in the seminaries. The Chautauqua Assembly began as a summer school for training Bible teachers. Later on, instruction was offered in all branches of knowledge, and in 1878 with the formation of the Chautauqua Literary and Scientific Circle, a much wider public was reached (200,000 members by 1895). It offered a program of continued education in the local community in the manner of a book or study club, with a four-year course ending in a certificate.[53] Chautauqua was a meeting place for social reformers of all stripes and varieties. It brought together clergy and college presidents, notables and "radical" social scientists. Through its opportunities for lecture courses and the writing of texts needed in the local study circles, men like Ely to whom the doors of the universities were temporarily closed found a platform and an employment base and were able to cultivate a broad spectrum of social contacts with prominent academics such as President Eliot of Harvard and Harper, future University of Chicago president, Herbert Adams of Johns Hopkins, and George Vincent, later Chicago sociologist, president of the ASS and president of the University of Minnesota.[54]

It was at Chautauqua in 1893 that the American Institute of Christian Sociology (successor to the Society of Christian

Sociologists founded in 1889) was formed. Its first backers and officers included distinguished clergymen like Bishop Vincent (father of George), Christian reformers and writers like the Reverends Washington Gladden and Josiah Strong, and social scientists like Ely, Commons, and Ulysses Weatherly (later president of the ASS). The object of the institute was "the application of the moral traditions and principles of Christianity to the social and economic difficulties of the present time."[55] Among its activities were listed "the publication of papers which relate to Christian sociology, the recommendation of courses of reading, the preaching of sermons, and delivery of addresses on sociological topics . . . the encouragement of local institutes for study and practical work, and the encouragement of the study of social science by founding libraries, scholarships, fellowships, and professorships. . . ."

The Chautauqua movement proved to be a powerful lobby for reform and for sociology. Partly through its influence, sociology as a course of study was introduced in the theological seminaries, and chairs of sociology and/or applied Christianity were instituted.[56] The reasons behind this innovation was explicitly stated by Charles F. Peabody, dean of the Harvard Divinity School: "The modern minister has a new demand made upon him. He is expected to be the advisor of his community in its charities, its temperance work, and in its varied social problems." Peabody himself introduced a course in social ethics at Harvard that dealt with charities and reform: "The theme is one which no minister can afford to neglect. . . . It is very fitting that a divinity school should give special preparation for this branch of a minister's work."[57] According to a report by Graham Taylor, the introduction of sociology in the sense of social ethics, charities, and corrections proceeded step by step:

The most diligent inquiry discovers scarcely any trace of attention to sociological topics in theological institutions prior to 1880. After that date, the work of regular instructors is found supplemented by volunteer representatives of reformatory and philanthropic movements. Then follow lecture courses by appointed lecturers . . . elective courses were offered at Andover (Theological Seminary) in 1887 on social economics and at Yale in 1892 on Christian Social Ethics. The introduction of sociology into the prescribed course was announced first by Hartford Theological Seminary in 1888. The establishment of the sociological department was initiated by the Chicago Theological Seminary in 1890.[58]

Sociological subjects and lectures were offered also in numerous summer schools and other institutes outside of regular universities which again brought together clergy, reformers, and social scientists on a common platform. The American Society for the Extension of University Teaching in the summer of 1893 in Philadelphia offered lectures on sociology and economics including "sociological statistics" by the Reverend Dike, "methods of sociological study" by the dean of the social settlement movement Robert Woods, "the city as a sociological workshop" by Dr. William H. Tolman of the New York City Vigilance League, and other lectures by E. A. Ross and William Lloyd Garrison.[59] The Society for Education Extension at Hartford, presided over by the Hartford Theological School's Chester Hartranft, opened in that city a School of Sociology that admitted only applicants with a bachelor's degree and offered a three-year professional course to train future managers of charitable and educational trusts for the work of practical and social reform. Its faculty claimed several ministers like the Reverend Dike and professors from leading eastern universities. The program announcement stated that "special attention will be paid to the investigation of social phenomena by the students themselves, and to the acquisition of practical experience through the various agencies now at work in several parts of the sociological field."[60] The American Institue of Christian Sociology operated a summer school of Christian Sociology at Oberlin that brought together as lecturers Samuel Gompers, Jane Addams, several clergymen-educators, and the Columbia economist J. B. Clark.[61]

No doubt stimulated by the spirit of the times and these educational efforts, the call went forth for "sociological investigation" by the parish clergy aided by its "splendid machinery and coteries of sympathetic workers." By sociological investigation was meant a simple fact-finding expedition on a local parish problem exemplified by the pamphlets of the Church Temperance Society of New York on the liquor problem.[62] Interest in religion and the church is also reflected in academic departments of sociology, as Faris has noted from the titles of early Chicago masters theses and doctoral dissertations.[63] Moreover, after World War I, the Institute of Social and Religious Research, with Rockefeller support, conducted from 1921 to 1934 a program of applied research on the Protestant church. The staff included Charles Luther Fry, who later wrote a manual on research methods, and Edmund de S. Brunner, prominent in the field of community studies and rural sociology. It was this Institute that sponsored the Lynds' Middletown study in 1925.[64] It should also be recalled that early volumes of the *American Journal of Sociology* gave space to "biblical" sociology and other topics of interest to the clergy.

There thus existed extensive and strong links between Protestant reformism and the rise of sociology in the United States. For sociology, the organizational network and movements described above represented a wide public forum in which sociological topics were discussed, courses taught, texts written and sold in large quantities, the recruitment of intellectually inclined people with a ministerial background into the new discipline assured, and a livelihood provided for reform-minded social scientists who were temporarily blocked from academic positions. Equally important, the reforming clergy was a powerful pressure group in favor of introducing sociology into universities, and through its respectability assured sociology a fair hearing among trustees and university presidents. For the Protestant church, sociology meant an emerging discipline more responsive to its needs and readier to provide its social activities with an ideological justification in the face of a hostile intellectual climate than any of the established disciplines. While in the 1880s there had been a strong association between the socially committed young economists and the Christian reform movement, economics as a discipline was rapidly professionalizing, was closed to entry by nonprofessionals, and occupied with its own intellectual problems. Sociology, the newer discipline, stepped into this vacant position, and, in need of backers and personnel, remained open for many more years. This explains the presence of so many former ministers among the ranks of the early sociologists. Men like Vincent, Hayes, Lichtenberger, Gillin, and Gillette could move into sociological studies and an academic career in their midthirties after a ministerial career start at a time when economics was already closed to them. Considering the low salary of ministers and the declining status of the clergy, sociology provided them with a more secure financial base and an opportunity for upward social mobility.

Yet, sociology's association with the Protestant and secular reform movements was also marked by an element of ambivalence. Sociology had to become accepted as an intellectual discipline and as a "science of society" in the university context. Too intimate an association with practical reform, applied ethics, and social betterment threatened to swamp and undermine the more basic concern of academic legitimacy. Thus Small, the most persistent promoter of sociology, literally walked a tightrope. On the one hand, in trying to enlist religious backers, he proclaimed that "the ultimate sociology must be essentially Christian,"[65] and that the "principles of ultimate social science will be reiterations of essential Christianity";[66] on the other hand, he wrote in the programmatic statement for the *American Journal of Sociology*: "To many possible readers the most important question about the introduction of this journal will be with reference to its attitude to 'Christian sociology.' The answer is. . . toward Christian sociology [this journal will be] sincerely deferential, towards alleged 'Christian sociologists', severely suspicious."[67] Small and other academic sociologists had to dissociate the new discipline from the revivalist style and preachings of the likes of the Western social messiah, Reverend George Herron, incumbent of the chair of Applied Christianity at Iowa College.[68]

social reform, the progressive
movement, and sociology

Even more crucial for the establishment of
sociology, its definition, early content, and preoccupations, was its link
with the secular reform movement and the Progressive movement. This
fact has been noted by many historians of sociology. Odum traced the
origins of American sociology to the joint influence of European thought
and the American background of social reform and practical (or applied)
sociology. He also documented the not uncommon organization and
career overlap between the early sociologists and social workers and
reformers.[69] Floyd House called philanthropy and social reform one of
the two major antecedents of American sociology, and observed that:

the sociology that was taught before 1920 in the colleges and universities of the
United States, or what was taught under that name, at any rate, was even more
strongly influenced and shaped by the humanitarian, philanthropic, and social
reform movements that were actually under way in the country during the nineteenth century [than by the European intellectual trends].[70]

As for Louis Wirth, the early sociology was an "omnium gatherum" and
hodgepodge of residual subjects, poverty, crime, insanity, marriage and
divorce, slums and other social pathologies that did not readily fit in
with the older established social sciences. He also noted that "social
workers, social reformers, prophets, and social critics, for want of any
other academic refuge, had identified themselves with the adolescent
science of sociology."[71] Sutherland, too, writes that "when universities
began to develop departments of sociology in the decade of the nineties,
many of them employed as sociologists persons who had attained prestige in the ministry or welfare organizations. . . . Of the authors of
articles in the *American Journal of Sociology* in 1895-1900, 25.3 percent were members of the National Conference of Charities and Correction, and/or the American Prison Congress; this percentage decreased to
4 percent in the volumes 1935-1940."[72]

Yet what these commentators do not suffi-
ciently emphasize is that without the active social support of various
reform groups and favorable Progressive public opinion, it is very doubt-
ful that sociology as an autonomous academic discipline would have
been established. It is also true, however, that because of this alliance it
threatened to become no more than an applied professional discipline of
the order of social work. This danger explains in turn the insistence of
the founding fathers on the "science of sociology," which was different
from applied or practical sociology, often culminating in an arrogant
sociological imperialism. It is significant that the consumers of early
sociology went far into shaping it beyond the title and content of the

sociology courses themselves. The vocational orientation of students, the early departmental collaboration with charity organization societies, the emphasis on textbook writing rather than genuine scholarship, the feelings of insecurity and inferiority toward more scholarly oriented disciplines in the universities, characterized early sociology and sociologists and have even to some extent come down to the present through the institutionalization within sociology of the often contradictory values of practical concern and social betterment and scientific objectivity and professionalism. The origin of sociology in reform also serves as a backdrop for the sharp reaction against preaching, muckraking, and value judgments that set in in the 1920s when sociology was more firmly established and professionalized, and was trying to thin out of its ranks the reformers and dilettantes who were no longer needed and were becoming a source of embarrassment to the discipline.

This is not the place to write at length on the spread of the reform movement in the United States; historians have performed this task comprehensively. Hofstadter writes that "Populists, Bryanites, muckrakers, progressives, followers of the New Freedom, men and movements transcending by far the influence of the socialists, single taxers and benevolent preachers, took up the causes of reform. . . . Previous reform and protest movements had been disjointed and uncoordinated uprisings of workers and farmers, now the middle class was drawn into the fray."[73] Elsewhere he describes the ferment of the Progressive era as urban, middle class, nationwide, bipartisan and concerned with urban problems—labor and social welfare, municipal reform, the interests of the consumer.[74] A high proportion of its leaders were well-to-do, native born, professional men and college graduates who formed an alliance with the reform clergy and were strongly helped by a "sort of informal brain trust of a creative minority of academic men including John R. Commons, Richard T. Ely, E. R. A. Seligman and Veblen in economics, Charles Beard and A. F. Bentley in political science, John Dewey in philosophy, Roscoe Pound in law, and Ross and Ward in sociology."[75]

Another important group were the journalists, a new brand of socially concerned reporter-reformers with a passion for getting the inside story. Their presence coincided with a revolution in journalism toward competitive mass circulation newspapers and nationwide magazines.[76] It will be recalled that both Giddings and Park had a presociological career start as newspapermen, and that Park even once described himself as "one of the first and humbler muckrakers."[77] Ross was a personal friend of Teddy Roosevelt and wrote one of the popular muckraking bestsellers of the period, *Sin and Society*, aside from being associated with just about every Populist and Progressive cause during his lifetime. Thirty percent of the members of the American Sociological Society in 1905 (and 20 percent in 1910) were also members of the National Conference of Charities and Correction (NCCC), among them Jane Addams, foremost reformer of the era and NCCC president in 1910; J. Brackett, its president in 1904; Edward T. Devine, editor of *Charities*, secretary of the New York Charity Organization Society, president of the New York School of Social Work, and NCCC president in 1906; Robert Paine, of the Peace Society, and NCCC president in 1895; Francis McLean of the National Consumer League; Robert A. Woods, leader of the social settlement movement; Carroll Wright, U.S. Commissioner of Labor; and several other settlement house workers, tenement reformers, and civic-minded men and women.

    The intellectual and organizational interpenetration between reform movement and early sociology can be traced through several sources: the American Social Science Association and its offspring, the NCCC; the social settlement movement; the survey movement; the Russell Sage Foundation; the schools of social work; and of course the university departments of sociology themselves. What the social reformers sought in their alliance with progressive social science was an ideological justification and scientific rationale and defense of their activities. They had

faith in the capacity of social science to translate ethics into action. They hoped to find in social science not merely a description of society but the means of social change for democratic ends. In the last two decades of the nineteenth century, academic sociologists and economists promised to provide such a body of information . . . [the professors] were the social engineers of their day.[78]

    The American Social Science Association (ASSA), organized in 1865 and stimulated by the example of the British Social Science Association, had for its purpose the advancement of education, prison reform, civil service reform, the Freedmen's Bureau, public health, infant welfare, prevention of crime, and the like, and also the promotion of the study of social science from history and jurisprudence to political economy. It had a distinguished set of officers and members, including at different times General Grant, Charles Francis Adams, Carroll Wright, several university presidents and numerous social scientists, that marked it and "social science" with a stamp of respectability. It published the *Journal of Social Science*. More important, the ASSA was the parent organization to a whole set of more specialized scientific and reform societies, such as the National Prison Association, the Civil Service Reform Association, the NCCC, and the American Historical, Economic, and Political Science Associations among others. These splits considerably weakened the ASSA, so that by 1895 it was primarily an association with eastern membership whose most energetic members were active in its offspring associations.[79]

    The principal reform organization, nationwide in scope and with a large membership, was the National Conference of Charities and Correction (NCCC, later called the National Conference of Social Work), with 300 members in 1888 but about 4500 members by 1908, many of them members of local and state boards of charities or charity organization societies. Its annual meetings were conducted in sections, on provision for the insane, provision for the feeble-minded and the blind, organization of charities, outdoor poor relief, municipal charities, immigration, reformation of the prisons, industrial training in juvenile reformatories, and care of dependent children. Promotional activities were carried out through study committees formed every year on which many distinguished professors and clergymen served. In the 1890s the NCCC saw its intellectual fate tied up with the emergence of sociology and championed the introduction of sociology into universities and colleges. In 1893 it established a "Standing Committee on Instruction in Sociology in Institutions of Learning," including Richard Ely, Albion Small, and Graham Taylor. This Committee sponsored an investigation addressed to the presidents of universities and colleges in the entire country the results of which were reported to the Conference in 1894 and published in its *Proceedings*.[80] This survey not only sought to find out how many institutions offered "sociology proper" as well as courses in "charities and corrections," the description of course contents, student enrollment figures, and so forth, but also solicited informed opinion about definitions of sociology, the reasons for its study, its relation to other disciplines, and opinions of its education value.

    Of the 146 institutions that replied (out of 421 queried), 24 offered sociology proper, with the University of Chicago offering a total of 31 courses in sociology and its allied practical fields. Henderson, Chicago sociology professor and later NCCC president, reported that "general sociology treats society in its normal light, whereas social pathology studies morbid conditions, remedies, etc." As for his students, "(they) have been visitors in charities, . . . and have taken censuses of the unemployed sleeping in the City Hall. . . ." Small defined sociology as "the philosophy of human welfare. As such it must be the synthesis of all the particular social sciences." The range of replies is well illustrated by the two extremes of an Iowa college president who named the Bible as his textbook on charities and corrections, the family, anthropology and ethnology, and the president of the University of Vermont who termed "the so-called sociology taught in our colleges, preached in our pulpits, and disseminated in our periodicals, crude, semicommunistic and harmful." The programmatic statement of the conference for 1894 hoped for a rapprochement between theoreticians of the science of society and social reformers:

[sociology] promises to be a subject that will henceforth receive more attention than in the past. It is hoped that students and teachers in institutions of learning and those whose relation to the subject is only theoretical will by means of this conference come into closer contact with the practical men and women who are at work along various lines of social reform, and that on the other hand the practical workers will receive inspiration and wise suggestions from meeting and hearing men who are devoting themselves to the study of the science of social life.[81]

This view was also put forward by Frederic Wines, Assistant Director of the Census, to a similar audience in an article on "Sociology and Philanthropy" when he wrote that "the philanthropist needs the sociologist . . . and the sociologist needs the philanthropist," and "I plead for a more intimate association and fellowship between professional philanthropists and sociologists."[82]

The twenty-second annual meeting of the NCCC had a section on "Sociology in Institutions of Learning" at which Giddings read a paper, and a Standing Committee on the Scientific Study of Social Problems was established, including Giddings, Farnam, the Yale economist and later president of the AEA, President Angell of Michigan, Simon Patten of the University of Pennsylvania, the ubiquitous Ely, and others, including clergymen. In 1896, A. D. Wright's presidential address on "The New Philanthropy" stated that

the New Philanthropy is slowly winning its way . . . (it) claims as its own the recent rise of the study of sociology in our institutions of learning. Philanthropy is thus raised to the rank of a science, the practical and the theoretical are yoked together, and a large number of able young men and women are looking forward to making it their life work.[83]

In fact among the founding fathers of U. S. sociology, in addition to Small and Giddings, Cooley and Ross also participated as speakers and/or committee members in the NCCC. *Charities Review*, the official organ of the New York Charities Organization Society (COS) for a number of years in the 1890s had the subtitle "A Journal of Practical Sociology." The monthly *Bulletin of the NCCC* gave frequent and sympathetic attention to sociology in its section on "Related Organizations," as, for instance, in its report on the newly formed Southern Sociological Congress in May 1914. Indeed, when in 1917 the NCCC moved to replace the antiquated term "Charities and Corrections" in its title and polled its membership for a new name, the second choice of the members (after the winning "National Conference of Social Work" that in fact was adopted) was the "American Sociological Conference."[84]

The identification of "sociology" with practical or applied sociology and social reform was the majority view even in academic circles and made the task of scientific and academic legitimacy a very delicate and difficult one for the early academic sociologists. It is only necessary to examine the connotations of the word "sociology" in books, publications, addresses, as, for instance, the contents of *The Bibliography of Selected Sociological References* prepared in 1893 by the City Vigilance League of New York for its members, and John R. Commons' *Popular Bibliography of Sociology*, whose bulk is taken up by references under such entries as Lodging Houses, Municipal Problems, Womanhood, The Slums, Temperance and Narcotics, after a passing reference to General Sociology, where works by Spencer, Ward, Giddings, De Greef, and Schaeffle are listed. The *Annals of the American Academy of Social and Political Science,* the journal that gave most space to the field of sociology, had in each issue from 1894 to 1900 a section entitled "Sociological Notes" under which the following subject matter was covered: Charities, College Settlements, Department of Labor, Domestic Service Question, Liquor Problem . . . School of Applied Ethics, Sociological Investigation, Tenement Houses, Theory of Sociology, Unemployed, and so forth. However, in 1902 the section was renamed "Philanthropy, Charity and Social Problems," and later yet became the "Department of Social Work." In 1898 the Academy devoted a part of its annual meeting to the "Study and Teaching of Sociology." It was in the *Annals* also that Ira Howerth reported on an inquiry "Among all the teachers of sociology in the United States" and others known to be deeply interested in the subject on the present state and status of sociology in the United States. It included the following questions: "which term do you prefer, social science or sociology? . . . is it a science? . . . in what department does it belong? what is its relation to political economy, history, political science, ethics?"[85] Forty replies were received, including those of Small, Cooley, Giddings, Ross, Henderson, and John Dewey. After looking over the diversity of opinion expressed on these matters, Howerth himself concluded that "this brief presentation of many conflicting opinions is far from satisfactory. . . . the inability of sociology to answer certain questions, scientific and pedagogic, only shows what every sociologist admits, that the science is in a more or less undefined and tentative position. It does not disprove the existence of the science." And Lester Ward in a review of the current conceptions of sociology wrote

(1) Sociology as Philanthropy. It is probably safe to say that this conception of sociology is the prevailing one with the public today . . . it is the housing of the poor, charity work generally, slumming, reform work in the neglected quarters of cities, settlement work, etc. Sometimes it gets beyond the tenement house and

sweating system and deals with consumers' leagues and cooperative stores. It includes such municipal reforms as public baths, gardens, and art galleries within the reach of the less well to do class. This cannot be called a system of sociology . . . but it is the common notion of what sociology or social science is, and is all the idea that the general public, the newspaper reporter and editor, or the average member of Parliament or of Congress has of it. . . . It is social work, often of a high order, and for the most part very useful, but is not sociology.[86]

Perhaps the clearest link of sociology with social reform can be gleaned from the content of the early sociology courses, the manner in which departments of sociology were established, the purposes for which sociologists were hired, and what they were supposed to add of value to the existing curriculum. Sociology made its entry into the competing universities without any intellectual or scientific program or content, in completely opportunistic fashion, in order to cater to students', reformers', philanthropists', and social workers' demand for vocational training before professional schools of social work were established. Small admitted as much when he later wrote that "sociology was a science without a problem, a name or a message. The many confident prophesyings in the name of sociology, but conflicting with each other, served not to mitigate the case but to aggravate it,"[87] and "the sociologists started out with the conviction that there was something for them to study, then went about to find it. They believed that there was more than the older social scientists taught. But what?"[88]

In the universities, some sociology courses were the successors of the earlier social science courses promoted by the American Social Science Association that have been described as a "hodgepodge of various odds and ends that deserved a place in a school of political science but that belonged specifically to none of the established social science subjects."[89] In the case of Cornell, President Andrew White recommended "a course of practical instruction calculated to fit young men to discuss intelligently such important social questions as the best methods of dealing practically with pauperism, intemperance, crimes, . . . insanity, idiocy and the like."[90] In 1884 Frank B. Sanborn, perennial secretary of the ASSA and the Massachusetts Board of Charities, was recruited to teach it. The course had a social problem orientation highlighted by visits to nearby asylums, prisons, and reformatories. The course was subsequently taken over by another instructor who added "the fundamental theory of sociology" to its content. He understood by that term what we would regard today as a mixture of biological sociology, paternalistic anti-laissez-faire ideology, and the social gospel.[91]

At the University of Michigan a School of

Political Science was opened in 1881, and soon offered courses on sanitary science, public scientific surveys, and social science that included everything from Plato's *Republic* to the usual catalog of social problems. In 1894 a department of political economy and sociology was formed after Cooley rejoined the faculty, and because of his interests a genuine theoretic sociology curriculum was offered. At Missouri the chair of sociology was established in 1900 largely through the influence of the State Board of Charities. At Iowa the sociology department grew out of the earlier department of applied Christianity after the radical revivalist Reverend Herron was fired. At Kansas, in 1889, the regents recruited Blackmar from Johns Hopkins: When he planned to call his new department "history and politics," they declined because "the people of Kansas would not tolerate a department of politics in the University as they had politics enough in the state already." Blackmar and the administration settled on the name "History and Sociology."[92]

Equally telling is how and why the two leading centers of sociology at Chicago and Columbia were established, for they were the leaders of American sociology well into the 1930s. With respect to Chicago, Small later wrote "there is no doubt in my mind that the rapid increase of academic attention to the subject of sociology in the United States must be credited very much less to the intrinisic merit of work done by the members of the new department at Chicago than to the general academic rivalry stimulated by Dr. Harper's aggressiveness."[93] Both Small and Giddings agreed that Columbia had no choice but to introduce a sociology section in its graduate school after Chicago had made its move.[94]

The aims of the department at Chicago outlined in its catalog were: "(1) the exposition of social relations and theories as will serve educated citizens. (2) train teachers in colleges. (3) train other vocations devoted to social service, including pulpit, platform, press, and the work of organizing enterprises for social improvement and (4) advanced student training."[95] While the department offered a wide range of courses both theoretical and applied, the vocational aims were strongly stressed throughout: " . . . the City of Chicago is one of the most complete social laboratories in the world . . . no city in the world presents a wider variety of typical social problems than Chicago . . . the organized charities of the city afford graduate students of the university both employment and training; the church enterprises of the city enlist students in a similar manner."[96]

Columbia responded to the Chicago challenge by hiring Giddings away from Bryn Mawr to strengthen the course work offered by Mayo-Smith and appointing him to the new professorship in sociology in 1894. The catalog of the Faculty of Political Science emphasized both the vocational aspects of the new subject and left no doubt that New York was equally if not better suited than Chicago for the purpose of acquiring practical experience in social problems: " . . . the term sociology, however, it may be defined, includes a large number of the subjects which are most seriously interesting to men at the present time. The effective treatment of social problems demands that they be dealt with both theoretically and concretely. A college located in the country must needs study these subjects in the abstract. Columbia deems it her duty and her wisdom alike to avail herself of the singular opportunity for practical work in this direction afforded by her location in the city of New York. It has therefore been determined greatly to enlarge the facilities for university study in sociology, and to bring such study into connection with the practical sociological work in this city. . . . It is in the city that the problems of poverty, of mendacity, of intemperance, of unsanitary surroundings, and of debasing social influences are met in their most acute form. Hence the city is the natural laboratory of social science."[97] Besides regular university courses and the statistical laboratory, the sociology program included field work and practical work in connection with the COS, the Brooklyn Bureau of Charities, the University Settlement Society, and the East Side House, where students would be trained in the work of investigating and reporting for applicants for relief, in friendly visits among the poor, and the like, six hours per week. As for the purpose of the sociology course, Columbia echoes Chicago: "It is believed that such study will be of the utmost value to future clergymen in training them for parish work in cities and factory towns, to journalists as professional training; to public men and ordinary citizens who may be called upon to direct the philanthropic and reformatory work of society. Still further there is a growing demand for trained men as trained superintendents or recruiters of COS and similar institutions . . . there will be growing demand for scientific statisticians in this country." The only early department of sociology that did not originate in connection with charities, philanthropy and reform, was at Yale because of Sumner's negative views on these matters. Philanthropy, social economics, and social reform were offered in the Yale Divinity School's Department of Christian Sociology.

      If one examines the comprehensive surveys on the status of sociology conducted by sociologists at the turn of the century, the above picture is further strengthened. After examining the 1901 course catalogs of U.S. colleges and universities, Tolman reports sociology being offered in 169 institutions.[98] His classification of courses is based on their titles as well as the catalog description, and includes many courses only peripheral to sociology (e.g., municipal institutions, civics) because they were taught in departments where sociology was also taught. Omitting the most obvious of these cases, the most frequent category of courses, with 95, was "General Sociology" (i.e., courses whose title was "outlines of" . . . , "principles of" . . . , or "introduction to sociology"). Second, with 57, was "social reform, practical sociology, social problems," to which should also be added 40 courses on the "sociology of dependent classes, charities," and 30 on "sociology of delinquent classes, criminology." These figures contrast with only 15 "advanced courses" mainly offered at Chicago, Columbia, and Yale and 6 courses in "field work," including the statistical laboratory work at Columbia. Seven years later the American Sociological Society sponsored an even more comprehensive survey under Small's direction. It was estimated that about 400 institutions by then gave some attention to sociology.[99] Sociology was offered most frequently in departments of "sociology and economics," "sociology," or "economics," but might also be found in association with every conceivable combination and nomenclature (including homiletics and Applied Christianity). Fifty full-time professors of sociology were by then in existence, though more typical was the part-time sociologist. The classification of courses presented is not decipherable as to content and comparable to Tolman's. Yet in contrasting the emphasis of theoretical to practical sociology, practical sociology (social problems, charities, the 3 Ds—delinquents, defectives, dependents) wins easily in 51 against 21 departments,[100] and a 3-page listing of the cooperative activities between academic departments and COS and other reform institutions leaves no doubt where the emphasis was. The survey also quotes answers to the last question on the schedule: "Express fully your judgment on the present tendencies of sociology. . . ." Of the 110 quoted responses, 43 expressed an opinion on the applied versus theoretical sociology issue (i.e., whether students preferred or demanded one or the other, whether the respondent himself stressed one or the other in his courses, and so forth). Of these, 34 stressed applied sociology, 7 stressed both, and 2 only (Sumner and Giddings) came out in favor of theory. Quite representative is the view expressed by Anna MacLean of Adelphi College, a Chicago Ph.D. in sociology: "General trend here seems to be along the line of greater interest in social work as a profession. Students want to do 'sociological work' instead of teaching. Theory makes no strong appeal. Ten of my students hold paid positions in New York."[101]

Small was therefore correct in his opinion that sociology became established in U.S. colleges and universities ahead of and without a central core of scientific method and theoretic content. The intellectual and "sociological" content of even the "general" and "advanced" sociology courses was not impressive. Most of instructors in sociology had not received any formal training in the subject matter and had but a marginal professional interest in it. They responded to a personal interest, student demand, and administrative pressures. Of the 118 instructors in sociology listed by Tolman, only 26 were ASS members in 1905; and of the 110 respondents quoted in Bernard's survey, only 20. The textbooks most frequently used at the time of Bernard's inquiry were Small and Vincent's *Introduction to the Study of Sociology* (based on Small's lectures, cf. below), Wright's *Practical Sociology* (a social problems text) and Giddings' *Elements of Sociology* (a Spencerian tract with a psychologistic orientation).[102] The dilemma of what to teach in a sociology course aside from practical topics had to be painfully faced by Small and all other sociology instructors. Writing in 1915, he said

It must be remembered . . . that in the early 1890s there was scarcely any available "helps" for the men who tried to get a hearing for sociology in the universities. There was no standard literature of any sort which could be used according to the classroom methods of the other social sciences. Each instructor was thrown upon his own resources. They were ridiculed by a hundred academic men to every one who was willing to consider them seriously. For several years my lectures were elaborations of Schaeffle with one eye constantly on Spencer and on Ward. This is a deliberate confession that during those years these writers got between me and the reality itself. While the emptiness of this work now almost makes my teeth chatter, I feel no conviction of sin for it. . . . I cannot see how transition from the older ways of thinking about human affairs to our present process conceptions could have been effected more promptly and surely than by using those writers for what they were worth.[103]

The early academic sociologists were textbook writers, not researchers or writers of scholarly publications. They responded to the demand for textbooks generated by mass education and competitive publishing houses. Ross managed to finance his worldwide travels partly from the sale of his textbooks.[104] Even the *American Journal of Sociology (AJS)* did not originate as a carefully planned intellectual undertaking in the manner of Durkheim's *Année sociologique*, and for many years down to World War I catered to a readership of progressive reformers as much as to professional social scientists. In Small's account, the *AJS* originated after a personal confrontation he had with President Harper. When Harper was unable to get a University of Chicago extension magazine going for which a budgetary appropriation already existed, he startled Small by suggesting that the sociology department undertake to publish a journal of sociology. While Small did not think he had sufficient intellectual resources for this purpose, "there was no room for doubt that Dr. Harper intended his suggestion as a 'dare'" that Small could not afford to turn down. Because there were not enough papers to fill the pages of the first volumes, "without the prompt and hearty cooperation of Ward and Ross, the enterprise could scarcely have survived its first year."[105] Fortunately, Ross had ready a manuscript version of his book *Social Control*, and agreed to its serial publication in 13 parts during the first 3 years of the *AJS*.

The early *AJS* was a curious blend of scholarly papers, Chicago Ph.D. dissertations, and popular articles designed for the Progressive public. While Small was able to enlist the cooperation of an impressive array of foreign advising editors, only Simmel actually published in it repeatedly. The easterners Sumner, Giddings and their students boycotted the journal for at least ten years, and after that their articles appeared only as a part of the ASS meetings and were also published in its *Proceedings*. Aside from the space devoted to Christian sociology, a special feature of each issue for several years was a typical muckraking exposé or social-reform oriented lead article with numerous photographs. The January 1897 number started with a photographic description of the "Smoky Pilgrims of Rural Kansas." Volume 3 (1897/1898) had two photographic lead articles on the "Junior Republic" ("an experiment in charity, penology, and pedagogy"), another one on "Character Building at Elmira," "The Social Value of the Saloon," and the "Possibilities of the Present Industrial System," as well as other reform-type papers on "The Illinois Child Labor Laws," "The Scientific Value of Social Settlements," and "The Stake of the Church in the Social Movement." The next volume had exposé articles on "Two Weeks in a Department Store" and "The Relief Care of Dependents" together with papers on welfare, social work, reform legislation, church and reform, and applied sociology. Volume 5 had a photographic lead article on "Model Public Bath at Brookline," and other similar articles, whereas in Volume 6 are found such titles as "The Sweating System in the Garment Trades in Chicago," "Public Outdoor Relief," "Prison Laboratories," "Work and Problems of the Consumers' League," and two on "The Saloon in Chicago." Volume 10 (1904/1905) was an exceptionally scholarly volume because the social science papers delivered at the St. Louis International Congress of Arts and Sciences were reprinted in the *AJS*. In Volume 13 a special 30-page "Review of Municipal Events" was added to attract the Progressive public, and was continued for a number of years. As late as the July and September 1910 issues one finds popular photographic articles on such topics as a "City of Vagabonds."

social research

The first social research techniques as well as the bulk of empirical social research up to the war were developed and

conducted mostly outside of the universities by social workers, philanthropists, public health and charity workers, journalists and reformers,
and some academic social pathologists, all of them loosely allied in the
social survey movement. Their models were the British researcher-
reformers and settlement workers, especially Booth. They were preceded by the muckrakers and the social gospel novel. Many were socially
committed, college-educated women, with no other outlet than to
channel their reforming zeal into charities and corrections, university
settlements, the social survey movement, and all the other reform causes
of the Progressive era from temperance to women's suffrage. The two
most remarkable of these were Jane Addams and Florence Kelley.

After a trip to Europe in which the squalor of
East London made a profound impression on her, Jane Addams opened
Hull House in Chicago. Settlements, first started in Britain, were houses
in the slums, staffed by college graduates, with the purpose not merely
to set a middle-class example to the poor, but to improve the neighborhood by organizing the working people, if necessary into pressure groups
and unions. A by-product of settlements was the collection and publication of social data on slum conditions with the goal of pressuring City
Hall into social improvements. Hull House received the sympathetic
support of some Chicago University professors like Dewey who came
to lecture at meetings of its Workingmen's Social Science Club.[106] One
of the early residents was Florence Kelley. She had been the first woman
ever to attend Cornell and was a specialist on socialist theory and the
British Factory Acts and inspection system.[107] While at Hull House, she
worked on a slum inquiry for the U.S. Commissioner of Labor, Carroll
Wright. Out of Kelley's and other residents' activities grew the *Hull
House Maps and Papers*, with the telling subtitle "a presentation of
nationalities and wages in a congested district of Chicago."[108] It contained a set of essays the most notable of which was Florence Kelley's
investigation of sweat shops. The maps were based on the house-to-
house enumeration for the Commissioner of Labor under Kelley's
supervision. They were block maps on which the ethnic composition
and average wage of residents were entered. The colors used to distinguish wage categories were the same as on Booth's London maps. The
techniques used by the researchers was for the most part participant
observation and differed from the muckrakers' exposés in that the settlement workers knew the slum dwellers through daily interaction. Even
Jacob Riis' *How the Other Half Lives*,[109] subtitled "Studies Among the
Tenements of New York," was based as much on talks with city officials
and employees of charity societies as on inquiries among the inhabitants
of the slums themselves. All such investigations were seen as stepping-

stones to social action. Jane Addams helped organize strikes when
appeals to City Hall failed to produce results. Florence Kelley became
Illinois' first factory inspector, studied law at night, and earned a law
degree because it was necessary for effective inspection work. Later she
went to New York where she founded the National Consumers' League
and through her activities on the New York Child Labor Committee,
the Pittsburgh Survey, the U.S. Children's Bureau, and other private and
public bodies had probably a greater hand in shaping legislation on child
and female labor, the minimum wage, sanitary ordinances in work
places, and other social problems than any other person at the time.[110]
Robert Woods, the informal leader of the set-
tlement movement in the United States, working out of Andover House
in Boston, was an active social researcher. Woods hoped that settlements
would eventually reclaim an entire blighted neighborhood. He and his
college-educated collaborators organized boys' clubs to take them off
the streets, cooperated with labor unions, and rubbed elbows with the
political bosses when necessary. Woods was influenced by the Fabian
socialists and Booth's work, and was the author of the first systematic
treatise on English social movements by an American.[111] He had the
notion that university settlements are "laboratories of social science."
The fruits of his investigations were published in *The City Wilderness*
(1898), *Americans in Process* (1902), and other books. These represent
the first systematic and empirical study of the processes of adaptation
of immigrants to city life and their assimilation in American society,
topics that later became of central concern to the Chicago sociologists.
The most professionally executed of the early
city investigations was W. E. B. DuBois' *The Philadelphia Negro* (1899).
DuBois, a Harvard Ph.D., had already conducted rural surveys for the
U.S. Department of Labor and was well acquainted with Booth's London Survey and the Hull House investigations. Hired by the University
of Pennsylvania for the study, DuBois for 15 months devoted all his
time to systematic field work among the blacks of Philadelphia, especially in the Seventh Ward, attending their meetings, churches, business,
social, and political gatherings, visiting their schools and institutions, and
most important of all conducting a house-to-house visitation in their
families.[112] For this purpose he used six census-type schedules that included questions on job discrimination. His results were summarized
and analyzed in clear tables, charts, and graphs throughout, and backed
up with systematic white-black comparisons. He followed Booth in
classifying households by their average weekly earnings into four categories and even compared Philadelphia blacks with Booth's London
working classes. He included typical family budgets for each category

of families. Kept from a well-deserved appointment at the University of Pennsylvania because of his race, he later organized a sociology department and "sociological laboratory" at Atlanta University. With this base of operations, he and his students conducted a whole series of empirical studies into the condition of different black social strata in the United States at the turn of the century, which represent a lasting contribution to American social history.

The social survey movement flowered in the decade of the 1910s especially after the Russell Sage Foundation was established in 1907. The Foundation supported Kellogg's Pittsburgh Survey with $15,000, the investigations by students in schools of social work, and investigations of women and child labor conducted under the direction of Florence Kelley at the Consumers' League. Russell Sage had close links with the COS of New York, the New York School of Philanthropy, and Paul Kellogg's *Charities and Commons* (later *The Survey*) magazine. The origin of the social survey idea was in the COS's effort to arouse public opinion for social reform. Its Tenement House Committee in 1899 arranged a public exhibit of models of tenements including 1000 photographs and over 100 maps, charts, and graphs, and a host of statistics that presented to the public "in accurate and scientific form the results of bad housing conditions upon the health and industrial welfare of the community."[113] The Pittsburgh Survey originated in 1907 with the COS Committee on Publications' desire to run a special issue of the *Charities and Commons* on steelworkers. After Russell Sage financing was secured, it was vastly expanded in scope and pushed beyond the goal of a quick journalistic survey. It was finally published in six volumes, crammed with social data and photographs, and topped by a civic exhibit in Pittsburgh itself to publicize its findings in charts and graphs, lectures and conventions, and at meetings of civic associations. In this connection, it is worth noting that the Russell Sage section concerned with this and other subsequent inquiries was called the Department of Survey and Exhibits. After Pittsburgh, a series of surveys on a smaller scale followed, the most notable of which was the Springfield Survey directed by the Foundation's Shelby Harrison. In the late 1920s a bibliography listed 2775 titles and projects in which the survey technique had been used in some manner.[114] But it is fair to say that not until the late 1930s and World War II was the survey technique methodologically perfected and systematically applied in professionally directed scientific research projects. It is only at that point that the present meaning of social survey designating a specific methodology emerged, rather than the earlier meaning of a community movement for the purpose of presenting a constructive program of social advance and for curing community social problems.

differentiation

If the early sociologists were not engaged in sociological theorizing and social research in the contemporary sense, they were busy building grand systems of universal theory and polemicizing with other disciplines about the proper scope and boundaries of sociology, and often attacking each other as well. Every observer of early U.S. sociology has noted these characteristic birth pains. Under the heading "Aspirations to Establishment," Shils writes about the early sociologists that the problem of legitimacy for academic newcomers forced them to devote much time to self-justification.[115] Louis Wirth noted that in 1915 much of the output of sociological writers was still devoted to programmatic pronouncements and apologetic essays, that "the attempt to legitimize sociology on the ground that it had a subject matter of its own, left sociology . . . the unenviable role of studying the trivial and neglected aspects of the social world," and that some sociologists assumed the role of "generalissimo" of the social sciences, and showed excessive concern with "building up a technical vocabulary and finding rationalizations for systems of classification and other abstract categories of thought" remote from the concrete reality of the social world.[116] Indeed, in a 1924 article, Small himself put forward similar views in a frank statement: "The true story of the American sociological movement would be a treatment of the theme 'Up from Amateurism.' . . . a humiliating proportion of the so-called 'sociology' of the last 30 years in America . . . has been simply old-fashioned opinionativeness under a new-fangled name."[117] And Small was equally explicit about the consequences of pressures for academic legitimacy:

Since the older disciplines exercised "squatters" rights over subject matter, to get a hearing the sociologists had to meet the conditions which they encountered in the only way that was open to them. . . . They had to appear in the name of "science" in order to get a hearing in court. . . . Whatever the logical character of the procedure, it was strategically necessary for these innovators . . . to gain ground by playing the academic game under the existing rules. Their instincts rather than deliberate calculation prompted them to speak for a "science" in the old uncritical sense, and having accounted themselves as the exponents of a "science" they were under bonds to make "good". . . . It was impossible a quarter of a century ago to make a different sort of entry into the sociological field.[118]

The observations of Shils, Wirth, and Small, as well as of others, could be extensively documented. For instance, a single early volume of the *American Journal of Sociology* has articles with the following titles: Henry J. Ford, "The Pretensions of Sociology," followed by Charles Ellwood's defense, "The Science of Sociology: A Reply," countered by Ford, "The Claims of Sociology Reexamined;"

two articles by Small, "The Sociological Stage in the Evolution of the Social Sciences" and the "Vindication of Sociology;" Simmel's "The Problem of Sociology;" a symposium on "The Psychological View of Society" with H. P. Fairchild, E. C. Hayes, E. A. Ross, and Carl Kelsey.[119] The most charitable statement one can make about the contents of these and similar articles is Shils' comment that "most of the sociology of the older generation of the 1920s has disappeared from the memory of most sociologists, and rightly so,"[120] a statement born out by a recent study of citations in introductory textbooks that reveals that only Sumner and Cooley (probably because of the usual references to *Folkways* in the chapter on "culture," and to the primary-secondary group distinction) are referred to with any frequency and consistency.[121] These evaluations can, however, be tempered by Merton's generalization that every science in the process of institutionalization goes through the early phases of intellectual and academic legitimation, which inclines its advocates in the direction of system-building, the rivalries of schools, the necessity to establish its autonomy from parent disciplines, the stress on its "scientific" nature, and the willingness to take on neglected subject matter.[122]

The era of maximum hostility between sociology and economics, the discipline from which it was differentiating, occurred in the middle 1890s, when in the words of a contemporary observer of the academic game, "just now sociology is being examined by boards of trustees. Has it a field of its own which will warrant the creation of a separate chair? Other scientists are watching the poachers upon their preserves. As one economist put it: 'the sociologist has no business in the field without the economists' consent.' It is a time for diplomacy. . . ."[123] At the annual meetings of the AEA, duly reported in its *Publications* and spilling out in polemical articles in the *Annals*, Giddings, Ward, and Small took on their critics, Patton, Ashley, and other economists. By the time of the founding of the ASS in 1905, relations between economists and sociologists had improved, but those between sociologists and historians had become strained. The AEA was most helpful in organizing the ASS.[124] Sixty-two percent of the 115 founding members of the ASS were AEA members, including all the prominent founding fathers of sociology. The founding of the ASS can be interpreted as a defense of disciplinary interests in the university context as well as a move to defend academic sociology from being swamped by the applied or practical sociologists and social reformers. The purpose of the association was set down in article 2 of the ASS constitution: "The object of this Society shall be the encouragement of sociological research and discussion, and the promotion of intercourse between persons engaged in the scientific study of society." It was, how-

ever, decided to allow social reformers entry at their discretion by providing for an open membership depending only upon payment of dues.
A circular of the ASS explicitly stated that "the new society . . . has
been founded with the hope of securing the active cooperation of scientific philanthropists as well as of persons engaged in academic institutions, of sociological writers as well as of sociological workers– of all
those who recognize the importance of the scientific aspects of sociology."[125]

Aside from the large membership overlap with
the AEA, 30 percent of the 115 founding members of the ASS were
also members of the National Conference of Charities and Correction.
Sixty-four had a clearcut academic affiliation (using the title professor
and/or reporting a university mailing address), 5 were prominent clergymen, 14 were prominent social reformers, including 6 presidents or
presidents-to-be of the NCCC, and 22 were professional economists
(university affiliation with economics departments), including 3 presidents-to-be of the AEA. Sixty-three percent of the members gave an
eastern address. In 1910, 5 years after the founding of the ASS, of 322
members, 50 percent had a clearcut university affiliation, 34 percent
were members of the AEA, and 20 percent of the NCCC. It should be
noted that ASS members did not terminate their AEA membership: of
the 44 members of the ASS in both 1905 and 1910 who had been members of AEA in 1905, 43 were still listed in the AEA in 1910. However,
the new society did not reach the majority of college instructors in
sociology. Of Tolman's 1901-1902 list of sociology instructors, only 26
of 118 were ASS members in 1905, and in L. L. Bernard's 1901 survey
on the status of sociology, only 20 of the 110 respondents quoted were
ASS members. In fact, even among the 28 Chicago sociology graduates
with a Ph.D. up to 1910, only 16 were members of the ASS in 1910. It
can be concluded that the ASS members in the first few years of its
existence were primarily economists and sociologists in universities and
colleges, supported by a smaller contingent of social reformers and
social workers.

Starting from this narrow and unpromising in-
tellectual base, sociology lifted itself by its own bootstraps to become
what it is today. This development can in part be attributed to the
multiple independent starts of sociology at several universities, which
increased the probability that at least one or two of the departments
would break away from the earlier unfruitful preoccupations. Personalities, as well as institutional factors, become important at this point.

After theological studies at Geneva, Göttingen,
and Oxford, and a presociological career in the ministry, Sumner occupied the professorship of political and social science at Yale where he

taught sociology and was a very popular lecturer. Yet Sumner, after the British manner, was not teaching at the graduate level. Small later commented that

several of his students have told me that in their day [Sumner] was lecturing on what might be described as the sort of opinions that ought to be held on things general by a Yale man. They added that no one was supposed to have "done" Yale as a gentleman should without having at least one course with "Billy" Sumner. . . . At that time (in 1907), when Sumner was elected second president of the ASS, he was not within my field of vision as even nominally a sociologist. . . . he remained the American echo of *laissez faire* as represented in England by Spencer.[126]

Hofstadter writes of him that "although clerical phraseology soon disappeared from his style, his temper remained that of a proselytizer, a moralist, an espouser of causes with little interest in distinguishing between error and iniquity in his opponents. . . ." In the columns of popular magazines and from the lecture platform "he waged a holy war against reformism, protectionism, sociology, and government intervention."[127] Donald Fleming quipped that "in Sumner's view, what *Social Classes Owe to Each Other* (1883) is nothing."[128] However, in the 1890s Sumner moved his attention more and more to academic sociology, labored on his vast *Science of Society*, and published *Folkways* (1906) upon which his present-day professional reputation rests. He was a founding member of the ASS, yet his relations with it and to other sociologists were hostile, to say the least, because he was totally opposed to their political and social ideas. A pupil of his who reedited *Folkways* wrote that Sumner used the term Science of Society instead of Sociology because "he detested with fury most of the work done under the latter name, most of its tendencies, and nearly all who taught it."[129] *Folkways* relies on ethnographic sources, the history of religions, classical studies, mythology and philosophy, and a few of the social Darwinist writers, to the exclusion of sociological writers. Aside from his two ASS presidential addresses, he steadfastly refused to publish in the *American Journal of Sociology* and to partake in promotional activities on behalf of sociology. At any rate, he died too soon in 1910 to have much of an impact on the ASS. After him, under Keller, Yale sociology became for a time little more than a cult of Sumner centered on the William Graham Sumner Club and the posthumous publication of *The Science of Society*.
Yet Sumner was a thoroughly honest man who lived according to his individualist philosophy and who put his position on the line by espousing unpopular causes to which he was firmly committed: the use of Spencer's *Study in Sociology* in his courses against the objections of President Porter, his outspoken oppo-

sition to the tariff, and his condemnation of the Spanish-American War.[130] And in his use of ethnographic and anthropological data in a comparative manner, he was foreshadowing a similar productive alliance between the two fields that can be traced through Thomas, Ogburn, Lynd, and the influence of the British social anthropologists upon sociological theory.

Lester Ward, first president of the ASS, professionally a botanist, and employed as a museum researcher by the U.S. government, did not get an academic position until 1906 at Brown, when he was already 65 years old and seven years before his death. He wrote a series of repetitious books in "cumbersome prose" and "barbarous terminology" that all contained the word "sociology" in the title and that were consistently ignored.[131] Ward came to sociology through his voracious readings in adult life. In the manner of Comte, he was an encyclopedist with a predilection for classifying the sciences in a hierarchic way (with sociology on top). At Brown, he taught a course called "The Survey of all Knowledge." During the year he managed to work up from astronomy and the physical sciences into the organic and psychic, and closed with an exposition of the laws and principles of sociology.[132] Of *Dynamic Sociology* (1883), Small reported that when Ward wrote it, "he had only the most meager knowledge that anyone else had worked in the same field."[133] Ward was not so much an original thinker as a great destroyer of the Social Darwinists' and biological sociologists' systems and pretensions, and a tireless propagandist for social reform and social planning opposed to the laissez-faire individualism of Spencer. At Brown, after Ward's death, James Q. Dealey led the department, and although he later became a president of the ASS in 1920, he had always been primarily and remained a political scientist.[134]

The most scholarly of the early sociologists was Charles Horton Cooley. The upper-class son of a Michigan Supreme Court justice, ICC Chairman, and dean of the Michigan Law School, Cooley first studied mechanical engineering at Michigan, wrote a Ph.D. in economics on the theory of transportation, and soon branched out into sociology. He was a withdrawn man, frequently ill, widely read, and because he never cared to assume administrative burdens was content to let sociology remain under the wing of the economics department at Michigan. In his manner of thinking, he had a preference for introspective contemplation in the style of the Scottish moralists and G. H. Mead and was not influenced to any extent by other U.S. sociologists. He distrusted large-scale research undertakings because of the tendency to select problems for which techniques were readily applicable rather than their importance for social theory and human understanding. He refused to hire at Michigan an empirical sociologist at a senior level. He defintely was not a department builder.[135]

Edward A. Ross, who came to occupy the chairmanship at Wisconsin for many years, was by far the most colorful, independent, widely traveled, and at 6 1/2 feet, the tallest of the early sociologists, but remained first and foremost a Populist, muckraker, and social reformer so typical of the 1890-1920 period. In his autobiography, he has very little to say about sociology and sociologists, but fondly recalls his political activities, which brought him into contact with William Jennings Bryan, Teddy Roosevelt, Justice Brandeis, Clarence Darrow, Roscoe Pound, Lincoln Steffens, and others. His travels, always followed by a book against social injustice, colonialism, landlordism, and other social evils, led him to China in 1910, to South America in 1913-1914, to Russia during the Revolution, to Mexico in the summers of 1922 and 1928, to Angola and Mozambique in 1924, to India, Indonesia, and the South Pacific. In Russia he interviewed Trotsky in 1917 and was caught up in the fighting during his trip on the Trans-Siberian railroad. In Angola he toured 32 villages and questioned members of road and field gangs, and followed it up with a scathing denunciation of Portuguese treatment of Africans, in particular the evils of forced labor. In Indonesia he was openly skeptical of officials who equated nationalism with communism. His procedure was to interview officials, notables, scholars, and missionaries, and then to follow up their statements by the method of direct observation.

Don Raphael in Mexico City tells me that there were no more contented or happy laboring people in the world than the 12,000 souls on his large sugar plantation in Morelos before the Revolution. Next week, I am in Morelos—he wouldn't dare set foot here—and am able to check his statements. I note how spring water for the hacienda buildings had been piped through the village but no faucet put in for them, so that 112 families have no drinking water save from the irrigation ditch. . . .[136]

As a result of his travels, his early belief in the natural superiority of the Anglo-Saxon "race"—widely shared at the time even among progressive thinkers—was shaken.

Differences of race mean far less for me now than it once did. Starting on my explorations with the naive feeling that my own race is right, all other races are more or less "queer," I gained insight and sympathy until my heart overlept barriers of race. . . . slowly I came to see that many factors besides disparity of natural endowment explain why this people has . . . higher culture while that people has a low culture. . . .[137]

Yet just to be on the safe side, he listed at the end of his autobiography 26 physical measurements of himself by a colleague and a complete psychoanalytic profile by a neuropsychiatrist who found him completely and thoroughly "normal" in a tongue-in-cheek report. Many of Ross' insights gained from his wide personal experiences were not systematically formulated. Recalling *Social Control*, which brought him his earliest professional success, he later wrote "in the 35 years since the book left my anvil I have scrutinized society in many countries, and the society which 'controls' does not look so global to me now as it did then. Not only do most laws at their passage reflect the outcome of struggle behind the scenes among pressure groups, but the same holds true of trends in public opinion and the deliverances of organized religion. Sooner or later the alert, well-led elements organize in order to mold social requirements to their wishes. The content of the code of social requirements, as well as the strictness with which obedience thereto is exacted, reveal an incessant tug-of-war among spokesmen of contending groups."[138] Ross was many things, but not a professional interested in closing sociology to outsiders and in making it a "science" at any cost. When an "excellent scholar" asked him to support a motion that the ASS "shall no longer strive to receive as large a membership as possible from philanthropic, religious, civic, and social reform groups," he retorted, "if we take pure sociology as our objective, heedless of current social problems and exigencies, our society will have from one to two hundred members and no influence. . . . [our] aim should be to bring to bear upon the outstanding social difficulties of our time the best possible technique of inquiry."[139]

If these founding fathers and their departments did not become centers for a reorientation of sociology, the same could not be said of Chicago and, to a lesser extent, of Columbia. But even Chicago was coasting along in the established pattern until World War I, and Columbia had a hand in the transformation of sociology in spite of, rather than because of, Giddings. Innovation had less to do with the brilliance and originality of ideas than with personality factors and the organizational aspects of the two universities and their environment.

columbia

Franklin H. Giddings was brought to Columbia in 1891 to develop the social problems area of the social sciences and to supplement Richmond Mayo-Smith in social statistics and social theory. Mayo-Smith, a member of Burgess' original German-trained team, was a conventional descriptive statistician dedicated to reform activities and out of touch with the newer British developments in mathematical statistics. He wrote two widely used statistical textbooks for economics and sociology students. His *Statistics and Sociology*, following the German moral statisticians, covers the usual topics of sex, age, conjugal condition, births, marriages, deaths, sickness and mortality, suicide, crime, race, and nationality, and reads like an international statistical almanac. Though he included the discovery of sociological laws by induction as part of the statistical field, he meant by them little more than statements of quantitative fact (i.e., the rate of suicide in England is 80 per 1 million inhabitants) or generalities (i.e., economic conditions are a cause of crime), and did not think the most relevant moral and social phenomena could be quantified.[140]

Giddings had greater ambitions as theorist and a penchant for quantification, for which he acquired a reputation in the histories of U.S. sociology out of proportion to his accomplishments. His stress on a scientific sociology led to a termination of the social work and practical sociology side of the Columbia sociology curriculum. His personal dogmatism, conceit, and prejudices alienated many prominent and influential members of the Columbia faculty who saw to it that sociology would not be expanded there before Giddings retired. Giddings himself contributed to it by surrounding himself with second-rate men who were no threat to his leadership. According to those who knew him personally, he was anti-Semitic and had poor relations with outstanding Columbia social scientists like Boas and Seligman because they were Jewish. He was proud of his dolichocephalic skull and believed that all genius and culture were carried by blond Aryans.[141] He was obsessed by anti-Germanism and anti-Bolshevism. According to Barnes

. . . for years his lectures were more often diatribes against his pet hates than calm sociological analyses. . . . he was a markedly dominant personality and very dogmatic in his views. He insisted upon doctrinal loyalty, not to say worship from his departmental colleagues. For this reason he surrounded himself with satellites rather than equals or professional rivals. In this way he stood at the opposite extreme from the other leading academic sociologist of his day, Dean Albion Small of Chicago, and was prevented from building up anything like the impressive department of sociology Small created at Chicago.[142]

A unique feature of the turn-of-the-century Columbia department was its statistical laboratory equipped with up-to-date computational facilities. As part of their training for a social work career, students were required to collect reports of the charities societies of New York City and put them into "scientific shape" by means of statistical tabulations and analyses.[143] Columbia and the COS collaborated in applied research from 1894 to 1903 through the COS Committee on Statistics that was headed at one time by Giddings and by Mayo-Smith, but this arrangement broke down shortly after Mayo-Smith died in 1901.[144] The annual reports of the COS contain detailed accounts of studies undertaken by Columbia sociology students on homeless men, the causes of unemployment, what became of the children in families aided by the COS, and similar topics. After this collaboration was discontinued, training in applied research was continued under the division of social economy with Edward T. Devine and Samuel Lindsay.[145] When the Russell Sage Foundation was formed in 1907, it received universal acclaim from social workers and academics alike, except for Giddings, who in an article entitled "The Danger of Charitable Trusts" wrote that "it would seem entirely possible that . . . the income of the Russell Sage Foundation would one of these days be devoted to the propagation of either anarchism or socialism, free trade or protection, neo-Malthusianism or the patriarchal family."[146] In this manner, Giddings constantly weakened the position of sociology in the potentially favorable Columbia and New York context.

Giddings had a reputation as a quantitatively oriented sociologist. In his 1901 statement in the Bernard survey on trends in sociology, he wrote

. . . the present tendency is to loaf and to generalize. I speak of the subject, not of any institution. We need men not afraid to work, who will get busy with the adding machine and the logarithms, and give us exact studies, such as we get in the psychological laboratories, not to speak of the biological and physical laboratories. *Sociology can be an exact, quantitative science*, if we get *industrious* men interested in it.[147]

Yet an examination of his quantitative work reveals that he himself was not abreast of the new British mathematical statistics, nor did he perform any empirical research in the modern sense. His *Inductive Sociology*, "a syllabus of methods, analyses, and classifications, and provisionally formulated laws," is actually an extremely elaborate and detailed scheme for the classification of statistical data. His provisional laws are in the nature of introspectively and deductively derived generalities. A good example is his second law of imitation, the law of refraction ("limitations are refracted by their media—words, customs, laws, religions, and institutions are modified as they pass from race to race and from age to age") or his law of sympathy ("the degree of sympathy decreases as the generality of resemblance increases").[148] In his later text of 1924, *The Scientific Study of Human Society*, not a research methods book in the contemporary sense, he did refer discursively to correlation and to Bowley, Pearson, Galton, and Yule, but did not apply their techniques to any concrete problem. His method of analyzing data consisted of presenting marginal distributions and inspecting them. As for the type of research he conducted, it is illustrated in the chapter on the "significance of casual groups" (groups incidentally assembled). In a study of such groups, a class of students was requested to answer questions on their leisure-time activities. From the frequency distribution to questions such as "How many times a year do you play a physical exercise game, mental exercise game, read a novel, go to the theater, the concert, to church?" Giddings concluded that "in the reactions of causal groups to situations, a spontaneous and approximately multi-individual response is basic, but is complicated by interstimulation and response, particularly by example and imitation. A consciousness of kind is always discoverable and usually is obvious."[149]

Giddings' only methodological innovation is an early attempt at converting ordinal data into a quantitative scale, a procedure he termed the "social marking system."[150] As a concrete illustration, he ranked ethnic and nationality groups in the United States according to the popular prestige order, from native-born of native white parents (scale position 0), native-born of foreign-born white (1), foreign-born, English-speaking (2), northwestern Europeans (3), southern Europeans and Latin American white (4), eastern Europeans (5), all other white (6), civilized yellow (7), civilized dark (8), to uncivilized (9). He then stated that there is a "scientific" way of checking popular markings by assigning one point each for the following attributes of these groups: if the parents are native-born, if self is native-born, if native language is that of the United States, if reared under Celto-Teutonic traditions and cultural influences, if reared under constitutional government, if of European stock and reared in European civilization, if from a race that has created an independent political state with a history, if from a race that has created a literature, if from a race that has independently raised above barbarism, if color lighter than yellow, lighter than red, lighter than brown, and finally lighter than black. Nor surprisingly, native-born of white parents again tops the list with the maximum 14 points. Similar "scientific" rankings were applied to religious groups (Protestants end up with 8 or 7 points, Jews with 1), education strata, and other population attributes, and were then applied to the 1880 and 1890 U.S. Census classifications of the population by race and nationality, from which Giddings concluded after computing various indices of heterogeneity that the American population is becoming more heterogeneous in ethnic composition.[151]

Giddings summarized his theoretic ideas centered on the principle of "consciousness of kind" in a paper at the 1903 AEA and American Historical Association meetings where his dogmatism and sociological imperialism antagonized historians.[152] In his view, men collectively respond to primary stimuli (common sentiments due to shared ethnic and racial background) and secondary stimuli (ideals, political beliefs, constitutions). Their collective response explains the phenomena of social conflict, adaptation and selection, modes of cooperation, the great processes of history, and the principles of social organization: "In a homogeneous group, the cooperation of individuals is spontaneous. Their organization may be democratic in form and in spirit . . . ," whereas in a heterogeneous group, "There are inequalities of energy and ability . . . the population is differentiated into leaders and followers." Such a population cannot spontaneously combine its efforts in cooperative undertakings. This must be brought about by "fear of torture, imprisonment, death, that is, despotic rule." Only after a large measure of assimilation has been completed might a monarchy or oligarchy replace despotism based on force. Democracy is feasible only in homogeneous populations. How is it then that the great American melting pot has nevertheless maintained a democratic polity? Ideals (secondary stimuli) "become a factor of chief importance in the higher forms of social causation" and overcome the limitations imposed by ethnic and social diversity.

Not impressed by this universal theory and irritated by Giddings' proclamation that only a history that is aiming at generalizations such as his or making use of his "laws" can be termed a "science," the historians present reacted sharply. George Burr replied:

I have listened with much interest to the speculations of Professor Giddings. . . . But if you ask me as a student of history for a verdict upon them, I can only make the plea which I think lawyers call "confession and avoidance." They are very fine, they may well be very true. But the thing of which Professor Giddings is talking is not history. . . . the philosophy of history which followers of Auguste Comte in France, England, and the United States prefer to know as sociology may well have for us its high use, if we can ever agree as to its province and its name.

Willis West echoed these sentiments:

. . . I have found no one who will accept as satisfactory the relationship between history and sociology set forth tonight by the sociologists. . . . sociologists can ill afford to fling these disagreeable missiles about so recklessly until they move into less breakable and less transparent houses than those that have so far sheltered them. . . .

In ironical tones he termed Giddings' exposition generous because he at least allowed to history the chronological arrangement of events. He concluded, "historians do object to any quaint assumption of a division of labor that tries to exclude them from reasoning about history."[153] Small and Ward who were present that evening came to Giddings' defense even while they were trying to placate the historians, but the damage had already been done.

Giddings' personality and prejudices were thus blocking the emergence of a really first-rate sociology department at Columbia. But some of his students, notably Ogburn, Chapin, and Odum, rose to prominence in American sociology and were instrumental in the subsequent transformation of sociology. Columbia was a great university with prominent scholars: Franz Boas in anthropology; Charles Beard in history before the New School schism; J. B. Clark and Seligman in economics; Dewey in philosophy. Ogburn's *Social Change* (1922) is heavily indebted to the anthropologists Boas, Lowie, Wissler, and Kroeber, and follows directly Boas in rejecting culture-change theories based on racial and biological theories and Giddings' "consciousness of kind" as explanatory principles. The new mathematical-statistical techniques that Ogburn and Chapin were to diffuse in American social science journals and that Giddings was only familiar with in passing they learned from Henry L. Moore, one of the first econometricians, who was on the Columbia faculty at that time and who frequently visited the statistical laboratory of Galton, Pearson, and Edgeworth in London.[154] Exposure to these newer techniques gave Columbia sociology students the opportunity to play a leading role in the introduction of quantitative techniques in sociology, an opportunity that they fully seized.

Of 21 articles and books published in 1922 or earlier on research methodology in the broad sense, Ogburn led with 5 and Chapin was second with 3, just as Stuart Rice, another Columbia graduate, was the statistical pioneer in political science, and Thorndike, at Teachers' College, was a leader in mental measurement in education research.[155]

British statisticians were first in the field with basic statistical texts that covered the subject matter through multiple and partial correlation.[156] In the United States the most comprehensive and advanced text based on the British models was F. C. Mills' *Statistical Methods* (1924). Mills taught business statistics at Columbia. In sociology, another Columbia graduate and faculty member, Robert Chaddock, published *Principles and Methods of Statistics* in 1925. This was a more elementary treatment than Mills', but gave detailed computational routines for correlation and regression, and instructions, complete with photographs, for the operation of key punch and countersorter equipment. In the field of research methods specifically, F. Stuart Chapin's *Field Work and Social Research* (1920) was the first "modern" textbook and already had an elementary exposition of random sampling, the preparation of interview schedules, coding, classifying, and tabulating data, including a photograph of a punch card, in contrast to earlier texts such as Carol Aronovici's *The Social Survey* (1916) and M. C. Elmer's *Technique of Social Surveys* (1917) that still had a chapter on "Publicity," that is how to organize a photographic civic exhibit of survey results to mobilize the citizenry for reform.

The newer quantitative techniques took a long time in penetrating the periodical literature. Here too Columbia graduates played a pioneering role. Until about 1910 the *Journal of the American Statistical Association (JASA)* all but ignored the new British mathematical statistics. This fact was recognized and sadly commented upon in the 1908 presidential address of the American Statistical Association.[157] The following year, however, Yule's text was reviewed, and the econometrician Warren Persons introduced to American social scientists and statisticians in the *JASA* the use of the correlation coefficient, the regression line, curvilinear regression, and their applications to time series. In 1914 and 1915 five Columbia graduates, Ogburn, Chapin, Chaddock, Gillin, and Gehlke, published in it empirical-statistical articles. In Volume 16 (1918/1919), Ogburn demonstrated the use of multiple regression equations in his analysis of the standard of living in Washington.[158] Finally, in the early 1920s the *JASA* began to publish routinely methodological and technical articles, especially on the problem of time series analysis, business cycles, index numbers, and correlation, written by mathematical statisticians and econometricians, to which Ogburn, Dorothy Thomas, Chapin, and Stuart Rice repeatedly made contributions of an applied nature.

        The *Political Science Quarterly*, edited at Columbia, was primarily historical and public law and government in orientation, but here again Ogburn as well as Stuart Rice introduced the application of regression and other quantitative techniques for the empirical analysis of electoral and legislative processes.[159] Stuart Rice also introduced these techniques in the pages of the *American Political Science Review* in 1926.[160] The *Annals of the American Academy of Social and Political Science* was in this period filled with articles on labor legislation, municipal reform, housing conditions, with occasional excursions into immigration and the black problem in the South and was similar to the *AJS* in this respect. As for sociology proper, the *AJS* proceeded only slowly and cautiously to abandon its social reform orientation and to concern itself with methodological issues and statistical applications, a task made difficult by the refusal of easterners to publish in it, except as part of ASS *Proceedings*. It was not until the late 1920s that empirical research papers (other than the muckraking type) were published in it routinely. The Columbia boycott was broken in Volume 16 (1910/1911) when John Gillin published a three-part paper on the "Sociology of Sects." Gillin, Chapin, and the Yale graduate H. P. Fairchild contributed papers in the following years. The first major methodological and statistical paper was Chapin's "Elements of Scientific Methodology in Sociology" (Vol. 20, 1914/1915) in which he referred to Bowley and Yule, discussed the concept of random sample, but concentrated on distributions and descriptive statistics primarily. While a brief note in Volume 21 (1915/1916) did illustrate the use of the correlation coefficient, [161] the most usual "methodological" articles in the *AJS* were concerned with the social survey movement and its relation to academic sociology rather than with bread-and-butter technical issues in the application of survey methodology. It was not until Volume 30 (1924/1925) that Chapin broke the ice on the new statistical techniques in a quantitative reanalysis of data published between 1910 and 1915 in the *AJS* by Chicago School of Civics and Philanthropy students on housing conditions in Chicago.[162] He illustrated and discussed the use of the correlation coefficient, regression equation, confidence intervals, nonlinear regression, and gave full computational routines. Specialized empirical papers oriented to testing a specific hypothesis in a quantitative manner as we know them today did not take up much space in the *AJS* until about 1926 when Pitrim Sorokin, Carle Zimmerman, Jerome Davis, George Lundberg, Read Bain, and others started publishing their papers in it, papers notably in the area of rural sociology.

In contrast to the *AJS*, the *Publications* of the American Sociological Society was a little more rapid in introducing quantitative techniques to sociologists. In 1911 (Vol. 6) Columbia graduate Gillin published "The Application of the Social Survey to Small Communities," and the rural economist G. H. von Tungeln provided a concrete illustration of it in Volume 13 (1918). In Volume 18 (1923), Ogburn applied multiple regression techniques to a problem in family sociology,[163] and that same year a committee on research started compiling for the ASS a list of research projects conducted by sociologists. The 1924 annual meetings had a section and committee on social research chaired by Ogburn. In 1925 a new Division of Statistics with Chapin in charge was formed, and the Division of Social Research was headed by Gehlke, another Columbia graduate. Meanwhile at the sections on rural sociology and on social research empirical papers were presented. From that time on papers on empirical social research became more or less routine at the annual meetings. Columbia graduates thus played a key role in the process of introducing and diffising up-to-date quantitative techniques within American sociology, a process that was greatly speeded up when Ogburn, the major innovator in this respect, accepted a professorship at Chicago in 1927 and had a decisive impact on faculty and students there, notably Burgess, Stouffer, Bogue, Duncan, Hauser, and others.

chicago

The Chicago department has been the subject of a recent book by Faris and it is therefore not necessary to repeat an

account of its outstanding accomplishments and leading figures.[164] My
interpretation of just how Chicago was able to break through from the
older to the present-day sociology differs from Faris' in a number of
respects. To be sure, as Faris contends, Small was a great organizer and
department builder lacking the dogmatism of Giddings and the individualism of Sumner, yet, except for W. I. Thomas, the pre-World War I
Chicago sociology department was not intellectually exceptional and
atypical with its emphasis on vocational training for social reformers
and social workers and on Chicago urban problems. The *American
Journal of Sociology*, as noted above, was not a very scholarly journal
and within sociology itself was mainly a publication vehicle for Chicago
faculty and students and Small's friends within sociology like Ward and
Ross. As at Columbia, it was the entire university setting that proved
decisive: its sheer size and intellectual and material resources, high salary
scales to attract outstanding scholars, a university president pushing
faculty research and willing to reduce teaching loads, the formation of
the interdisciplinary social science group that made for a mutually bene-
ficial collaboration between political scientists and sociologists, and the
university's special relationship with the Rockefellers who provided the
Chicago social scientists with ample research funds. Last but not least
was the impact of Park, a man dedicated to social research, an outstanding teacher with the ability to motivate others and the willingness to
help their work, and with a clear idea of what sociology was all about
and the drive and means to realize his conception.

Brought to Chicago by Harper in 1892 to
develop sociology, Small was sensitive to the fact that he had to make
good on such an unprecedented opportunity. He was the number one
tireless "promoter" and booster of sociology as Barnes so aptly put it.
He himself did no empirical research. He was a historian of social
thought and instrumental in presenting the ideas of the German historical school of economists, the philosophers of history, and the conflict
theories of Gumplowitz and Ratzenhofer to American social scientists.
Others at Chicago in the early years were Small's student George Vincent, son of a president of the Chautauqua Assembly, who later left the
department for the presidency of the University of Minnesota and later
president of the Rockefeller Foundation, and Charles Henderson, essentially a social reformer who handled the practical and vocational training of students in collaboration with city welfare and charitable
agencies and who wrote one of the earliest handbooks for practical
sociologists, the *Catechism of Social Observation* (1894). W. I. Thomas,
the fourth member of the faculty and second Ph.D. student under
Small, was not much influenced by Small or Henderson. He later wrote
that "I remember that Professor Henderson, of sainted memory, once

requested me to get him a bit of information from the saloons. He said that he had never himself entered a saloon or tasted beer."[165]

Thomas himself was cut of different wood. After he had studied language and philosophy in Germany and taught English at Oberlin for three years, he went to Chicago and earned a Ph.D. degree in 1896. It was not until his postgraduate years that his intellectual interests took a decisive turn when he became fascinated with folk psychology through Wilhelm Wundt.[166] He then turned to a study of ethnographic sources, from which resulted *The Source Book for Social Origins* (1909), a compilation and systematic classification of anthropological materials. It is interesting to note that the Durkheim group was doing the same sort of work in France at this time in the pages of the *Année sociologique*. The subsequent *Polish Peasant* was an application of the ethnographic method to contemporary materials and in Read Bain's estimation was "a monumental instance of the revolt against 'armchair' sociology."[167] Park himself acknowledged that "Thomas' work established the tradition of research at Chicago . . . lifting American sociology from its concern with 'social problems' to a concern with theoretical problems."[168] He was fired from Chicago in 1918 after being arrested on a charge involving violations of the Mann Act, despite Small's support and a subsequent dismissal of the charges. It was a severe loss, but did not diminish his intellectual influence among Chicago students who were responsible for electing him president of the ASS in 1927, though he was not on the official ballot. Thomas later freelanced in social research in New York supported by various foundations.

The Polish Peasant in Europe and in America, written in collaboration with Florian Znaniecki and published in five volumes between 1918 and 1920, was singled out for review by the Social Science Research Council in a 1938 conference as the most important piece of American sociological research up to that time. In an autobiographical note at the conference, Thomas himself described the origins of the study. He was concerned with the process of immigration and the changes that immigrants experienced as they moved from rural-peasant Europe into the urban-industrial United States. In 1908 he received a $5000 research grant from Helen Culver, the heiress who also had backed Jane Addams' Hull House at Chicago. In journals of folklore he found no data on peasants aside from trivia such as the coloring of Easter eggs and their superstitions. The lack of data forced him into field work. He settled on studying Poles because of the availability of records and because they were the most disorganized of all immigrant groups in Chicago. During eight periods of field work (the University of Chicago was exceptional in allowing faculty to absent itself for research purposes), he assembled altogether 8000 documents, including the files of a journal that published peasant letters covering a 20-year period. In 1914 Znaniecki, who was trained in philosophy and headed the Bureau for the Protection of Emigrants in Poland, was recruited as collaborator when he was inadvertently stranded in the United States at the outbreak of the war.[169]

       The *Polish Peasant* was ambitious in scope. It tried to capture the totality of social change for an entire population group in the process of being absorbed into American life. Many of the subsequent concerns of the Chicago tradition were present in that work: immigration, assimilation, family disorganization in an urban setting, culture change and nationalism, an emphasis on process rather than on structure. Methodologically it exemplified the Chicago style of open-ended research, stronger on the side of discovery than on the side of proof. In a 1928 note to Park, who had asked him about his method of study, Thomas described this research style in the following way: "It is my experience that formal methodological studies are relatively unprofitable. . . . progress in method is made from point-to-point by setting up objectives, employing certain techniques, then resetting the problems with the introduction of still other objectives and the modification of techniques. . . . some of us, in connection with some experience, raised a question, 'What would happen if we were able to secure the life records of a large number of persons. . . .?' After some experimentation, yourself [Park], Shaw, and others have been interested in the preparation of very systematic and elaborate life histories. In this connection it is noted that the behavior of young persons is dependent upon their social status and the regions in which they live. Studies are then made from an ecological standpoint. It is discovered that children brought into the juvenile court are predominantly from certain localities in the city. The rate of delinquency is related to gang life and gang life is related to localities. Thrasher then makes a study of the gang from this standpoint. As comparative observations multiply, Shaw undertakes to determine how the cases of boys brought in the juvenile court for stealing are connected with gang life and determines that 90 percent of these boys did their stealing in groups of two or more. In the search for the causes of delinquency, it then appears that the delinquent and nondelinquent are often very much alike. . . . at present, we have introduced the plan of using nondelinquent groups as a control in connection with studies of the causation of delinquency. . . . we move from point to point without necessarily making any formidable attempt to rationalize and generalize the process. It is only . . . since we abandoned the search for standardized methods based largely on the work of dead men, that we have made the beginnings which I have indicated."[170] This statement

illustrates at once both the strength and weakness of the Chicago researchers. On the positive side, collaboration by faculty and students
in a joint and continuous research enterprise, guided more by partial
results and a feel for social processes emerging from the investigation
itself than by premature research plan with clearly formulated hypotheses and study design; on the negative side, a tendency to underestimate
the power and flexibility provided by quantitative methods when properly used. Shils has observed in this connection that Park's students did
not use Bogardus' social distance scale or Thurstone's attitude measurement technique, though both were or had been associated with Chicago
and their techniques were applicable to research on ethnic groups undertaken by the Chicago researchers.[171]
                    The central figure in the Chicago breakthrough
was Robert Ezra Park.[172] He was recruited by Thomas after a chance
meeting at Tuskegee Institute and joined the faculty in 1914 when he
was already 50 years old. After college, Park went into newspaper work
where he was in charge of the city desk for the Sunday edition and
acquired a wide knowledge of city life and city problems. After continuing his education in Germany under Simmel and Windelband and at
Harvard where he was an assistant in philosophy to William James, he
became "sick and tired of the academic world, and wanted to get back
to the world of men." The opportunity for it came after a meeting with
Booker T. Washington. Park became his secretary at Tuskegee Institute
for the following seven years during which he got familiar "with the life,
and customs, and the condition of the Negro people." Thus before entering a late academic career, Park recalled that he had "covered more
ground, tramping about in cities in different parts of the world than
any other living man. Out of all this I gained among other things a conception of the city, of the community, and the region, not as a geographical phenomenon merely, but as a kind of social organism." The
important fact here is that these varied experiences were acquired on
top of an already systematically schooled mind, so that Park's reaction
to them was at a theoretical level, not just at the level of humanitarian
concern. At the same time, not being part of the academic world and
not having to concern himself with problems of legitimacy and with
intellectual controversies, he was freed from the pressures and conven-
tions that so often dry up the imagination and the willingness to take
intellectual risks.
                    At Chicago, Park "lived research" and took
under his wing promising students with whom he spent long hours in
conversation, often supplying them with the central framework and
ideas for their dissertation. Park had a talent for formulating research
problems. His 1915 paper "The City, Suggestions for the Investigation

of Human Behavior in the Urban Environment" contains much of the
research program that was subsequently undertaken at Chicago. He was
well read and open to ideas from all quarters. In his 1915 paper he refers among others to C. H. Cooley, Walter Bagehot, W. I. Thomas, W. G.
Sumner, Lord Bryce, Emile Zola, Robert Woods, and the Pittsburgh
Survey. The 1921 *Introduction to the Science of Society* edited with
Burgess, that became the basic sociology reader for many years, shows
him drawing on the European tradition of Simmel, LeBon, Dicey, Sorel,
Durkheim, Tönnies, as well as to a lesser extent on some Social Darwinists and on all of the founding fathers of American sociology and
the pragmatist philosophers. The arrangement and choice of topics in
that text represent a radical theoretical departure from the earlier
"social problems" oriented sociology texts and the "grand-systems"
emphasis of Giddings and Ward. Park stressed social processes: social
contacts, social interaction, social forces, competition, conflict, accomodation, assimilation, collective behavior, social control. In the typical
Park style, each chapter had an up-to-date bibliography and a long list
of questions for discussion and further research, many of them still
eminently topical and researchable.[173]

In his theoretical approach Park parted with
the atomistic and psychological approach then exemplified by Giddings
to rejoin the mainstream of European social action theory. He wrote
that

While it is true that society has this double aspect, the individual and the collective,
it is the assumption of this volume that the touchstone of society, the thing that
distinguishes a mere collection of individuals from a society, is not like-mindedness,
but corporate action. We may apply the term social to any group of individuals
which is capable of consistent action . . . directed to a common end.[174]

Park saw in the city a "laboratory" in which human nature and social
processes could be most conveniently and profitably studied.[175] Reviewing the state of social research in 1921, he wrote accurately that "sociological research is at present in about the situation in which psychology
was before the introduction of laboratory methods. . . . A great deal of
social information has been collected merely for the purpose of determining what to do in any given case. Facts have not been collected to
check social theories. Social problems have been defined in terms of
common sense and facts have been collected for the most part to support this or that doctrine, not to test it. . . . "[176] It is this state of affairs
that Park and his collaborators set out to change.

The work of the Chicago school, already comprehensively described and illustrated in Faris and in Burgess and
Bogue's recent compilation,[177] did not represent a radical break with

established social research techniques. They rather adopted and systematized methods already in existence, applied theoretic concerns to research problems, and conducted research on a wide interdisciplinary front with a large number of adequately financed faculty and students participating. For instance, the concept of the city as a "laboratory" or "workshop" had been a widely discussed idea for almost twenty years.[178] The problems of immigration, ethnic groups, and social disorganization in a big city had already been studied by Robert Woods in Boston and at Chicago by students in the School of Civics and Philanthropy, but in the popular photographic social survey style.[179] Scholarly research based on painstaking field work, making use of graphs, maps, charts, and tables, and focusing on Chicago immigrant neighborhoods and ecologically distinct areas, had already been part of the best of the Chicago dissertation tradition.[180] Working relations with Chicago social agencies had already been established. It was especially in its organizational aspects that the Chicago research of the 1920s differed from the previous atomized efforts.

      The Chicago department was responsible for an innovation that greatly advanced continuity and cumulation in social research: The integrated series of student dissertations concentrated the collective effort of students on the same topics—urban sociology, ecology, the contemporary Chicago scene. Elsewhere the German tradition of students picking idiosyncratic topics under loose faculty supervision was followed. The unique Social Science group provided a favorable setting at Chicago for interdisciplinary collaboration and division of labor in research. The total social science faculty with Mead, Sapir, Merriam, Park, and others had an impact upon students outside of their specialties. The pragmatic influence in the philosophy department meant a relative lack of resistance by the older humanities to social science research. The faculty club was a live center for the exchange of ideas and interdisciplinary discussions. In particular, the sociologists were able to forge an alliance with the political scientists who were academically more established and hence in a better position to raise research funds in the university and with the foundations. What the political scientists sought in return was the sociologists' longer experience and greater skill in empirical research.[181] In political science the presence of an older and entrenched political theory and public law orientation acted as a break to innovation in an empirical direction. In the early 1920s, however, Charles F. Merriam at Chicago led a nucleus of his colleagues in an attempt to establish an empirically grounded "science of politics." It is their efforts through the American Political Science Association's Committee on Political Research that led to the creation of the Social Science Research Council in 1923. Merriam gathered about him a group of able younger scholars receptive to his novel conception of political science, Harold Gosnell, Harold Lasswell, V. O. Key, Jr., Quincey Wright, Leonard White, Gabriel Almond, David Truman, Avery Leiserson, and others, who implemented their intellectual program with a series of empirical investigations into politics, electoral processes and voting, city government, corruption and machine politics, and other topics that were carried out contemporaneously with the Chicago sociologists' own research program. It was this Chicago political science group, following the depression and World War II, at a time when many of them had achieved senior positions in their profession, that set the stage for the "behavioral" reorientation of their discipline.[182]

The interdisciplinary aspect and broad range of the entire Chicago research enterprise can be followed in the Chicago symposia held from time to time to describe and evaluate the entire program.[183] Starting in 1923, the university set up the Local Community Research Committee which supported faculty and student research with contributions from and in cooperation with civic clubs, social agencies, and foundations. These resources were vastly augmented when the Laura Spellman Rockefeller Memorial (later Rockefeller Foundation) under Beardsley Ruml made considerable funds available for the Social Science Building and the appointment of research professors. The building became a workshop of 200 social scientists devoted to research and graduate activities crossing departmental lines. The Chicago spirit of active faculty research is well captured in the following novel formulation

. . . the University Professor who accompanies a police squad on a series of midnight raids . . . or who comes to know by personal contact a large proportion of the precinct captains of the city is a more intelligent and useful instructor than one who reads of these things in books. To the extent that graduate students, in the role of research assistants, also participate in those contacts, . . . stimulation and intensification takes place.[184]

The university administration not only encouraged faculty research, but made it publicly visible through the publication of the symposia and a handbook entitled *The University Faculty*, in which comparisons of research output were presented by department, and even by professors according to rank.

University of Chicago policy on social science research and its unique organizational structure bore the fruits the administration expected, and in sociology led to the empirical breakthrough and first transformation of U.S. sociology that are described elsewhere.[185] Chicago sociologists dominated American sociology from the early 1920s up to about World War II. In the 11 years from 1924 to

1934, 9 ASS presidents were Chicago faculty members and/or Chicago graduates. Sociological fields not developed by the Chicago nucleus of the early 1920s, such as the quantitative and methodological specialties, were put in charge of Ogburn who was recruited from Columbia in 1927. Chicago established a successful satellite system throughout the Middle West. Its graduates would spread out to staff the universities there, including the chairmanships of sociology departments, and the most promising and outstanding graduates would be recalled to top positions in Chicago. This system of rewards and mobility was exceedingly successful while it was expanding because of the increase in number of departments and of faculty positions in the 1920s, although Chicago did not succeed in penetrating Columbia and Harvard, its chief rivals at the total university level. However, when the depression hit, the reward system stopped expanding, and even shrank, especially, in the state universities of the Middle West. The very success of the Chicago department made for a surplus of qualified and prominent Chicago graduates who hoped to rejoin its faculty at this critical time. This sudden contraction of opportunities for professional advancement led to rivalry and bitterness between some members of the Chicago group itself and even more intensely within the entire sociological profession where Chicago dominance within the ASS and its grip on the job market at a time of scarce opportunities for the placement of graduates was resented. The consequences of the depression for the sociological profession and the anti-Chicago sentiments that it brought to the fore are responsible for the 1935-1936 changes within the ASS that for a time even threatened to split it into two hostile camps, in particular for the founding of the *American Sociological Review*.

a new professional ideology

While the Chicago school managed to reorient American sociology away from the earlier sociological imperialism, system building, and charities and corrections emphasis, the development of sociology between 1920 and 1940 was not an unqualified success. The Chicago transformation had an impact only upon the minority of sociologists trained at a handful of leading universities. A gap between the leaders of sociology represented by these institutions and the vast majority of teachers of sociology in the United States was increasingly evident. Moreover, the Chicago school remained to some extent parochial in its emphasis, especially when the depression, labor conflict, and the rise of European fascism and nazism came to dominate national and international concerns. It neglected the problems of social class and stratification and the fundamental questions of authority, social order, and the mass society.

To be sure, from the point of view of increased student enrollments and sociology courses, autonomous sociology departments, greater acceptance of the discipline in the academic world, participation in interdisciplinary bodies, foundation- and government-sponsored research, sociology made important strides. Bernard reports that in 219 universities and colleges that had been surveyed in 1909, the number of sociology courses had increased from 815 to 3420 in the 1940-1944 period, and that in a total of 441 institutions over 5000 sociology courses were offered in the 1940s.[186] Sociologists were actively participating in the Social Science Research Council; they were collaborating in prestigious interdisciplinary projects such as the President's Research Committee on Social Trends. Yet, outside of a few elite institutions and their satellites, the field remained oriented to teaching and vocational training in social work and served as a repository of leftover subject matter as it had in the earlier period. In Bernard's survey of 1940-1944, about 50 percent of all sociology courses taught in the United States were either elementary, or dealing with such topics as family and marriage, criminology, penology and delinquency, social disorganization and poverty, social betterment, and social control and the control aspects of other social problems.[187] Surveys of the interests of members of the ASS and the annual census of the ASS Committee on Research show that a majority of members were not engaged in any research at all, and that the earlier concern with social problems, social work, and the family persisted.[188] Most teachers of sociology were not members of the ASS. While the society had grown to 1021 members in 1920, it still had only 1034 members in 1940. In the late 1920s, a special rate for students boosted membership temporarily to about 1500, but these gains were wiped out during the depression. Even among ASS members, a 1942 study reported that 25 percent did not consider themselves primarily sociologists.[189]

Faced with the consequences of the overexpansion of sociology in terms of competent and professionally trained manpower, the inertia of the majority of teachers of sociology and the continuing problem of academic recognition, some of the leaders of U.S. sociology responded by severing the earlier alliance with the social reform and Progressive movements and by forging a new professional ideology. After World War I, the reform movement was weak in any case and no longer needed to help introduce sociology in additional institutions of learning. Indeed such an alliance was increasingly embarrassing so far as achieving higher status and gaining rewards within the academic world. The exclusive reference group for many sociologists became the professional scientific community in the university. This meant that the visible signs of a science, notably the use of quantitative techniques, were championed to the exclusion of "softer" techniques, although this was done under the banner of creating a truly "scientific" sociology. To gain access to research funds and to participate in inter-disciplinary collaboration and advisory positions at all levels of govern-ment, sociologists stressed that their theories and techniques were value-free and politically neutral, especially since sociology and socialism still tended to be confused in the public view.

Gillin's ASS presidential address of 1926 al-ready reflects the emergence of the new professional ideology as a weapon to be used to eliminate the "undesirables" from sociology:

In certain of our institutions it has unfortunately been true that sociology has been advocated by men who had no adequate understanding of scholarship. In their hands it was a mess of undigested, unsystematized, unscrutinized generalities which made a popular appeal to sophomores and attendants at Chautauquas. . . . While some of these, unfortunately, are still with us, the application of the scientific method and the increased emphasis upon objective data have been acting as selective agents in consigning these enemies of sociology to a deserved innocuous desuetude. Doubtless we shall have to put up with some of them longer, inasmuch as there is no sociological orthodoxy and no sociological inquisition or holy office by which these fellows can be eliminated. Emphasis upon rigidly scientific methods will attend to them.[190]

In this view, quantitative techniques are a weapon in the hands of some sociologists to purge from the profession others who have become an inconvenience for its continued rise.

Perhaps the clearest statement of the new professional ideology, the stress on value-free sociology, the separation of the roles of scientist from that of the citizen and reformer, and the emphasis on limited, specific, and quantitatively oriented sociological research that would in small increments build up a scientifically founded sociology, was provided in the writings and addresses of William F. Og-burn, the Progressive of the 1910s who in later years represented the pinnacle of achievement for sociologists: Columbia professor hired by the University of Chicago, Chairman of the Social Science Research Coun-cil, Director of Research of the President's Research Committee on Social Trends, President of the American Sociological Society and the American Statistical Association, vice-president of the American Asso-ciation for the Advancement of Science, and many other honors and distinctions. For Ogburn, the matter of objectivity was simple: ". . . a multiplication table should be reliable both for the Tory and the Com-munist . . . ," and the same ideal was relevant for sociology.[191] In his 1929 presidential address, he stated that "sociology as a science is not interested in making the world a better place to live," although sociologists as human beings (and Ogburn himself) may be deeply committed to producing knowledge that is relevant to human progress and as citizens may wish to participate in ameliorative activities.[192] Sociology will grow into a science "by the accumulation of bits and pieces of new knowledge" meticulously verified by the application of quantitative techniques. In the future, nearly every sociologist will be a statistician. "In the past the great names in sociology have been social theorists and social philosophers. But this will not be the case in the future. . . . a scientific sociology will be quite sharply separated from social philosophy, for it will be recognized how much social philosophy is a rationalization of wishes." At the conclusion of his address he stated in poignant terms that, "The happy ending for a scientific sociology will be its achievement. It will be necessary to crush out emotion and to discipline the mind so strongly that the fanciful pleasures of intellectuality will have to be eschewed in the verification process; it will be desirable to taboo ethics and values (except in choosing problems); and it will be inevitable that we shall have to spend most of our time doing hard, dull, tedious, and routine tasks. . . . it is not necessary for a scientist to be a scientist all of the time. He can temporarily shut the door to his laboratory and open for a while his door to the beauty of the stars, to the romance of life, to the service of his fellow men, to the leadership of the cause, to the applause of his audience, or to the adventure in the great out-of-doors. But when he returns to his laboratory he will leave these behind; although there is a beauty, a romance, a service, a leadership, and an adventure of a kind to be found in the laboratory."[193] No statement of the subsequently dominant professional ideology of American sociologists has since been expressed in more moving and eloquent words.

Ogburn's view did not remain unchallenged. In particular, Robert MacIver's 1930 presidential address, "Is Sociology a Natural Science?" was a reply to Ogburn and his supporters.[194] An even more radical critique of the new professional ideology was provided by Robert Lynd in *Knowledge for What.*[195] Lynd objected to sociology moving in the direction of accomodation with the American establishment and the influential public and the resulting uncritical acceptance of how American society was organized, how it operated, and what its crucial problems were. In their desire for collective professional mobility and recognition, sociologists hid behind the façade of value-free social science that spared them the risk of radical social criticism and unpopular suggestions for the remedy of social problems. Techniques developed in advance of substantive subject matter dictated the choice of problems to be investigated. Lynd expressed misgivings about the laissez faire organization of social research in which research topics were chosen because of personal convenience and quick rewards while important areas of national concern were left uninvestigated.

It is important to realize that the controversy over the professional ideology appropriate for sociologists was not identical with, though it was often confused with, some other methodological controversies pitting the advocates of qualitative and quantative techniques against each other. Neither MacIver nor Lynd was opposed to empirical social research or to quantitative techniques as such. On the other side, Ogburn and some of his supporters like Dorothy Thomas admitted that statistical techniques could easily be abused and that other techniques provided indispensable insights into sociological subject matter. Yet, basically, for Ogburn, both intellectualism and a concern with practical social problems and social engineering were the major obstacle to a cumulative science of society, while Lynd watched with dismay the fragmentation of sociology into an anarchy of limited and specialized research areas (the "empirical radicalism" often commented upon by Europeans) shedding no light on the major controversies of the period.

Despite grudging recognition of the validity of Lynd's views, it is primarily the orientation expressed by Ogburn that has become institutionalized within American sociology as our professional ideology. Whether this ideology has served sociologists well so far as collective mobility for the profession, higher academic prestige and public esteem, and the creation of a scientific sociology are concerned, is a difficult matter to establish and one upon which certain doubts can be expressed and have repeatedly been expressed.[196] Yet there can be little doubt that with its institutionalization sociology severed the remaining tenuous links with its modest and obscure origins.

notes

1   Joseph Ben-David, "The Scientific Role," *Minerva*, 4 (Autumn 1965), 15-54; Ben-David and A. Zloczower, "Universities and Academic Systems in Modern Society," *Archives Européennes de Sociologie,* 3 (1962), 45-84; and Ben-David and Randall Collins, "Social Factors in the Origins of New Science," *American Sociological Review,* 3 (August 1966), 451-465.
2   Louis Wirth, "American Sociology, 1915-1947," *American Journal of Sociology, Index to Volumes 1-52*, pp. 273-281.
3   Robert K. Merton, "Social Conflict over Styles of Sociological Work," *Transactions of the Fourth World Congress of Sociology,* 3 (1959), 21-46.

4 Edward Shils, "The Contemplation of Society in America," in Arthur M. Schlesinger, Jr., and Morton White, eds., *Paths of American Thought* (Boston: Houghton Mifflin, 1963).

5 Albion W. Small, "50 Years of Sociology in the United States, 1865-1915," in *American Journal of Sociology, Index to Volumes 1-52* (1895-1947), p. 225.

6 Richard Hofstadter, *The Age of Reform* (New York: Vintage Books, 1955).

7 Paul Samuelson, "Economic Thought and the New Individualism," in Schlesinger and White, *op. cit.*, p. 227.

8 Max Lerner, "The Triumph of Laissez-Faire," in Schlesinger and White, *op. cit.*, p. 153.

9 Richard Hofstadter, *Social Darwinism in American Thought* (Boston: Beacon, 1955), p. 5.

10 *Ibid.*, p. 6.

11 *Ibid.*, p. 41.

12 *Ibid.*, p. 43.

13 *Ibid.*, pp. 22-23, 45, 48.

14 Richard Hofstadter, "The Revolution in Higher Education," in Schlesinger and White, *op. cit.*, p. 275.

15 Abraham Flexner, *I Remember* (New York: Simon & Schuster, 1940), p. 46.

16 Abraham Flexner, *Universities: American, English, German* (London: Oxford University Press, 1930), p. 47.

17 Bernard Berelson [*Graduate Education in the U.S.* (New York: McGraw-Hill, 1960), p. 11] reports that during the nineteenth century about 10,000 Americans went to Germany for graduate study, relatively few to France.

18 Richard T. Ely, *Ground Under Our Feet* (New York: Macmillan, 1938).

19 Flexner, *Universities*, p. 47.

20 Ely, *op. cit.*, p. 100.

21 Flexner, *Universities*, p. 80.

22 Flexner, *I Remember*, p. 49.

23 R. Gordon Hoxie *et al.*, *A History of the Faculty of Political Science, Columbia University* (New York: Columbia University Press, 1955), pp. 1-70.

24 Frank L. Tolman, "The Study of Sociology in Institutions of Learning in the United States," *American Journal of Sociology*, 7 (1901/1902), p. 815.

25 *Ibid.*, p. 823.

26 Flexner, *Universities*, p. 184.

27 Howard Odum, ed., *American Masters of Social Science* (New York: Holt, Rinehart & Winston, 1927), p. 157.

28 Small, *op. cit.*, p. 204.

29 Robert E. Faris, *Chicago Sociology, 1920-1932* (San Francisco: Chandler, 1967), p. 23.

30 Quoted in Richard Hofstadter and Wilson Smith, eds., *American Higher Education, A Documentary History*, Vol. 2 (Chicago: University of Chicago Press, 1961), p. 759.

31 Alvin Johnson, *Pioneer's Progress* (Lincoln, Neb.: University of Nebraska, Bison Books, 1960), pp. 120 ff.

32 Edward A. Ross, *70 Years of It* (New York: Appleton, 1936), p. 47.

33 *Ibid.*, p. 64

34   Ely, *op. cit.*, p. 184.
35   Ely, *op. cit.*, pp. 183-184.
36   Albert Somit and Joseph Tanenhaus, *The Development of American Political Science* (Boston: Allyn & Bacon, 1967), pp. 25-47.
37   Ely, *op. cit.*, pp. 121, 131-146.
38   Small, *op. cit.*, p. 215.
39   Joseph Dorfman, *The Economic Mind in American Civilization*, Vol. 3 (New York: Viking, 1949), pp. 205-227.
40   Samuelson, *op. cit.*, p. 228.
41   Hoxie *et al.*, *op. cit.*, p. 176.
42   Hofstadter, *Age of Reform*, p. 200.
43   R. C. and G. Hinkle, *The Development of Modern Sociology* (New York: Random House, 1954), p. 3. See also biographical data on ASS presidents in Howard Odum, *American Sociology* (New York: Longmans, 1951).
44   Henry F. May, *Protestant Churches and Industrial America* (New York: Harper & Row, 1949), p. 138.
45   *Ibid.*, p. 116.
46   *Ibid.*, p. 185.
47   *Ibid.*, p. 6.
48   Hofstadter, *op. cit.*, p. 152.
49   *Ibid.*, pp. 150 ff.
50   *Ibid.*, p. 152.
51   For full details, consult May, *op. cit.*, *passim.*
52   First edition, 1897.
53   W. D. P. Bliss, *Encyclopedia of Social Reform* (1897), "Chautauqua Assembly."
54   Ely, *op. cit.*, pp. 70 ff.
55   *Annals of the American Academy of Social and Political Science*, 4 (1893-1894), 194 (hereafter cited as *Annals*).
56   May, *op. cit.*, pp. 194-195.
57   Tolman, *op. cit.*, pp. 823-824.
58   *Ibid.*, p. 825.
59   *Annals*, 4 (1893/1894), 193.
60   *Annals*, 5 (1894/1895), 134-135, 449.
61   *Annals*, 6 (1895), 184.
62   *Annals*, 5 (1894/1895), 818.
63   Faris, *op. cit.*, p. 10.
64   Cf. *The Institute of Social and Religious Research. 1921-1934.*
65   May, *op. cit.*, p. 216.
66   Walter R. Houghton, ed., *Neely's History of the Parliament of Religions* (Chicago, 1894), p. 580.
67   *American Journal of Sociology*, 1 (1895-1896), p. 15.
68   May, *op. cit.*, p. 249.
69   Odum, *American Sociology*, pp. 10, 17, 51 ff, 71, 386, 397.
70   Floyd House, *The Development of Sociology* (New York: McGraw-Hill, 1936), p. 220.
71   Wirth, *op. cit.*, p. 273.

72   Edwin Sutherland, "Social Pathologies," *American Journal of Sociology,* 50 (May 1945), 429.

73   Hofstadter, *Social Darwinism,* p. 119.

74   Hofstadter, *The Age of Reform,* pp. 131-133.

75   *Ibid.,* p. 154.

76   *Ibid.,* pp. 186-199.

77   Odum, *American Masters of Social Sciences,* p. 132.

78   Arthur Mann, *Yankee Reformers in the Urban Age* (Cambridge, Mass.: Harvard University Press, 1954), p. 102.

79   On the ASSA, see Small, *op. cit.,* pp. 211 ff., and Odum, *op. cit.,* pp. 43, 57-58, 68.

80   David Fulcomer, "Instruction in Sociology in Institutions of Learning," *Proceedings of the National Conference of Charities and Corrections,* 21 (1894), pp. 67-78 (hereafter cited as *NCCC*).

81   *NCCC,* 21 (1894), pp. iii-iv.

82   *National Bulletin of Charities and Corrections,* 3 (1899), May issue.

83   *NCCC,* 23 (1896), pp. 1-12.

84   *Bulletin of the NCCC,* February 1917.

85   "Present Condition of Sociology in the United States," *Annals,* 5 (1894/1895), 112-121.

86   Lester Ward, "Contemporary Sociology," *American Journal of Sociology,* 7 (1901/1902), 477.

87   Albion W. Small, "A Decade of Sociology," *American Journal of Sociology,* 11 (July 1905), 2.

88   Quoted in George Lundberg *et al., Trends in American Sociology* (New York: Harper & Row, 1929), p. 21.

89   *Ibid.,* p. 8.

90   Frank L. Tolman, "Study of Sociology in Institutions of Learning in the United States" part 1, *American Journal of Sociology,* 7 (1901/1902), 800.

91   "Loyal service due from the weak to the strong, the protecting service due from the strong to the weak, etc. . . ." *Ibid.,* p. 804.

92   For details, cf. Tolman, *op. cit.,* pp. 810-830, and Small, "50 Years of Sociology . . . ," pp. 200-201.

93   Small, *Ibid.,* p. 205.

94   *Ibid.,* pp. 203 and 208.

95   Tolman, *op. cit.,* part 2, *American Journal of Sociology,* 8 (1902/1903), 116-117.

96   *Ibid.*

97   Tolman, *op. cit.,* part 1, pp. 806-813 for the Columbia catalog.

98   Tolman, *op. cit.,* parts 1 and 2.

99   L. L. Bernard, "The Teaching of Sociology in the United States," *American Journal of Sociology,* 15 (1909), 164-213.

100   *Ibid.,* p. 191.

101   *Ibid.,* p. 195.

102   *Ibid.,* p. 212.

103   Small, "50 Years of Sociology . . . ," p. 210.

104   Odum, *American Sociology*, p. 13.
105   Small, "50 Years of Sociology . . . ," pp. 218-219.
106   Jane Addams, *Twenty Years at Hull House* (New York: Signet Books, originally published 1910), p. *ix.*
107   Josephine Goldmark, *Impatient Crusader* (Urbana, Illinois: University of Illinois Press, 1953), p. 11.
108   New York: T. Y. Crowell, 1895.
109   New York: Scribner, 1894.
110   Goldmark, *op. cit.*
111   Arthur Mann, *op. cit.*, pp. 115-123.
112   Philadelphia, 1899, pp. 1-4.
113   Elisabeth G. Meier, *A History of the New York School of Social Work* (New York: Columbia University Press, 1954), p. 14.
114   Allen Eaton and Shelby Harrison, *A Bibliography of Social Surveys* (New York: Russell Sage, 1930).
115   Edward Shils, in Schlesinger and White, *op. cit.*, pp. 393-394.
116   Wirth, *op. cit.*, pp. 273, 277.
117   Albion W. Small, "Some Contributions to the History of Sociology," *American Journal of Sociology*, 30 (November 1924), 332.
118   Small, "50 Years of Sociology . . . ," pp. 225-229.
119   Vol. 15 (1909/1910).
120   Shils, *op. cit.*, p. 393.
121   Read Bain, "The Most Important Sociologists," *American Sociological Review*, 27 (1962), 746-748.
122   Robert K. Merton, "Social Conflict over Styles of Sociological Work," *op. cit.*, pp. 24 ff.
123   *Annals*, 5 (1894/1895), 714.
124   For details, see "The Organization of the ASS," *American Journal of Sociology*, 11 (1905/1906), 555-569.
125   *American Journal of Sociology*, 11 (February 1906), 681.
126   Small, "50 Years of Sociology . . . ," p. 184.
127   Hofstadter, *Social Darwinism*, pp. 54-55.
128   In Schlesinger and White, *op. cit.*, p. 129.
129   Lyon Phelps, in *Folkways* (Boston: Ginn, 1940 edition), p. *x.*
130   Hofstadter, *op. cit.*, pp. 20, 64.
131   *Ibid.*, p. 70.
132   Odum, *American Masters of Social Science*, p. 61.
133   Small, "50 Years of Sociology . . . ," p. 154.
134   Odum, *American Sociology*, pp. 116-119.
135   On Cooley, cf. Odum, *ibid.*, pp. 110-111, and R. C. Angell's Introduction to Cooley's *Social Organization, and Human Nature and the Social Order* (New York: Free Press, 1953).
136   E. A. Ross, "Getting at Significant Social Situations in Foreign Countries," in *Publications of the ASS*, 17 (1923), pp. 161-167.
137   Ross, *Seventy Years of It*, pp. 276-277.
138   *Ibid.*, p. 96.
139   *Ibid.*, p. 180

140   Franklin H. Giddings, *Statistics and Sociology* (New York: Macmillan, 1891), pp. 9, 18, 26.
141   Johnson, *Pioneer's Progress*, pp. 122, 163-164, and Hoxie *et al., op. cit.,* pp. 291-292.
142   H. E. Barnes, *An Introduction to the History of Sociology* (Chicago: University of Chicago Press, 1948), pp. 763-764.
143   Tolman, *op. cit.,* pp. 811-812.
144   Elisabeth G. Meier, *op. cit.,* pp. 5-6.
145   Hoxie *et al., op. cit.,* p. 289.
146   John Glenn *et al., Russell Sage Foundation, 1907-1945* (New York: The Foundation, 1947), pp. 15-17.
147   Bernard, *op. cit.,* p. 196.
148   Franklin H. Giddings, *Inductive Sociology* (New York: Macmillan, 1901), pp. 106-108.
149   *Ibid.,* pp. 114-117.
150   *American Journal of Sociology,* 15 (May 1910), pp. 221-240.
151   One of his indices of relative heterogeneity is actually the statistical formula for the mean of a distribution, not a measure of dispersion.
152   Frank H. Giddings, "A Theory of Social Causation," *Publications of the American Economic Association,* 3rd series, 5:2 (May 1904).
153   *Ibid.,* pp. 190-196.
154   Hoxie *et al., op. cit.,* p. 186.
155   Hornell Hart, "The Prewar Upsurge in Social Science," *American Sociological Review,* 14 (1949), 605.
156   Arthur Bowley, *Elements of Statistics* (1901) and *An Elementary Manual of Statistics* (1910); G. Udny Yule, *An Introduction to the Theory of Statistics* (London: Griffin, 1911).
157   S. N. D. North, "The Relation of Statistics to Economics and Sociology," *Journal of the American Statistical Association,* 8 (1908/1909), 431.
158   William F. Ogburn, "An Analysis of the Standard of Living in the District of Columbia in 1916," *Journal of the American Statistical Association,* 16 (1918/1919), pp. 374-389.
159   Ogburn and Delvin Petersen, *Political Science Quarterly,* 31 (1916), 300-317. Ogburn and Inez Golta, "How Women Vote," *Ibid.,* 34 (1919), 413-433. Stuart A. Rice, "The Behavior of Legislative Groups," *Ibid.,* 40 (1925), pp. 60-72.
160   Stuart A. Rice, "Some Applications of Statistical Methods to Political Research," *American Political Science Review,* 20 (1926), pp. 313-329.
161   F. A. Dewey, "An Application of Statistical Method," *American Journal of Sociology,* 21 (1915/1916), 334-338.
162   F. Stuart Chapin, "The Statistical Redefinition of a Societal Variable," *American Journal of Sociology,* 30 (1924/1925), 154-171.
163   William F. Ogburn, "Factors Affecting the Marital Condition of the Population," *Publications of the ASS,* 18 (1923), pp. 47-59.
164   Robert Faris, *Chicago Sociology, 1920-1932* (San Francisco: Chandler, 1967).
165   Quoted in H. E. Barnes *op. cit.,* p. 794.

166   Odum, *American Sociology*, p. 144.

167   Quoted in Barnes, *op. cit.*, p. 804.

168   Quoted in E. H. Volkart, ed., *Social Behavior and Personality* (New York: Social Science Research Council, 1951), p. 85.

169   Herbert Blumer, *An Appraisal of Thomas and Znaniecki's Polish Peasant . . .* (New York: Social Science Research Council Bulletin No. 44, 1939), pp. 103-104.

170   Quoted in Blumer, *op. cit.*, pp. 166-167.

171   Edward Shils, "The Present Situation in American Sociology," *Pilot Papers*, 2:2 (June 1947).

172   On Park, see the autobiographic note in R. E. Park, *Race and Culture* (New York: Free Press, 1950); Faris, *op. cit.*, pp. 28-53; and E. W. Burgess and D. J. Bogue, *Contributions to Urban Sociology* (Chicago: University of Chicago Press, 1964), pp. 2-9.

173   R. E. Park and E. W. Burgess, eds., *Introduction to the Science of Society* (Chicago: University of Chicago Press, 1921), p. 662, question 33, "In what ways does race conflict make for race consciousness?"; question 35, "Is the heightening of race consciousness of value or of disadvantage to a racial group?" question 36, "How do you explain the present tendency of the Negro to substitute the copying of colored models for the imitation of white models?"

174   *Ibid.*, p. 42.

175   R. E. Park and E. W. Burgess, *The City* (new ed.; Chicago: University of Chicago Press, 1967), p. 612.

176   Park and Burgess, *op. cit.*, p. 44.

177   Cf. note 172.

178   Cf. *Annals*, 4 (1893/1894), 193; *Annals*, 5 (1894/1895), 584-586; *Proceedings of the NCCC*, 21 (1894), 313-320; as well as the catalog statements of Chicago and Columbia quoted earlier.

179   Cf. the series on the housing of immigrant ethnic groups by Edith Abbott, Sophonisba Breckinridge, and others published in the *American Journal of Sociology*, 16 (1910-1911), pp. 289-308, 433-468.

180   Cf. J. M. Gillette "The Cultural Agencies of a Typical Manufacturing Group in South Chicago," and Charles Bushnell, "Some Social Aspects of the Chicago Stock Yards," *American Journal of Sociology*, 7 (1901-1902), pp. 145-170, 188-215, 289-330, 433-474, 687-702.

181   Conversation with Harold Lasswell, March 25, 1968.

182   Somit and Tanenhaus, *op. cit.*, pp. 88-129.

183   T. V. Smith and Leonard D. White, eds., *Chicago, an Experiment in Social Science Research* (Chicago: University of Chicago Press, 1929); Louis Wirth, ed., *Eleven Twenty-Six, A Decade of Social Science Research* (Chicago: University of Chicago Press, 1940); and Leonard D. White, ed., *The State of the Social Sciences* (Chicago: University of Chicago Press, 1956).

184   Smith and White, *op. cit.*, pp. 44-45.

185   Faris, *op. cit.*, and Burgess and Bogue, *op. cit.*

186   L. L. Bernard, "The Teaching of Sociology in the United States in the Last 50 Years," *American Journal of Sociology*, 50 (May 1945), 535.

187   *Ibid.,* pp. 545-546.
188   See among many reports George Lundberg, "The Interests of Members of the ASS in 1930," *American Journal of Sociology,* 37 (November 1931), 458-460, 620.
189   Robert Myers, "Some Notes on the 1942 members of the ASS," *American Sociological Review,* 8 (1943), 203-206.
190   John L. Gillin, "The Development of Sociology in the United States," *Publications of the American Sociological Society,* 21 (1927), p. 25.
191   Quoted in Odum, *American Sociology,* p. 151.
192   William F. Ogburn, "The Folkways of a Scientific Sociology," *Publications of the American Sociological Society,* 24 (1930), p. 2.
193   *Ibid.,* pp. 6, 7, 10.
194   *Publications of the American Sociological Society,* 25 (May 1931), pp. 25-35.
195   Princeton: Princeton University Press, 1940.
196   As one highly qualified observer put it: "The issues which concerned Small and Tolman are still alive . . . [Elbridge Sibley, *The Education of Sociologists in the United States* (New York: Russell Sage, 1963), p. 18].

index

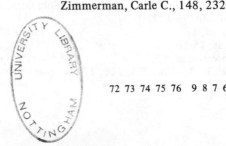